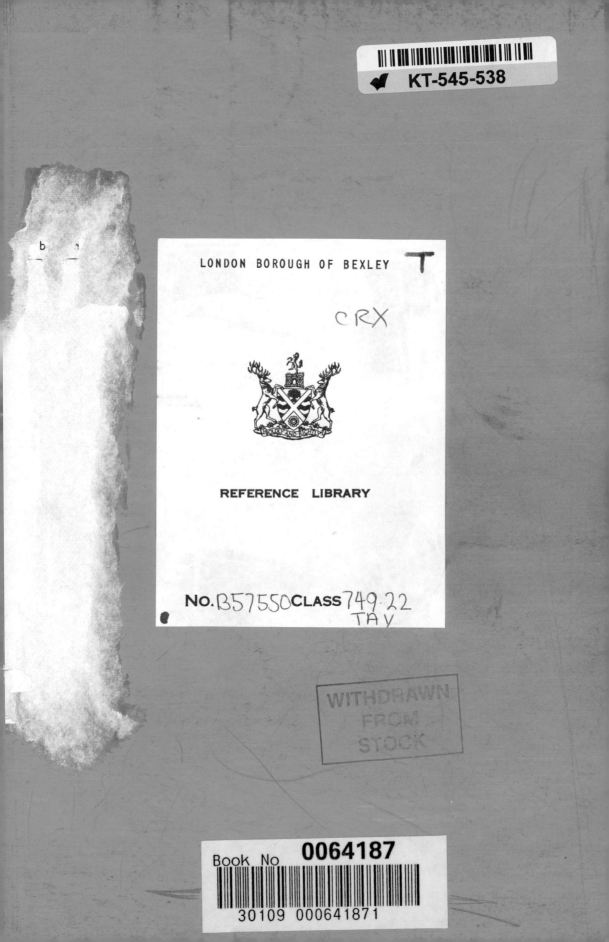

English Furniture

from the Middle Ages to Modern Times

Japanned bedstead made, probably by Thomas Chippendale after a design in *The Director*, for the 4th Duke of Beaufort. c. 1754.

English Furniture

from the Middle Ages to Modern Times

Margaret Macdonald-Taylor

London

Evans Brothers Limited

Published by Evans Brothers Limited
Montague House, Russell Square,
London, W.C.1

First published 1965

Set in 12 on 13 point Walbaum
and printed in Great Britain by
Butler & Tanner Ltd, Frome and London
7/5023   PR 2968

Contents

For permission to reproduce the photographs in this book the author and publishers are indebted to the Victoria and Albert Museum and to the Council of Industrial Design.

Foreword

More people than ever before are becoming interested in that fine heritage of furniture made by English craftsmen in the past and preserved through the centuries. Some people are fortunate enough to have inherited original pieces, some are able to follow the path of the collector or connoisseur of antiques. All of us can see in our museums much to delight us, whilst many of us enjoy the modern pursuit of visiting country houses open to the public where furniture of various historic periods appears to advantage in a natural setting. Some knowledge of period styles can add much to anyone's pleasure and appreciation; it can also help one to see how past ideas have been revived in more recent times, and in contrast to see to what extent modern designers have moved right away from tradition, creating something quite fresh. The whole story, brought up to the present day, if told in full, can contain an immense amount of detail. Too much detail however can confuse the picture and make the story rather indigestible for people coming new to this entrancing study. This book is therefore intended to give a general idea of the subject, with a few more detailed descriptions of suitable individual examples.

To help the general reader, the book has been designed deliberately in two parts. In the General Survey, characteristics of the style prevailing in successive periods are given; this is followed by chapters dealing separately with beds, chairs and so on. No great stress is laid in this account of English furniture on the part played on design by foreign influences; rather the object is to concentrate on the recognizable features generally associated with certain definite periods of development. In assessing contemporary trends there is naturally the difficulty raised by living in the midst of them, so it is only possible to select what seem the most striking innovations. These indeed can be followed in pieces displayed in retail shops, and very specially in the exhibitions arranged at the Design Centre in the Haymarket in London.

PART ONE

General Survey

CHAPTER ONE

The Medieval Period

The story of English furniture begins during the rather primitive times of the Middle Ages, and progresses through the period of gradual improvements under the late Tudors and early Stuarts until the Restoration, after which conspicuous advances were made. From the late seventeenth century onward design and craftsmanship reached a very high standard, culminating in the grace and elegance of the later eighteenth century. Then, with the Regency period, there set in a decline which became more and more marked during the Victorian era with the onset of mass production coupled with a marked uncertainty in taste. This uncertainty continued until quite recent times; but after the Second World War fresh stimulus was given to creative invention, with the advent of new materials and changes in social conditions.

Before tracing in detail the changing fashions in the design of specific classes of furniture, chairs, cabinets, tables, and so on, it is useful to give some account of the characteristics which prevailed at certain periods in the history of furniture generally. One may also take note of the social conditions which have influenced not only design and craftsmanship, but also the different pieces of furniture which were to be found in the houses of the time. For this purpose, after the somewhat negligible medieval period, the story is divided into eight main historical periods. These may be called Tudor and early Stuart, later Stuart, Queen Anne and early Georgian, mid-Georgian, later Georgian, Regency, Victorian and Twentieth Century.

During the very early years it is evident from contemporary documents, such as inventories and wills, that few people had much furniture at all. Society during the Middle Ages was mainly feudal, many people living out their lives attached to some great aristocratic household, or serving the Church in some monastic establishment. Castles and manor houses appear to have contained only the bare necessities of living, mainly to be found in the great hall in which two long tables for meals, of the removable board and trestle type, accompanied by long forms for seats with perhaps a chest or two, were the main furniture. On the dais at the far end, reserved for the use of the owner and his family and the occasional honoured guest, there was another table also accompanied by a long form or perhaps by a backed settle. A form of sideboard resembling a cupboard with two or three tiers of solid shelves above stood nearby; from it dishes of food and cups of wine were served. All such pieces were stoutly made of oak with little refinement in the way of decoration, but with perhaps some hint of Gothic tracery in the panels. Rich persons were content to display their wealth in the form of articles of a more movable kind, gold plate and tapestries, for example, which could be safely stored away in troubled times. Even the rich man's own bed could be easily dismantled, consisting as it did of a light wood framework of posts and top entirely covered in material and draped with curtains which closed it in like a tent at night. In contemporary illuminated manuscripts such beds are depicted, apparently used for reclining at ease by day; often there seems to be little else in the room but a chest.

Hardly any provision was made for the comfort of the retainers, although it must be remembered that much time was spent out of doors in various occupations during the day, and that, with very little artificial light available, people regulated their lives very much by the duration of the daylight hours. Wars, both at home and abroad, and the recurrence of plague such as the Black Death were long responsible for the continuance of such near-primitive ways of living. It was only as the country became more settled under the Tudors, and wealth began to be distributed amongst the trading as well as the land-owning classes of the community, that some advances were made. At the same time, ideas from the Continent were more warmly welcomed and standards in furnishing began to improve.

During the later years of the fifteenth century the increase in the growth of manufactures at home and trading abroad greatly encouraged higher standards of living. English merchants not only were in business at Calais, but were familiar with the riches of the immensely important trading centre of Antwerp. The English abroad, too, could see with their own eyes the comfortable homes of the burghers of the Low Countries and the kind of furnishing usual in them. At home, when Henry VIII succeeded to the wealth piled up by his careful, not to say parsimonious father, he set about living like a true Renaissance prince with his palaces richly furnished from Italy or Spain. Judging by the Royal inventories he owned pieces of furniture richly coloured and gilded, finished with luxurious upholstery. Cardinal Wolsey rivalled him in magnificence, both of these personages being great collectors of Flemish tapestries used to decorate their rooms, and also of the newly-fashionable Turkey carpets which were chiefly used to spread over the long table of the period. Except for a number of tapestries such glories have in the main long vanished; indeed few pieces of furniture, including the humbler types used in the homes of lesser folk, have survived. A wooden bedstead, an armchair or two, a simple rectangular table, a cupboard for food, a chest and a form or settle, comprised the range of pieces used by ordinary folk. This simple furniture was usually made of native oak and surviving examples show little ornamentation. Where decoration occurs it is carved, taking sometimes the form of linen-fold where the piece is panelled, such as a chest, and sometimes as Gothic tracery; on doors to food cupboards this 'tracery' is pierced for ventilation. During this early Tudor period there was also some intrusion of Italian Renaissance motifs, such as the baluster, the head or bust in profile set in a roundel or a lozenge, and arabesque designs; these usually took the form of carved ornamentation.

CHAPTER TWO

Tudor and Stuart Furniture

During the reigns of Elizabeth I and the first two Stuart kings a greater advance in civilized ways of living becomes distinctly noticeable. Such a development may be traced in architecture, interior decoration and furnishing. The medieval way of life, so much of it centred in the great hall with only a few rooms in addition for the owner's special use, had now largely disappeared. Houses were planned and built with more rooms which ensured more privacy for members of the family and guests, and which were even beginning to be intended for special uses. The new long gallery, for instance, for indoor exercise in inclement weather, became a notable feature. Here, however, it would seem there were few pieces of furniture. The hall, chiefly left to the servants, had a number of long tables and forms for their use at mealtimes, and perhaps a cupboard or two. Bedrooms were less frequently used as living-rooms and were still comparatively bare of furniture beyond the necessary bed, a chest for clothes and linen, a livery cupboard and perhaps a child's cradle and a small side table. It is in the increasing number of 'parlours' that more pieces of furniture were placed. Throughout the house oak panelling lined the walls creating rather a dark effect, but enriched by hangings of colourful tapestry or needlework, and further enlivened by the embroidered upholstery.

The furniture in use during this period was generally of a very solid type and was mainly of oak, although elm was often used for the tops of dining tables. Chestnut, beech and deal also occur in inventories, e.g. for tables or livery cupboards, whilst walnut (probably imported) seems to have been used for specially important pieces. Cedar is also mentioned. Carved ornament was lavished on important pieces, the chief motifs being strapwork, gadrooning and acanthus leaves. Inlay, using native woods, such as apple, cherry, holly and poplar, introduced some contrast of colour and tone; sometimes mother-of-pearl may be seen in furniture where the design has been influenced by contemporary work in the Low Countries. Inlaid ornament usually took the form of chequer patterns, or of simple

14

floral sprays arranged rather stiffly in a flat manner. It is interesting to note that during the sixteenth century there was a fairly steady flow of Flemish craftsmen into England, and that printed books of designs, of ornament especially, had from mid-century been coming from Flanders and had found ready acceptance here. The ideas of such designers as Vlederman de Vries and Collaert had introduced the native English craftsman to the use of such ornamental motifs as strapwork and grotesque figures, besides the arabesques and more classical forms, e.g. the column and pilaster derived from Renaissance Italy.

Some developments in structure may also be observed, for instance chairs were no longer of the early box-like form but had legs connected by stretchers. Chests were now always of framed construction (i.e. with posts, rails and panels) instead of being made of solid planks. The dining table often had a top which could be extended at each end to give extra seating space at meals. This was a distinct advance for the family eating in the dining parlour, where naturally there would be less space than in the old hall. Between meals the table could be used for other purposes, and indeed in many cases would be a very decorative piece of furniture. A conspicuous feature of this period is the bulbous support, introduced from the Low Countries, and used for open shelves, tables and bedposts.

Although rooms of this period were sparsely equipped according to modern ideas, there were more chairs than formerly since the chair was no longer the exclusive and privileged seat of the master of the household. Stools were being used in greater numbers to supplement the long form. The day-bed for relaxing and reclining during the day appeared for the first time; it is mentioned not only in contemporary inventories but also in *Twelfth Night* where Malvolio says:

'Calling my officers about me, in my branched velvet gown; having come from a day-bed, where I have left Olivia sleeping,—'

(ACT II, SCENE V)

Hanging shelves, sometimes enclosed with a door formed of open balusters, were provided for temporary keeping of food, usually for refreshment at night in bedrooms, whilst small tables began to be made for occasional use; playing at cards had become very fashionable in Court circles, so a small table with a folding flap was convenient for this amusement. By mid-seventeenth century tables of gate-leg type were being introduced and were soon to displace the long rectangular one for dining. Although many more persons than formerly could read and write, books were not yet being printed in sufficient quantity to stimulate the need for bookcases; that was to be a later refinement, and proper desks or bureaux were also still to come. A simple portable type of writing desk resembling a box with a sloping top or lid was fitting for most purposes. Whilst the bedstead was draped with curtains as before, some upholstery began to appear for seated furniture. In general, loose cushions were used in quantities, often covered with some brightly-coloured fabric, more often still with rich embroidery in silk perhaps enhanced still further with gold thread. Now also, some chairs might have some slight padding fixed to the back and seat, this padding being covered with velvet or leather, or with 'Turkey Work', and often being finished with a fringe. The day-bed was provided with a loose mattress and a round bolster upholstered very often in velvet, or some other decorative material.

All the furniture already mentioned was of English workmanship even if it was influenced by foreign ideas in design and ornamentation, but it should be recorded that persons of wealth and position were in the habit of importing some very decorative pieces from abroad, chiefly through Antwerp which continued to be the great trading centre of Europe. Chests and chairs were bought but most conspicuous of all were the handsome cabinets made in Holland, which were inlaid with tortoiseshell and ivory or veneered with tortoiseshell and inlaid with silver and brass. Some idea of the appearance of these splendid cabinets may be gained from pictures of Dutch interiors painted by such seventeenth-century artists as Terborch. Sometimes, too, one reads of fine looking-glasses being brought from Venice to decorate the walls of some wealthy Englishman's home. These cabinets and looking-glasses, like the chandeliers of rock crystal, the inlaid marble tables on gilt frames and other exotics, were a foretaste of the increasing luxury which was to follow soon after the Restoration.

Later Stuart Furniture

Since the period of the Civil War naturally saw some disruption in the pursuit of the arts generally, and since the Puritan régime of the Commonwealth tended to discourage much enterprise in this field, it would be natural to expect a revival once conditions became more favourable. This indeed was so and to a most remarkable extent. The year which saw Charles II restored to the throne may be said to be a great landmark in the history of the social scene. New houses being built were lit by tall and narrow windows arranged regularly along the façade in true Renaissance style, whilst indoors this influence was felt in the decorative treatment of chimney-pieces, doors and wall panelling, following the initial lead given by Inigo Jones in early Stuart times and now promoted further by the taste and genius of Sir Christopher Wren. The new type of windows, fitted with sliding sashes during the reign of William and Mary, imparted a definite symmetry to the interiors of rooms which were mainly panelled in oak, although in much larger panels than before, and now arranged above a dado or chair-rail moulding. In the state rooms of royal palaces or the mansions of the aristocracy walls were often hung with tapestry above chair-rail height, or lined with a rich fabric of glowing colour, crimson damask for example, or blue bordered with gold.

The taste for luxury and display so typical of the Court (where, it has been said, Charles' ministers of state and his mistresses vied with one another in the splendour of their furnishings) naturally spread among other classes of people, who imitated the wealthy to the best of their more modest means. There was indeed almost a revolution in the general way of life. This naturally found expression in furniture and now many pieces destined for special use appeared which had hitherto been lacking. Chief among these newcomers were chests of drawers in which people could keep their clothes with more convenience. There was also an early form of bureau for writing at and for keeping papers and documents in handy fashion, besides cabinets fitted with very small drawers for jewels, miniatures, collections of coins and other small objects. It also became necessary to have a glazed bookcase in which to assemble a small library, for books were now being written and printed in greater quantity. A dresser, the ancestor of the sideboard, was added to the furnishing of many a dining-room enabling the servants to carry out the service of meals with more ease and dignity.

A new fashion, too, had arisen which put the traditional rectangular table into retirement for a long time. It was now the mode to arrange the company in groups at various small tables, and for this purpose the gate-leg table with its oval or circular top was especially suitable. The inventory, taken in 1679, at Ham House near Richmond in Surrey refers to eight small tables of cedar in what was then called the Great Dining-Room.

Light-weight stands for candelabra, and brackets for small clocks or some ornament, were among the more decorative pieces to appear in public rooms, whilst the grandfather or long-case clock became an established favourite in many homes during the late Stuart period.

English craftsmen were now making mirror plate more successfully, so that the looking-glass to hang on the wall became a prominent feature with a natural place ready for it between the tall windows of saloons, where one of the new side tables could stand under it. Here also chandeliers, suspended from the centre of the ceiling and fitted with several branches, were about to become decorative and useful adjuncts to the furnishing of fine interiors. Single chairs as well as armchairs were more common from now onward, whilst the settee proved a welcome innovation, and the day-bed with its structure following chair design was in common use. Canework was used for seats and backs. Another refinement was the use of movable screens, either to keep off draughts or to mitigate the heat of the fire.

As the taste for luxury spread, the design of upholstered furniture with greater use of padding was developed. The high-backed winged armchair, with its over-stuffed frame and its ear-pieces to ward off draughts, together with the settee of similar design, were most conspicuous examples of this increase in comfort. Stools and the long forms for a number of people were also now upholstered and covered in keeping with the other furnishing, e.g. the window draperies, or the splendid hangings of the bed. Elaborate fringes were used for bordering the fabrics.

When William and Mary came to the throne the new Queen brought with her the current Dutch passion for collecting Oriental porcelain, so that glazed cabinets had to be made to show off such treasures to advantage. Every lady with pretensions to fashion must now have her 'China cabinet', but it was not until the time of Chippendale that any remarkable pieces were made for this purpose.

All these developments and innovations in furniture were carried out in a variety of new treatments introduced from abroad, which in the main brought more colour into rooms. It is true that oak, beech and solid walnut continued to be used, but a fine walnut veneer, light in tone and attractive in figure, was gradually introduced where it could be suitably employed. On the flat surfaces of tables, chests of drawers, clock-cases and important cabinets and bureaux marquetry patterns of lively design, set in panels of dark wood, were combined with the veneer to give a rich effect. Lacquerwork of black and gold decorated with Chinese motifs was fashionable as a finish to some cabinets which were already designed in Oriental style. Very wealthy people could indulge the taste, brought from France, for finishing some furniture in silver. At the French Court furniture was actually made of solid silver; in England looking-glass frames, small tables and decorative stands might, instead of being solid, be wholly plated with the precious metal richly wrought. Other pieces were elaborately decorated with silver plaques or fitted with silver mounts. Gesso was used in conjunction with carved ornament to achieve more refined effects, and there was much use of gilding, or sometimes of silvering, for very decorative pieces of furniture. Handles, locks and hinges were usually of brass and became noticeably more decorative in this period.

In form, furniture tended in general to develop from the earlier more solid type with rather coarse mouldings and a good deal of spiral turning, to more graceful designs with more subtle outlines. There was much use of foliage in carved ornament, with amorini, cherubs' heads, birds, flowers and fruit, often combined in generous exuberance. In marquetry, sprays of flowers and leaves with a bird or two made bright patterns of light-coloured wood and ivory, white or stained green, all set in panels of a dark contrasting background. English craftsmen proved themselves equal to working in the new techniques and their work reached a very high standard, especially in marquetry. Carving, too, became very accomplished, inspired by the immensely skilful work of Grinling Gibbons, who proved himself a master of realistic design carried out with the greatest fidelity to natural forms, birds, flowers, leaves, fruit, mingled in drops or festoons all showing great refinement of touch. Whilst his work was mainly associated with interior decoration, i.e. in great houses such as Hampton Court Palace, his style and achievement gave a lead also in the field of good furniture. Here limewood was the usual wood employed. Designs of a most elaborate kind were used for the carved and gilded stands made for lacquer cabinets, and frames for pictures and looking-glasses were often intricately and finely modelled.

Names of individual craftsmen begin to emerge, chiefly from Royal accounts where orders for the refurnishing of Royal palaces are recorded in interesting detail. The name of 'Thomas Roberts, Joyner' appears regarding the supply of various pieces of furniture, whilst there are 'William Shearer, Mercer' for crimson velvet, 'Thomas Carr, Fringmaker', and 'Richard Bealing, Upholsterer'.

The latter's charges naturally included the cost of making up but there is also mention of certain materials, e.g. 'curl'd hair and linnen to stuff in'. Earlier, in accounts running from Michaelmas 1690 to Michaelmas 1691, the name of John Pelletier occurs describing himself as 'carver and guilder' and asking for payment for making several tables and large stands. This entry serves to remind the historian of the decorative arts that the Revocation of the Edict of Nantes in 1685 sent many Huguenot craftsmen flying from France, to seek refuge and work in neighbouring Protestant countries such as Holland and England. Daniel Marot was one of these Huguenot refugees and although he attached himself to William of Orange and was concerned in work for him on the Continent, there is not conclusive evidence that he actually provided furniture for English clients. His book of designs (published in Amsterdam in 1712) showed he had been ready to tackle any problem, whether in interior decoration or furniture, or even the layout of garden parterres. Altogether the period of the later seventeenth century was one of great encouragement and patronage for makers of furniture who met the demand with enthusiasm, and adopted and adapted fresh ideas from abroad with notable success.

CHAPTER THREE

The Queen Anne,
Georgian and Regency Periods

Early in the eighteenth century there began an era of much domestic building in the grand manner, apart from the lesser houses which followed the simple brick and stone style initiated by Sir Christopher Wren. First came Sir John Vanbrugh with his stupendous designs for the Earl of Carlisle at Castle Howard in Yorkshire, and for the nation's hero, the Duke of Marlborough, at Blenheim Palace in Oxfordshire. By the 1720s and 1730s other men appeared on the scene; the most important were Colin Campbell, the Earl of Burlington, and William Kent, all declared followers of the Italian architect Andrea Palladio and the tenets of Inigo Jones. Large mansions for the grandees, such as Sir Robert Walpole and the Earl of Leicester, arose to the designs of these men, which were outwardly less dramatic than Vanbrugh's compositions but internally had, in the chief rooms at any rate, something of the same large scale and grand manner. There was much use of stone or marble for doorways and chimney-pieces which were strongly architectural in style, whilst mural painting or huge tapestries decorated the walls. In many rooms there was colour, with crimson damask, or figured velvet in colours on a white ground which covered the main part of the walls. Otherwise, rooms were lined with wood panels arranged in a definite scheme, painted in olive green, or blue, or brown or perhaps white, and enlivened more or less with gilding which was used to pick out details of carving. Such was the setting, varying only according to the resources of the owner, for the furniture of the time.

Queen Anne and early Georgian

This period was distinguished during the earlier years by the development of the characteristic curvilinear style in furniture, popularly associated with the label 'Queen Anne', and mainly carried out in a veneer of warm-toned walnut. These curving forms continued to a great extent in the years following, but after Sir Robert Walpole, when Prime Minister, removed in 1733 the tax on imported timber, mahogany from the West Indies and Honduras gradually came into fashion and eventually displaced walnut altogether. At the same time there was some modification in the use of curved lines in furniture. Throughout the early years of the eighteenth century the design of simple pieces could be adapted from the more ornate examples made for the rich, but during the 1730s the genius of William Kent created furniture for great houses which was both too magnificent in style and treatment and too monumental in size to form a model for the design of humbler furniture in such a vein. This furniture of Kent's therefore stands in a class by itself.

Chief among new articles introduced during this period were the folding card table, and the bureau with sloping top which sometimes had a two-doored cabinet over it. The chest or coffer for clothes gradually went out of fashion as the chest of drawers became firmly established, and the double chest of drawers, or tallboy, was introduced. Console tables began to be placed between windows under decorative looking-glasses. Pedestals, often called 'terms', were made and on them were placed the busts or bronzes which now formed an important part of the English gentleman's collection of art objects. Bookcases were to be made in increasing quantities towards the middle of the century.

The curvilinear style referred to as characteristic of so much work of this period depended a great deal on the use of the cabriole leg, now used as a support to all types of seats and tables. Since its curved shape made the use of stretchers inconvenient, these disappeared from all such pieces. Curves, too, were characteristic of the shape of the chair back and seat, and for the tops of cabinets and looking-glasses, and presently for the corners of the new card table.

In ornamentation, since the fine-figured walnut chosen for veneer could form the chief decorative element, marquetry soon went out of use and the main effect was obtained by plain panels outlined with a narrow border of herring-bone veneer. Carving was used very sparingly, for example on the 'knee' of the cabriole leg, and perhaps a touch on the chair back and with some restraint in the design of looking-glass frames and frames for pictures. Otherwise the style is notable for the carefully designed proportions of the whole piece, and for the refinement of the mouldings where these were required, e.g. to the tops of cabinets and bookcases and in the design of clock-cases.

Although walnut veneer in all its beautiful simplicity held the field, the taste for lacquerwork had not been entirely abandoned; it was however carried out in a more brilliant colour key than before. Instead of the rich but dark tones of the raised gold and black lacquer of the later seventeenth century, a glowing vermilion became a favourite for the main ground and was eminently suitable for an important piece, such as the tall bureau-cabinet or for the long-case clock. Emerald green was also in vogue and, more rarely, blue; on all such grounds the chinoiserie ornament was raised and gilded. This treatment is occasionally found on other pieces, notably chairs and day-bed frames; here it is not so suitable since it shows to less advantage than on flatter surfaces.

Silvering as a finish to very decorative pieces also went out of fashion. Gilding continued in use, and indeed during the historic periods never went out of favour at any time for decorative pieces of furniture intended for the more important rooms. At this time touches of gilding were used on certain small carved motifs, especially on looking-glass frames of walnut veneer. Gilt gesso continued to be employed for the minuter details associated with carving, to achieve more delicate treatment as found in the finish of pier glasses and the tops of the more extravagant forms of side tables often designed to accompany them.

With William Kent the name of a specific designer of furniture comes to the fore. He was a man of considerable versatility. Architecture, interior decoration and mural painting, as well as sculpture and landscape gardening, were among his pursuits. Kent was the fortunate protégé and intimate of such artistocratic connoisseurs of architecture and the arts as the Earl of Burlington and Thomas Coke, Earl of Leicester. He had spent several years in Italy, studying and making sketches of buildings, and thus came to know at first hand the fine palaces of Venice and the luxurious villas of the nearby mainland. The decoration of such Venetian interiors was sumptuous, but the furniture contributed little to amenity. The number of pieces placed in saloons was very limited, to allow space for the crowds which frequented the assemblies and entertainments. The furniture indeed seemed designed to enhance further the brilliance of the interior decoration rather than to accommodate human beings. William Kent, therefore, when he turned to the designing of furniture for the great houses of English noblemen showed a preference for a style of almost baroque grandeur. When he was concerned with case furniture he displayed a strong leaning towards the use of architectural forms, e.g. columns, with the full architrave, frieze and cornice of the classic orders, topped by a pediment. His huge side tables were mostly

23

designed to stand under the pier glasses, or in other significant places along the walls of halls and saloons. Their great marble tops were supported on frames composed of heavy and elaborate open-carved forms, e.g. animals or birds and swathes of foliage, associated with armorial bearings. They were weighty in appearance, but also so weighty in actuality that they formed immovable parts of the interior decoration. It need hardly be added that such pieces were richly gilded. So, too, were the various forms of seats, single chairs, settees and numerous stools; these again were elaborate in form and usually upholstered in richly patterned velvet, either imported, perhaps from Venice itself, or of English manufacture in the same style. Some of Kent's settees appear more like ample thrones or chairs of state, formal rather than designed for the comfort of the person. They, too, were almost immovable. A contemporary writer, criticizing the sacrifice of comfort to ostentatious display, singles out Kent for this fault and speaks of the fashion among grandees for having reception rooms large enough to accommodate up to a hundred persons, but containing little more than a couple of tables and six or eight chairs by way of furniture.

Mid-Georgian

In the mid-Georgian period, across the middle years of the eighteenth century, the chief wood in use for furniture was mahogany and pieces were made in a variety of styles, designated respectively by contemporary designers as the 'French Taste', the 'Chinese Taste' and the 'Gothick Taste'. Each style had clearly identifiable character-istics. At the same time more examples of the smaller types of furni-ture came into use. This period is also notable for the publication of books of designs, particularly that celebrated work *The Gentleman and Cabinetmaker's Director* (1754) by Thomas Chippendale. This book was so successful that it appeared in two further editions; thus London fashions spread much more quickly than formerly among provincial makers, who were enabled to supply furniture, in a simpler version of the latest fashions, to the lesser gentry, local tradespeople and others with pretensions to gentility.

In the field of interior decoration some variation was also apparent, in modifications of the strongly architectural treatment of doors, windows and chimney-pieces, which had prevailed for so long in the larger houses and in a lesser degree in smaller ones. Across the Channel the French had, in the 1720s, been developing a light and somewhat fantastic style of interior decoration to which the term rococo is applied. In this the use of the classic orders was banished, and instead there was fine panelling with delicate applied mouldings, following irregular outlines and diversified with light foliated scrolling forms. Looking-glasses and 'branches' for lights were incorporated with this panelling, and the gilding of the ornamental motifs lit up the over-all colour of white or delicate grey. This fashion did not have time to take a firm hold in England, for Robert Adam was shortly to come upon the scene and exert his own strong influence upon the decorative arts. However, in the 1740s, at Chesterfield House in Mayfair, Norfolk House in St James's Square, and else-where, such décor expressed the beginning of a swing away from the taste for ponderous grandeur seen in the more architectural forms. Wallpaper, too, was beginning to rival fabric for lining the walls of rooms above chair-rail height. Generally speaking makers of wall-papers were content to imitate the designs of contemporary damasks, brocades and velvets, but in contrast there was the painted 'Chinese landscape' variety which was either imported from the Far East by the East India Company, or copied at home in similar style by English hands. This, with its delightful finely-drawn trees set with exotic flowers and long-tailed birds, forming a continuous but not strictly repetitive pattern around the room, combined well with the rococo treatment of the chimney-piece and gave a romantic air to the bed-room or lesser saloon for which it was mostly used.

During this period certain innovations and developments in furni-ture took place. Among newcomers were the centre table and the open hanging shelves both of which were intended for the display of porcelain. For the now fashionable habit of drinking tea there was the circular-topped table on its tripod support, and the small stand for the tea-kettle. Another small occasional piece was the so-called breakfast table for one person only, designed with folding flaps to the top and having a shelf underneath partly enclosed with lattice-work. Some refinements introduced to assist in making the toilet included the provision of a small table with a box-like top specially fitted with a mirror and tiny compartments for cosmetics, and a stand for washing or shaving made to carry a basin and fitted with a soap drawer. In the dining-room there was the new tripod dumb-waiter with its tiers of circular shelves; the dining table itself now returned to the tradi-tional rectangular form, but with new modes of extension. Elsewhere in the house beds were now of a more normal height, whilst stools were fewer in number than in the preceding period. Day-beds and long forms had gone out of fashion and long settees were now very often designed to hold, not merely two persons as before, but three or even more. The bookcase became an important piece of furniture and the doors to the upper part were glazed with bars carefully spaced. The chest of drawers often had a two-doored cupboard added above with a pull-out slide between top and bottom parts on which to rest clothes, the whole piece now forming a wardrobe.

The general character of mid-Georgian furniture displayed less use of curving form, although the cabriole leg continued to be used with modifications. A very distinct change appeared in the shape of the chair back which now took on the lines commonly associated with the name of Chippendale; the seat too ceased to be curved in plan, whilst the tops of case furniture, e.g. bookcases, tallboys, wardrobes and the like, were finished with a broken pediment. Very conspicuous indeed was the change in the design of looking-glasses and wall-lights or girandoles, their frames of carved gilded wood taking on the freest of rococo forms. These were the most extreme expression of the 'French Taste' which otherwise tended to show itself in slightly more elaborate shaping of the cabriole leg, and the decoration of the frames of upholstered chairs and other seats. The more elaborate forms of chair back likewise showed something of this spirit.

The 'Chinese Taste' chiefly consisted of the intrusion of Chinese motifs used both as constructive and ornamental forms, such as the pagoda roof and the Chinese lattice, together with a suggestion of the bamboo shape in the lines of legs and stretchers. Pseudo-Chinese figures, dragons and long-tailed birds, give an added touch of the exotic to rococo looking-glasses and wall-lights. It is true that the architect Sir William Chambers had visited the Far East and produced some designs for 'Chinese' furniture, which appear to be based on the use of bamboo. He informed his public that he had taken them from the models which seemed to him the most beautiful and reasonable, adding that 'some are pretty and may be useful to our cabinetmakers'. His drawings, however, appear to have nothing in common with the chinoiserie pieces made by Western cabinet-makers whose furniture clearly has basically a distinctly European character, with Oriental motifs superficially added to or involved in the design, giving this furniture the very engaging flavour of fantasy peculiar to it.

The 'Gothick Taste' was even slighter in character, and mainly took the form of the use of Gothic window tracery patterns, adapted for open chair backs and for the arrangement of glazing bars to book-cases. Again, pieces of this nature had no real resemblance to furniture of the medieval period, but merely carried some hint of Gothic ornament. It was not a taste that appealed to many people, although Horace Walpole in his famous villa, Strawberry Hill, at Twickenham, cultivated medievalism with fervour and may well have been the first to indulge in the 'Gothick Taste'. At this time understanding of Gothic forms was very superficial and their limited use in Georgian furniture was no more than playing with a new idea in a search for variety.

During the mid-eighteenth century, except for the gilding of the more important furniture, mahogany gave its colour and character to most pieces. Its fine figure gave great distinction, as a veneer, to table tops and the flat surfaces of case furniture; used in the solid for supports, for chair backs and for mouldings, it was a splendid medium for refined carving. Tougher and stronger than walnut, it could be used successfully for the delicate-seeming intricacies of open-carved splats to chairs, and it allowed the use of more elaborate and at the same time finer and more detailed ornament elsewhere. This can be seen in the friezes to cabinet tops, the frieze rails of decorative tables and in applied ornament in general, as well as in the outlines of cornices and other mouldings. Marquetry remained out of fashion, and incidental touches of gilding were less frequent. Marble, mostly red-veined, and its counterfeit scagliola in rich combinations of colours, were both used to give added richness to tops of decorative side tables. Although the rococo element in design was derived from French sources, English cabinet-makers did not copy the copious use made by French craftsmen of elaborate ormolu mounts. Brass handles and lock plates were more decorative than in the previous period, but lacked the flamboyance that characterized French work.

Ornamental motifs, other than the Chinese ones already referred to, include the acanthus and other foliage, wave scrolls and the Greek key or fret, all carved.

For upholstered furniture there was a noticeable decline in the use of wool embroidery in gros and petit point. Instead, fabrics such as fine woven silk damasks and brocades were in favour for the best pieces of furniture, the patterns being in designs of smaller scale than in the earlier years of the eighteenth century. Dyed leather and printed chintz offered a further choice. Ornamental fringes were never used.

Mid-Georgian furniture shows a high level of good craftsmanship, and in the most elaborate pieces displays outstanding quality. More names of actual makers are now to be found recorded, especially of those working in the London area, although it is evident that a thriving trade was also being carried on in the provinces. There the work was not necessarily of a regional character, but tended to consist of the production of simplified versions of the more elaborate fashionable styles. In doing this local makers were helped, as has been said before, by the publication of Chippendale's book in which it can be seen he was careful in his plates to provide for the same piece a simple design and a more decorative alternative side by side.

Some of Chippendale's contemporaries may be mentioned. Mathias Darly (died c. 1781), a man of varied activities, produced in 1750 *A New Book of Chinese, Gothic and Modern Chairs*. In 1754, as a partner in the firm of Edwards & Darly, he was concerned with Edwards in another publication *A New Book of Chinese Designs*. H. Copeland, designer rather than furniture maker, published with Mathias Lock in 1768 *A New Book of Ornaments*. These two men were both concerned with designs in Chippendale's *Director*. Thomas Johnson is recorded as having brought out designs for *Twelve Girandoles* in 1755, followed by *One Hundred & Fifty New Designs* in monthly parts between 1756 and 1758, whilst W. Ince and J. Mayhew produced *The Universal System of Household Furniture* about 1763. There was therefore, as never before, a considerable fund of ideas in circulation for the more ordinary makers of furniture to draw upon, which encouraged a high all-round level of good taste.

Late Georgian

During the late Georgian period there was more activity in the field of domestic architecture than there had been, especially in connection with the building of fine mansions in different parts of the country. These continued to show classical features on the exteriors, which together with the traditional sash windows, imposed symmetry and regularity still on the façade, and to a great extent also on interior design. The chief architect of the period was Robert Adam whose strongly-defined style dominated the scene, and in particular affected the appearance of interior decoration and furniture, since he applied his genius and energy to designing and controlling everything down to the smallest detail in any house with which he was concerned. He was in fact responsible for a reaction in taste, a swing away from the varied fancies of the rococo, Chinese and 'Gothick' tastes, to something which was characterized by more controlled lines, allied to greater delicacy in ornamentation, and which made use of certain distinctive motifs derived from classical architecture. Hence evolved the style which is usually termed neo-classical, and which in furniture was to be carried out in rather more variety of materials, with a general tendency towards lighter effects in colour.

Adam owed his inspiration to his study at first hand in Italy of the works of classical antiquity, and was evidently influenced by the light reliefs seen in Roman stucco work. Other stimulus was also provided by the results seen in the excavations at Herculaneum and Pompeii, where the brilliant mural decoration of houses and villas revealed a style full of novelties. Adam's designs, however, did not slavishly copy ancient Roman forms; he used and adapted them in a fresh manner which was particularly successful in his treatment of interiors. Here he practically abandoned the use of columns and pedimented entablatures for doors and windows, and began to make greater use of plaster-work instead of wood panelling for wall decoration. The colour scheme for walls and ceiling alike was mainly carried out in pastel shades of blue, or of pink and green, relieved by raised ornament in white. Fine examples of such treatment may be seen at Osterley Park House and Syon House in Middlesex. Pictures in oils, usually classical subjects, often formed part of the design, and together with the rich dark tones of the mahogany doors saved the effect from being one of insipidity. Sometimes the walls of a fine drawing-room might be lined with a soft-coloured damask or velvet, or be hung with contemporary French tapestry in more brilliant colours. Other interiors again, such as those designed by James Wyatt, were treated in imitation of painted Pompeian decoration, for example with arabesques in bright colours on a light background. Looking-glasses continued to play an important part in interior decoration between the windows as before, but were also beginning to take a more constant place over the chimney-piece, whilst carpets were, as far as possible, woven to echo Adam's ceiling design, or chosen to harmonize with the general colour scheme.

The furniture arranged in these newer interiors was mainly characterized by straighter lines and a greater air of elegance. Not only were architectural forms, e.g. the pediment, no longer used, but many pieces became smaller in size and looked less weighty owing to the decline in the use of carved enrichments, now supplanted by the revival of marquetry and lacquer and some use of painted decoration. Satinwood replaced mahogany as the fashionable wood for furniture, especially for pieces for drawing-rooms, and this again contributed to the lighter effect.

Among the newer objects characteristic of the period were the tall pedestals to hold vases, busts or candelabra, placed about in halls, staircases and larger rooms, whilst the more fragile tripod stand, modelled on classic Roman originals, was a more elegant support for candelabra in the finer saloons. A new small occasional piece was the folding Pembroke table, also the nest of very small tables called quartettos. Commodes, designed in close imitation of the French piece so named, had some vogue, often being placed between windows under pier glasses. In this connection it is interesting to note the French terms introduced into English usage during the second half of the eighteenth century, such as fauteuil, bergère (often spelt burjair), and confidente (confidante). French Louis XVI influence was especially noticeable in the lines of much of Adam's furniture, not only in commodes, but also in chairs and sofas. In the dining-room, the sideboard table was now flanked by two pedestal cupboards each with a large urn on top, and fitted variously for the butler's use. This arrangement was, by the later 1780s, to be combined into one piece of furniture raised on six legs, the sideboard proper, although the urns ceased to be an essential part of the composition.

The straighter aspect of the furniture of this period is due, not only to the lack of pedimented tops and to the cleaner line resulting from the abandonment of applied carving in favour of flat surface treatments, but also to the use of a tapered leg instead of the curved cabriole, as a support to chairs and tables. This was either square and plain, except perhaps for some fluting or a narrow line of inlay, or was of column or baluster form, perhaps with a little ornamentation. Even the oval chair back introduced from France had, despite its curved shape, this same clean outline. Chair backs in general showed some variety in design, within the prevailing outlines, whether square, oval or shield-shaped, but the exuberance which had appeared in Chippendale's more extravagant versions of the rococo was now calmed down to a more restrained elegance.

Gilded wood naturally continued to be used for the most important pieces of furniture with mahogany, inlaid with some reticence, still in favour for the dining-room. Elsewhere satinwood, with its glowing yellow colour and the typical rippling figure in the grain whence its name is derived, was a new and pleasing material. Used as a veneer this figure showed to great advantage, and was further enhanced by marquetry decoration which returned to fashion. The marquetry patterns were not now formally enclosed in panels of a dark contrasting wood, but instead were more lightly strewn about the surface of the piece, and were carried out in very soft tones. This presented a more delicate effect than that of the marquetry style prevailing during the Restoration period. Sometimes painted motifs were used in conjunction with the satinwood veneer, or, again, appeared on other pieces which were entirely painted. The soft blues or greyish greens of the painted background set off prettily the natural colours of flower bouquets or garlands of olive leaves. Scagliola, like the marble it counterfeited, was now less fashionable for table tops, but in his design for cabinets, Adam is known to have used it much after the French way of using Sèvres porcelain, i.e. as small decorative plaques, thus obtaining some contrast with the satinwood veneer by yet another means. For mounts, the French use of ormolu was not imitated to any great extent; handles and plates, where they occurred, were usually more simply designed in brass and some pieces were even designed without them, the key appearing to be the sole means of opening a cupboard door or drawer.

Ornamental motifs were various, including those of classical derivation such as the ram's head, urn, vase, sphinx, gryphon, patera (flat ornament or rosette) and the Greek honeysuckle or anthemion. Fluting, reeding, segmental fan shapes and a reserved use of foliage were all employed, whilst festoons of drapery and garlands of husks appear suspended from ribbon bows.

Books of designs continued to be put before the public. Most notable was the volume entitled *The Works in Architecture of Robert and James Adam, Esquires*, published in three volumes in 1773. This included, in addition to plans and elevations of houses and drawings of interiors, a quantity of designs for furniture for certain of Adam's clients, such as the Earl of Bute at Luton Hoo in Bedfordshire and Mr Child at Osterley Park. Here can be seen a varied number of pieces which well illustrate the Adam style. The style of furniture associated with the name of George Hepplewhite (died 1786) may be seen in the book published in 1788 by his widow, and called *The Cabinet-Maker and Upholsterers' Guide*. This seems to have been sufficiently successful to encourage two further editions in 1789 and 1794. Another name well-known today is that of Thomas Sheraton, who, whilst he does not seem to have traded as a maker of furniture, yet had enough confidence to publish a book of designs: the *Cabinet-Maker and Upholsterer's Drawing Book*, which appeared in 1791, 1793 and 1802.

Regency

In the history of architecture and the decorative arts the first decades of the nineteenth century are today known as the Regency period, more as a matter of convenience than of real accuracy. Since the unfortunate George III was not continuously incapacitated by madness from carrying out his kingly functions, the Prince of Wales was only called upon at intervals to act as Regent. Nevertheless, the label Regency is a handy one, since already practically the whole of the eighteenth century has had to be divided up into Georgian units, early, middle and late, and some relief from this nomenclature is necessary in view of the Hanoverian attachment to this particular name.

The new houses of the period owed a good deal to the lead given by John Nash, who favoured the use of stucco as an exterior finish to buildings. Against this, white or cream in colour, a new feature appeared in the form of light ironwork balconies and verandahs, usually painted black, thus introducing a new kind of patterning in the design of the exterior. Most new domestic building activity was no longer concerned with the design and erection of very large mansions for the wealthy. In general that demand had already been met by the end of the eighteenth century, but there now was a great extension of terrace building for less important people, both on new estates arising about London itself, and in towns such as Cheltenham which was becoming a fashionable health resort, and Brighton which was even more fashionable owing to the patronage of the Prince Regent. In such terrace houses the bow-windowed front was a very characteristic feature, an extension to the room space which had not been seen since the Jacobean period. This feature tended to dominate the room inside and to concentrate window lighting from the end of the room only, instead of along the side from a number of sash windows, which had been the general usage for over a hundred years. This, as will be seen, affected not only the interior design but also to some extent the furnishing.

Interior design showed practically no use of architectural features, with rare exceptions such as at Carlton House, the palatial London home of the Prince of Wales. His other house, the Royal Pavilion at Brighton, was decorated with such an extravagant mixture of Oriental fantasies that it stood completely outside the main development in style. In normal room design doors and windows were framed with a simple architrave moulding, and the chimney-piece, of white or black marble, was simple in form and was surmounted by a chimney-glass. Walls became extremely plain, for there was neither wood panelling nor plaster enrichment to divide up the surface. The pastel colour schemes, so characteristic of the preceding era, were superseded by richer and more sombre effects, with warm crimson or dark green predominating as the key colour, whether on the walls or for the window draperies. This taste for dark tones extended in a most marked manner also to the furniture where darker woods were employed, with the minimum of decoration added. The general character thus became much more solid on lines that became increasingly more heavy in shape, not to say clumsy in proportion. For these developments English taste was indebted to French influence to a great degree, in a style which was to be the basis of yet more massive pieces of furniture during the early Victorian period.

The date of Robert Adam's death may be said to mark the climax of fine design and craftsmanship in the applied arts in England. It also coincided with the beginning of the Revolution in France, which had among its side effects the dispersal by the new regime of all the contents of the Royal palaces, and these pieces of Louis XV and Louis XVI furniture were eagerly bought at auction by wealthy English connoisseurs; among them was the Prince Regent himself who became a noted collector. The French, on the other hand, were seeking fresh inspiration in design and achieved a new style at first called 'Directoire', and later 'Empire' when Napoleon assumed the ultimate title. This style was based on the design of furniture of classical antiquity and owed something to Napoleon's interest in archaeology. The intrusion of the Egyptian sphinx as a decorative motif may also be attributed to this source. Furniture of classical times however had been limited to a very few pieces and displayed no variety of form or treatment, so it could offer few models for the early nineteenth-century designer looking for new shapes. Furthermore, the original pieces available were in marble or bronze and were not easily translatable into wood. Indeed no attempt was made to adapt them to this medium, and leading designers claimed that their pieces closely followed Greek or Roman furniture. The most conspicuous feature which in fact did derive from antique sources was the curious support compounded of a cat or lion head, and hocked or plain animal leg found on ancient Egyptian and Roman examples. Versions were also made in wood of the Roman marble tripod table. The general outline of the armchair, and the design of the sofa, also followed the classical original. Otherwise the shapes were mainly severely rectangular, the necessary fashionable 'antique' touch being given by the ornamental motif used.

Changes or developments typical of the Regency period in furniture include the introduction of the long sofa, with low back curved over at one end, which was meant for one person only to recline upon (like the ancient Roman at dinner), and which was accompanied by a small footstool. Another new piece was the whatnot, a stand of several open shelves for displaying ornaments; stands for plants also appeared more frequently. The davenport, a small writing desk, was a characteristic piece, and the so-called sofa table with a new type of folding top also came into use. Since the bow window had superseded the traditional range of windows, there was not the same need of pier glasses which used to be placed between them. The new looking-glass was of a distinctive circular shape, fitted with a convex mirror plate which gave a diminished reflection. This piece might be used as a chimney glass, or take a prominent place in the centre of a long wall. The dining table was once again altered in shape, now having a circular top fixed on a central pedestal support. Bedsteads in the French style became more fashionable than the traditional four-poster type. Instead of standing out at right angles from the wall the Regency bed was arranged alongside it, and was long and low in design.

The woods most frequently used included a rich mahogany, somewhat brighter in hue than that of the Chippendale period; this was much used in the solid. For veneer there was the dark tone of rosewood, whilst zebra wood with its strongly-contrasting figure produced a particularly striking effect. Marquetry was no longer fashionable and there was nothing to relieve these dark colours but the brass ornamentation of inlaid or overlaid motifs, used with great economy. Brass also appeared for the open-trellis doors of cabinets, and for the tiny pierced galleries added to the tops of some pieces. White marble was used to some extent for the tops of side tables and low cabinets and similar furniture. Canework was reintroduced, chiefly for the backs and seats of chairs and settees. Some furniture was made of beechwood, painted black to conform with the general trend. Such pieces, instead of carrying brass ornamentation, were painted in gold with motifs such as the Greek fret, or else parts of the structure were picked out in gold. True gilding was now mainly reserved for looking-glass and picture frames, and from this time onward it was much less used than in the great days of luxurious display of the seventeenth and eighteenth centuries. The wealthy who wished to be surrounded by splendid furniture already possessed quantities of inherited English pieces, or had begun to make collections of fine French eighteenth-century examples.

English Regency furniture, limited though it was in scope, could be made in styles suitable for most houses, not necessarily for those of the rich only. The shapes, except for the curious cat-headed support, were mainly simple, even if severe, and the small repertoire of ornament made no great demand on skilful craftsmanship, since the motifs of cast-brass could be supplied by manufacturers. These motifs were very limited, the chief being the Greek anthemion or honeysuckle, whilst a certain use was made of narrow inlaid brass lines and occasionally of stars. The Egyptian sphinx head was used as a mount, sometimes with the two feet added at an appropriate distance.

Ideas were again spread through the publication of designs. Thomas Hope of Deepdene in Surrey, a gentleman of means, was one of the enthusiasts for the new style and was particularly fervent in his support of great care in copying from ancient models, with an archaeological attention to detail. To further this ideal, he not only had furniture made for his own house, but published in 1808 a book of designs entitled *Household Furniture*. These designs were by no means universally applauded, as they were criticized for being much too large and heavy for ordinary or general use. More acceptable to the public were the designs of George Smith in *Collection of Designs for Household Furniture and Interior Decoration in the most Approved and Elegant Taste* which appeared in 1808, and his *Cabinet-makers' and Upholsterers' Guide* which was published in 1826.

One significant trend which must be recorded was the tendency to put more pieces of furniture into rooms. Jane Austen in her novel *Persuasion*, published posthumously in 1818, describes, in her dry way, how at Upper Cross the ladies were filling the parlour and giving it 'the proper air of confusion' with 'a grand pianoforte and a harp, flower stands, and little tables, placed in every direction. . . .' Here indeed is an indication of what was soon to come. The careful orderliness which gave grace and a sense of spaciousness to the eighteenth-century interior is nearly at an end, and the overcrowding of rooms which was to be so typical of the Victorian age is now in sight.

CHAPTER FOUR

The Victorian Period

When the young Queen Victoria succeeded to the throne in 1837 the period known as the Industrial Revolution had already begun. Of all the changes upon the social scene throughout the centuries, this was to be the one which by its nature affected furniture and the decorative arts most profoundly. With the introduction of machinery for so many processes of manufacture, and the rise and increase in production by mass methods, the old standards of design and craftsmanship were to decay rapidly. Furthermore, real patronage was no longer in the hands of a cultured class noted for its informed taste. Instead, most furniture, with but a few exceptions, was henceforth to be made in factories to be sold in shops to the casual customer. Hitherto, fine furniture had been made to please an aristocratic and discerning taste, and had been designed in many cases to be placed in particular positions in the rooms of special clients. Also it had been made to high standards of workmanship in every detail. These conditions meant that even the simpler pieces made for humbler people reached a notable level in design and finish. Books of furniture design, the work of such men as Chippendale and Adam, numbered in their lists of subscribers members of the aristocracy and gentry. During the nineteenth century, especially after 1860, published work took the form of trade periodicals circulating among manufacturers and retailers, who were themselves mainly persons of somewhat limited education and outlook. Also, there were as yet no magazines of any real standard to encourage the intending buyer to think critically and appreciatively before going to the shops to choose new possessions. The purchasers came from the new middle classes established by the Industrial Revolution, growing in numbers as the population increased and prosperity became more widespread. The rich aristocracy already had much fine furniture inherited from times of fine production, or were continuing to buy expensive and splendid eighteenth-century pieces suitable to their great houses. The new middle classes, on the other hand, were building suburban villas for themselves, of differing sizes according to their view of what was appropriate to their social standing. All these houses required re-furnishing throughout, and provided a great opportunity for manufacturer and shopkeeper to supply these needs.

The story of English furniture, therefore, will henceforward be concerned, with rare exceptions, with mass-produced pieces mainly for sale in the middle-class market. With regard to quality another factor may be noted. As England became increasingly urbanized and country folk left the villages to work in the factories, those of humbler station in life were inevitably cut off from the scenes of more refined living, which people of earlier generations had observed at close hand when the 'big house' had offered a situation and a livelihood for many of them. With these changes in the social structure the new classes in the towns had no such advantage, and were therefore dependent on what was provided for them by the manufacturer, who was himself suffering from the limitations of his own situation. The new middle class too, certainly during the first half of Victoria's reign, showed itself only too anxious to conform to those ideas commonly in circulation, being as yet uncertain of its own social standing. The whole world engaged in the manufacture of furniture and other articles for the home was without guidance over the question of design, whilst production had changed from the status of an art to that of an industry. Only a few architects took any interest in furniture design and on the whole their influence was negligible. As the century progressed, it becomes clear how uncertainty of taste and judgment affected furniture, with no designer of talent coming forward to produce ideas and no special patron to encourage them.

In the early Victorian period, styles tended to be very conservative, in striking contrast to developments during the second half of the nineteenth century. They were limited in the first place to copies of certain aspects of Regency design, secondly, to a compound of Louis XIV grandeur and Louis XV rococo called by the trade the 'old French style', and thirdly, to the so-called 'Elizabethan style' which was a mixture of such details as strapwork and spiral turning that bore little resemblance to the original. It will be noted that the word 'style' now appeared to possess a sales value, and was continually applied throughout the Victorian period. These three trends continued until mid-century, although the Government School of Design and some local schools had been established by the Board of Trade in 1837. After 1850 there is ample evidence of a search for new ideas, but it took the form of looking back to the past and trying to make furniture after every possible kind of previous 'style', Continental as well as English. Since there was the same poverty

37

of invention abroad there was no fund of fresh ideas available from the Continent, a fruitful source in earlier periods.

The dependence on ideas from the past was fostered to a great extent by the establishment of museums, in which collections were being gathered together for public viewing. This followed the stimulus given to the applied arts by the 'Great Exhibition of the Works of Industry of all Nations' (1851), in which they were given a foremost place. The word 'Industry' is perhaps significant. The chief museum, called the Museum of Manufactures, and ancestor of the present Victoria and Albert Museum at South Kensington, was opened in 1852 as a result of the combined efforts of the Prince Consort and Mr (later Sir Henry) Cole. Thus there were two official attempts to improve standards, first by providing schools of design and later by setting up museums containing examples of old and modern applied art. These attempts, however, failed to produce any creative result in design. In the event, and very noticeably where furniture was concerned, all that was achieved was an insensitive adaptation of past styles lacking in any sense of proportion or understanding of the use of ornament. As a result a kind of 'museumitis' set in from which the country was to suffer for nearly a hundred years.

One or two voices, however, were crying in the wilderness, such as that of William Morris (1834–1896), who with his friends and associates attempted to improve the standard of design, but their influence was only limited. Towards the end of the century matters began to mend to a limited extent with the inauguration of the Art-Workers' Guild (founded 1884), and of the Arts and Crafts Exhibition Society which held its first exhibition in 1888. Such activities, and those of the Home Arts and Industries Association, revived interest in the neglected handicrafts and encouraged practice in them. This was in direct contrast to the machine production of such goods as furniture, pottery, etc., in industrialized centres, where work was carried out under the factory system and where there was no opportunity for the expression of any individual artistic contribution. The short-lived Art Nouveau, during the later years of the nineteenth century, was another attempt, in the hands of a few leaders such as Voysey and Rennie Mackintosh, to improve the quality of design and workmanship in the applied arts. Thus the Victorian era is seen to be divisible into periods each with its own general characteristics, the first conservative and somewhat limited, the second crowded with a multitude of ideas derived from the past and resulting in confusion. Each period will now be surveyed in turn.

Early Victorian

During the earlier Victorian period modified Regency ideas still held the field to some extent in architecture and furniture design. The Gothic revival was reflected to a limited extent in domestic architecture, where what is sometimes called 'parsonage Gothic' manifested itself. This produced houses of irregular plan and would-be picturesque character, with steep roofs finished with Elizabethan barge-boarding and having windows fitted into openings of vaguely medieval aspect and arrangement. Other houses appeared plainer, with the 'Gothic' trimmings omitted. Rooms tended to be square or oblong in plan with the fireplace in the centre of one long wall, and the window or windows at one end. The bay window, segmental or rectangular in plan, was a great favourite although it tended to concentrate natural light in one part of the room only. Since the Victorians were far from being sun-worshippers and the Victorian housewife dreaded, with reason, the effect of direct sunlight upon her carpets and upholstered furniture with their impermanent dyes, this cannot have been considered a great disadvantage at the time.

Interior decoration continued to favour rather strong and often sombre colours, the walls being covered from picture rail to skirting board with wallpapers printed in all-over repeating patterns, large in scale and robust in hue. The fireplace, its shelf often disguised with a pelmet of coloured fabric, contained a cast-iron grate which required constant blacking by a servant; in the main reception rooms it was surmounted by a wide and tall chimney-glass in a narrow gilded frame, curved across the top. In the drawing-rooms, parlours and other sitting-rooms, there was very little orderly arrangement of the furniture which continually increased in quantity, beyond the limits of use and necessity.

Some changes and developments may be noted. In the dining-room the traditional rectangular table came into use again and with its chairs arranged around it in the centre of the room it provided some formality. In the bedroom the four-post bed had returned to favour, being more serviceable than the Regency bed in the French style. The Victorian bed once again was placed in the traditional manner at right angles to the wall facing the fireplace. A dressing table on which was placed a separate toilet glass was normally placed in the window area, whilst a plain wash-stand accommodated two sets of ewers, basins, etc., in a convenient corner. Large wardrobes fitted with drawers and trays inside tall doors made their appearance. In the drawing-room there was no commanding piece of furniture to guide arrangement, so chairs, sofas, ottomans and quantities of occasional tables began to crowd the floor. It is true that the piano gradually became an important possession. However, the nature of its design, dictated by the need for encasing the strings and providing keyboard and pedals, could not produce an object comparable with a cabinet or bookcase. The cabinet indeed remained as an item of furniture, but was not seen to great advantage, since the walls became increasingly crowded with pictures. Furthermore, English people were beginning to think less in terms of formality, even in the large mansions, and more in terms of comfort and ease. Gone were the days of the royal or aristocratic *vie de parade*, for which great suites of rooms had been designed during the seventeenth and eighteenth centuries, when a few pieces of furniture had been stiffly arranged along the walls, controlled by the regular position of the sash windows. A formal life which, it will be recalled, was imitated to a lesser degree by the smaller gentry. Now, however, the celebrated *confort anglais* was being established, with emphasis on warmth, freedom from draughts and provision for more comfortable upholstery, since the middle classes were to lead a more sedentary life in the suburbs, the outdoor sporting life of the country gentry not being available to them. The arrival of gas lighting, and presently of electricity, made this sedentary life indoors more agreeable with longer evenings of leisure possible after dark, especially in the winter.

The Victorian middle-class woman aspired to be thought a 'lady'. This meant giving an appearance of complete idleness with little time apparently spent in household tasks or their supervision. Daytime hours were passed in small social activities at each other's houses, with more pretentious parties for mixed company in the evening. The furniture she bought for her home may be divided into three categories or styles, as already indicated. First may be mentioned those pieces related to Regency precedent in their massive size and proportion, but lacking the brass mounts and typical ornament such as the anthemion motif. Secondly there were the pieces in the 'French style' which evolved during the 1830s, in which the framework of mirrors, seats and so on were garnished with carved scrolls and shell motifs on furniture of curving outlines. Thirdly there was the 'Elizabethan style', for which oak was the wood chosen and which depended on the somewhat indiscriminate use of carved strapwork patterns applied wherever they would conveniently go, for example, on case furniture such as sideboards. However, the Victorian designer's knowledge of the original true Elizabethan furniture was far from

40

being reliable, since he introduced features such as spiral turning and openwork cresting into chairs, which definitely belonged to the later seventeenth century; furthermore, these were combined with seat and back panels covered with coarse Berlin wool-work embroidery of tent or cross-stitch on canvas, carried out in the rather garish colours typical of this work. Parallel with this was the production of spurious 'Elizabethan' furniture, by the unscrupulous method of cutting up original pieces and then putting together various parts to form a new object. The more highly-carved portions (even sometimes of interior panelling) were chosen, and thus a great deal of later sixteenth- and seventeenth-century work seems to have been first mutilated and then transformed into Victorian sideboards, cupboards, etc. Needless to say the results did not have the proper aspect and proportion of Elizabethan or Jacobean furniture.

Much furniture during this period was made of rosewood or mahogany, used in the solid for preference, since veneers and marquetry had gone out of fashion and indeed were for the time being regarded as cheap and meretricious. An exception was the occasional use, for smaller pieces of furniture, of amboyna wood or of bird's-eye maple, both with a distinctive figure of yellow with warm brown spots. Perhaps the most characteristic development in design was in the chair which by degrees took the form known as 'balloon' back. The desire for extra comfort also appeared in the shaping of stuffed upholstered seats. These were made in a manner which showed the upholsterer in control of the form, with the fundamental framework completely obscured. Amorphous shapes were devised with swollen backs and roll-over arms, the rounded curving outlines merging into one another with no feeling of structure, for example in the sofa, the 'sociable' and the easy chair. A new piece was the ottoman, a long seat with neither back nor sides. Upholstery fabrics included woven horse-hair cloth, mostly dyed black, for hard wear, and finer materials for those seats destined for the drawing-room and the use of company. The covering fabric was usually 'buttoned' down all over the surface. The disregard of structure seen in much upholstered furniture was also evident in some of the very elaborate case furniture, such as richly carved cabinets or cupboards in which a wealth of ornamentation obscured the real form.

Mid-Victorian

Between the Exhibition dates of 1851 (London) and 1867 (Paris) there was a short transitional period before all the variety and complexities of the later Victorian period established themselves. The furniture displayed at the various International Exhibitions was naturally enough specially made for the occasion; the designs were apparently calculated to impress and astound the beholder, and were not intended to indicate the normal range of the firm's work. Such pieces, expensive and over-elaborate, could indeed hardly set trends for furniture in general. However, it is interesting to note one significant departure from the usual run of massive early Victorian pieces, which occurred at the Paris Exhibition of 1855. This took the form of a return to the Louis XVI style, with decorative veneers such as satinwood and tulip-wood, together with a revival of marquetry and the use of brass mounts. This was allied to the elegance and elaboration of design associated with the name of Sheraton, a noted admirer of the Louis XVI style in his day. At Paris, Messrs Jackson and Graham, the English cabinet-makers, won a 'Medal of Honour' on this occasion for a fine cabinet in which these characteristics were fully realized. This was but a foretaste; the furniture trade was to follow this revived 'Sheraton style' in due course. Wealthy English people could afford to have copies made in France of fine eighteenth-century French pieces, e.g. the copy of the 'Bureau du Roi Louis XV' (now in the Wallace Collection, London) made for the Marquis of Hertford. Others could afford to buy the expensive furniture on which elaborate carved ornament had been lavished, much of it the work of the so-called 'Warwickshire school' of carving. This local art practised in the Midlands was capable in the 1850s of producing pieces of furniture which were more like monumental sculpture than objects of real use in the home. A typical example was the impressive sideboard to be seen in the dining-room at Charlecote Park. A fair amount of furniture in this elaborate style was made for the local notables, and included various items, tables, chairs, mirrors, etc.

Aside from these rich extravagances, some changes in style were discernible elsewhere with simpler lines emerging and a more architectural form, whilst rococo ornamentation was less fashionable although lingering on cheaper work. Where carving was used on the less elaborate pieces there was a tendency to confine it within panels, thus not obscuring the shape. Large pieces of mirror plate, due to improved methods of production, were introduced into furniture, e.g. the backs of sideboards.

New materials came into use, notably papier-mâché and metal. The first could be used for smallish pieces or for larger flat surfaces. In metal, cast-iron was first in the field when the great foundries of

Coalbrookdale in Shropshire and the Carron Company in Stirling-shire, Scotland (and other lesser companies elsewhere), tried to popu-larize it, especially for garden furniture, and for such pieces as the new hall-stand which was fitted up for the reception of hats, umbrellas and so forth. Designs advertised for seats, tables and other room furniture have a somewhat fearsome appearance, and it may be doubted if they were ever in fact put into production. More welcome was the use of brass tubing for bedsteads, which came from Birmingham, already a centre for providing brass poles for curtains, fenders for the fireplace and other household objects. This brass tubing (iron too was sometimes used) brought about new types of design, arising out of the use of the material which was to some extent free of traditional influence.

Meanwhile, the influence of the Gothic revival in architecture was spreading into the world of furniture, and one or two architects tried their hand at furniture design. This new style received the label of 'Early English' or 'Modern English Gothic', and began to supersede the 'Elizabethan' style. In general it may be said this was intended to be a return to medieval methods of construction, the parts being 'joined', i.e. pegged together, instead of being secured with glue, and precluded the use of veneers. In addition it meant the use of many Gothic motifs, often assembled together in a rather incongruous manner. Furniture made in the 'Early English' style was often more profusely, indeed more violently, ornamented with Gothic architectural features, crockets, pinnacles, tracery and crenellations, than any pieces in the 'Gothick Taste' of the Chippendale period. In fact, it was the basic Victorian shape overlaid with these elaborations which were applied to chiffoniers, pedestal dressing tables, sideboards and even the upright piano. Such 'Early English' pieces were designed on the post, rail and panel type of rectangular construction.

The names of designers connected with this style include those of Eastlake, Webb and Talbert. The architect Pugin (1812–1852) was a kind of precursor, for he designed the Medieval Court at the Crystal Palace (1851). Philip Webb (1831–1915), an architect, was the chief designer for the firm of William Morris who was himself an advocate of the medieval type of work, and was in favour of simple methods of construction. Webb designed some pieces with flat surfaces which he intended should be decorated by artists, such as Burne-Jones. Bruce Talbert designed for various firms; some of his furniture was meant to be inlaid with tiny light and dark chequer ornament. William Burges (1827–1881), another architect, designed a quantity of furniture in the Gothic manner for his aristocratic patrons, the

Marquess and Marchioness of Bute. All this medievalism was chiefly to the taste of a special type of client, and distinct from the stream of Victorian trade furniture which had not wholly abandoned curving forms. Charles Eastlake (c. 1878) was talking of 'Art Furniture', i.e. those pieces designed by such people as Webb; he was also expressing scorn and contempt for the trade productions which he considered combined great ugliness with the least comfort.

Later Victorian

The variety of styles characteristic of the later Victorian period was now about to appear. From the 1870s onward the furniture industry was to become increasingly important, with the benefits gained from improvements in machine processes aiding mass production. Carving, for example, could be done by machine, merely requiring a little finishing-off by hand which could hardly be called craftsmanship. A glance through trade periodicals of the second half of the nineteenth century shows furniture designers ranging over all the past period styles available to them. 'Henri Deux', 'Louis Seize', 'Italian Renaissance', 'Sheraton' and many other romantic labels were given to various pieces of furniture, cabinets, sideboards, beds and settees. Sometimes careful line drawings, to scale, of original pieces were published in these papers, but the factories seem to have allowed themselves a pretty free hand in adapting old forms to nineteenth-century use. Many pieces became lighter in appearance than in the earlier Victorian period and were manufactured, not only in the woods of traditional use, but also in other types of material. Bentwood furniture, chiefly chairs, made its appearance, and brass and iron for bedsteads were triumphantly successful.

It is interesting, too, to note the influence of English life in India upon furniture, the canework and rattan pieces suited to a hot climate finding their place, not only on the liners in which Indian Civil Servants, the military, the doctors, the missionaries, travelled to and fro, but also in conservatories, verandahs and gardens at home. Bamboo also had its day. A new development in mass-produced furniture was the provision of 'suites' of furniture, particularly the bedroom suite which comprised the dressing table, wash-stand and wardrobe. All these pieces were made at prices to suit different purses, both in regard to the style (more or less ornate) and also the wood employed. Mention must be made of a curious development in design, the addition of corner shelving to various pieces of furniture. These recesses, for the collections of bric-à-brac so dear to the Victorian heart, were prominent on display cabinets for the drawing-room and even appeared in the design of the overmantel to the chimney-piece, where various little shelves were combined with a number of mirrors.

An exotic newcomer among 'styles' was that derived from Japan. This first appeared during the 1860s with the passion for collecting Japanese prints, pottery and lacquerwork. E. W. Godwin, an architect, designed furniture (c. 1880) in the Japanese style, which was characterized by narrow spindly supports to slender pieces composed of light shelves and small rectangular cupboards, sometimes carried out in ebonized wood. Furniture manufacturers in general, however, made pieces less true to the Japanese original and with less happy results. The *Furniture Gazette* in 1876 was advertising to the trade Japanese bamboo furniture (described as 'elegant') for the drawing-room, including tables and whatnots. Bamboo furniture could be made for sale at moderate prices; sometimes the bamboo was used alone, sometimes in combination with other woods.

Not only were all the above varieties of styles being followed, but also good copies of Adam, Hepplewhite and Sheraton designs in another class of work. There was of course at this time (the 1870s and 1880s) the start of the 'antique' trade, and the practice initiated by some firms of tricking up old mahogany furniture with bandings and small pateras or medallions of satinwood, to catch the current taste.

Towards the end of the era, the many gifted individual designers and craftsmen who were inspired by the Arts and Crafts Movement produced individual pieces of furniture of fine quality. Here the emphasis was on a return to hand-craftsmanship, and these designers ignored completely the great need for producing good designs which could yet be carried out by mass production methods. Their work, too, tended to be expensive for the purchaser. Notable designers included George Jack, Sydney Barnsley, W. R. Lethaby, C. R. Ashbee and Ernest Gimson. Lethaby (1857–1931) was an architect whose furniture was simple, the wood unpolished, although he did include some use of floral marquetry. Gimson (1864–1919), another architect, designed pieces which were simple and light, with some decoration of the large plain surfaces.

Art Nouveau appeared contemporaneously with the Arts and Crafts Movement, and was in effect a new style of ornament. This consisted in the main of the use of naturalistic forms, such as trees, flowers, foliage, etc., and sometimes included slim female figures, which seemed to have stepped from pictures of the pre-Raphaelite school. Translated into furniture, Art Nouveau meant the use of floral motifs, in which trees, or tulips on long thin limp stems, were the chief outcome, carried out in paint or inlay, or even applied as beaten metalwork decoration. The lines of the furniture itself might take on the character of the drawn-out curves (for example the tulip stem), unsuitable as a structural form made in wood, and hence unconvincing and weak in appearance. Charles F. Voysey (1857–1941) and Charles Rennie Mackintosh (1868–1928) were architects who designed in this style. Voysey's furniture was usually plain and designed on straight lines, often with a heart-shaped motif pierced in the back splat of a chair. Mackintosh's furniture tended to have an exaggerated slenderness, e.g. where the tall narrow uprights to chair backs gave a curious look, out of proportion, to the design. The cleavage between the artist-designer and the manufacturer was now complete, although some of the furniture designed by architects occasionally influenced design in the trade. The restrained taste shown by the architects, however, suffered some transformation, being too simple for the industry, who overloaded the original design with much ornamentation. Here the Victorian ideal of beauty, meaning ornamentation, and not fine lines and proportion, was still in force.

CHAPTER FIVE

The Twentieth Century

As the twentieth century began, some changes were taking place in domestic architecture, but new ideas in furniture were not conspicuous until the 1930s. The Second World War brought years of austerity, with 'utility' furniture only being made, and this was succeeded by a period in the 1950s when fresh stimulus began to come from abroad. In the early part of the century, many houses were being built in a new kind of 'cottage' style, with steepish roofs and gables, and a return to casement windows. In interior decoration, light-coloured wallpapers were used, in designs smaller in scale than before, whilst the woodwork was often painted white. The fireplace, with its brass-hooded iron grate, smaller now and set in a surround of coloured tiles, was surmounted by a number of open shelves and small glazed cupboards for the accommodation of ornaments. This was especially characteristic of the drawing-room and the 'best' bedroom. Rooms with casement windows, horizontal in effect and often irregularly placed, gave less opportunity than ever for a formal arrangement of furniture; indeed the rooms of the Edwardian house were as crowded as those of the Victorian had been. Cabinets, stands and numerous small tables were set about, to display quantities of bric-à-brac, 'souvenirs', photographs in silver frames, and every kind of useless object, particularly in the drawing-room and the lady's boudoir. The dining-room, because of its use, maintained the traditional orderly arrangement of dining table and chairs in the centre of the floor, with the sideboard against the wall nearest the door. Armchairs and a low settee were sometimes placed near the fireplace. Furniture for the drawing-room, sitting-room and bedroom was light-weight in appearance, whilst that for the dining-room tended to be more solid. Manufacturers continued to offer ample choice in the woods used for their furniture, but the wilder extravagances of style had more or less settled down to a type of design related to the simpler forms associated with the name of Sheraton.

The cult for collecting 'antiques' continued to increase, and after the First World War was well established. Magazines encouraged the amateur and the connoisseur alike in this pursuit, whilst the periodicals chiefly intended for women readers were making special features of articles on the decoration and furnishing of the home. Furniture trade shows had of course been held during the later Victorian period, but a new type of exhibition was introduced with the Daily Mail Ideal Home Exhibition (1908), which was held annually in London and was open to the general public. Here houses were specially built and furnished, and in addition there were special exhibits of interiors and of furniture itself. These annual shows attracted large crowds of people, many of whom might otherwise have had no chance to see current ideas, being perhaps reluctant to enter shops and see for themselves if they had no intention of buying.

During the 1930's distinctive developments were taking place in architecture with the increasing use of steel and concrete in building. The resulting style was characterized by severe clear lines bereft of decoration externally. The aspect of interiors was affected in sympathy. This meant an entirely new fashion for having rooms in which the accent was on light and space; there were large amounts of window area, walls free from too many pictures and other objects, and floors uncluttered by superfluous pieces of furniture. A craze for 'off-white' colour schemes lasted until the Second World War broke out. Architects frequently designed interiors in which fitments took the place of certain pieces of furniture, e.g. the cabinet or bookcase in the sitting-room, the sideboard in the dining-room, and the dressing table and the wardrobe in the bedroom. The more general installation of bathrooms, and the provision of wash-basins with hot and cold water in many bedrooms led to the banishment of the wash-stand and its accompanying towel horse for ever. The wood fitments, except for the wardrobe, were usually low in height and arranged along one or more walls of the room. Occasionally they took the form of a low partition, e.g. the fitment used as a sideboard might divide the dining space of a living-room from the sitting space. All these fitments were painted as part of the general colour scheme, usually very light in tone.

Garden furniture was beginning to come into its own as a particular class of furniture, now that most people began to appreciate sunshine, and the fashion for tanning oneself, or sunbathing, encouraged the spending of more of the leisure hours out of doors. In previous times, people had been content with a simple wooden seat from which to admire the view, although there was an attempt to popularize cast-iron seats in the nineteenth century. These however had mostly been used in municipal parks. In the first half of the twentieth century some developments took place, particularly between the two World Wars. Besides the plain folding deck chair and armchair, both fitted with striped canvas upholstery, there were folding metal tables, painted green. These had a hole in the circular top, through which the pole of a gaily-striped garden 'umbrella' could be thrust into the ground. Swing settees were slung from a metal frame at each end which also supported a canopy of fabric overhead. These pieces were upholstered in coloured cretonnes and chintzes printed with bright flowers.

The Second World War brought a period of austerity in which very little furniture was made, and most of it had to conform to standards of 'utility design' laid down by law. These pieces were of the plainest and most economical kind. The use of building 'board' was resorted to as much as possible in view of the shortage of timber, reserving wood for the actual structural parts, e.g. corner posts and so on. After the war, some developments took place in the 1950s, but the furniture trade in general continued as before to make quantities of 'suites' and other pieces in the usual bewildering array of designs. The kitchen, which between the wars had begun to attract the attention of the designer with regard to fitted cupboards, was now increasingly catered for. This meant not only the supply of equipment such as cookers, refrigerators and eventually dish-washers and clothes-washing machines, but also the supply of varieties of kitchen cabinets. Coloured enamel finishes were popular, and working surfaces were given heat- and water-resisting finishes. In some homes kitchen and dining-room were combined and the working space might be divided off from the dining space by a fitment which combined kitchen apparatus on one side with a type of sideboard on the other.

The 'open plan' in domestic architecture encouraged further the use of certain fittings as pseudo-partitions, separating the whole ground floor area (in extreme cases) according to use. The 'partitions', which were often partly open on both sides, therefore usurped the place of traditional storage furniture in the same way that the fitments of the 1930s had done. Not that all houses were of this kind, however; the furniture trade could continue to compete for the patronage of the public as before.

Fresh ideas in furniture design came from abroad in the mid-twentieth century, chiefly from the Scandinavian countries and Italy. Such furniture was usually very plain and rectangular in shape, sometimes veneered with exotic woods, particularly those examples imported from Denmark and Sweden. All were small in size, and tended to be low in height. Furniture from Italy tended to be more colourful, e.g. tops of tables and sideboards might be finished in imitation of marble in dark rich hues, either painted or in a plastic finish of some kind. Supports were generally slight and spindly, attracting the label of 'stick furniture' to much of this class. Other new ideas included the use of metal, painted white or in colours, for certain chair frames, and the use of synthetic rubber upholstery for seated furniture, which thus lost the clumsy look which had so often accompanied the use of internal springing.

The great popularity of television viewing after the Second World War encouraged a demand for more settees, usually comfortably low, to accommodate a number of viewers; very low tables for books, drinks and snacks accompanied these seats. It was some little time before English manufacturers adopted the new styles and ideas, which they had perforce to carry out in cheaper materials than were used for the most fashionable pieces imported from abroad. Likewise in continuing to follow certain traditional models, substitutes had to be used, for example, coloured plastics to imitate walnut veneers. Generally speaking, English furniture after c. 1950 can be described as having reached a better standard of design, on the whole simpler and more unified than during the Victorian period, but with no outstanding characteristics which could qualify it for the label of a style. With modern means of communication and methods of publicity, the newest ideas, wherever they came from, can rapidly spread about the countries of Europe and the United States of America, so that style, if any, is international.

PART TWO

Classes and Characteristics

The bedroom at Osterley Park House, Middlesex, designed by Robert Adam, c. 1775. The general colour scheme is soft olive green, with oyster-white and pale rose-pink. Late Georgian period.

CHAPTER SIX

Beds and Cradles

The bed was one of the first pieces of furniture to be made by man for his convenience and comfort, and examples of great antiquity exist today, but chiefly because they have been found in tombs. The interesting objects which came to light at various times from c. 1800 onward during excavations in Egypt readily come to mind. Something also was known about the beds used by the ancient Romans when Pompeii, which had lain buried for centuries, was rediscovered in 1745. None of this knowledge was available, however, to people in medieval England. The Romans had indeed brought something of their civilization with them when they occupied Britain, but all was lost in the dark ages which followed.

It is clear that during the Middle Ages only the very rich had beds of any consequence, lesser folk sleeping as best they could. Anything worthy of the name of furniture belonged to persons of wealth and high social position, owing to the conditions of the times. Even so, the few pieces owned by the rich were designed to be dismantled easily in case of need, due to the unsettled way of life prevailing. This particularly applied to the bed, which, judging by records in old wills and inventories, consisted of a framework to support the mattress and to carry the hangings. The hangings, in fact, were the most important part, being made of the finest and richest stuffs obtainable, such as woven tapestry, coloured damask, or even, in special cases of luxury, of cloth of gold. The bed presented the appearance of a tent, with its canopy and headboard covered with material and its matching curtains drawn close around on all three sides at night. Such beds can be seen illustrated in old manuscripts, where they are depicted standing in a kind of sitting-room. They were evidently used, with the curtains drawn back and looped up, for seats during the daytime, since chairs were not only crude in character but also very scarce. The material for the hangings must have looked extremely rich in the original brilliant hues, the design sometimes incorporating motifs from the armorial bearings of the owner. These important beds are those of which records remain, since as their

upholstery made them costly and valuable, they were carefully described in wills and inventories for the information of the heir.

Cradles for young children would seem to have been simple affairs,
woven of osier—like baskets; but for very important little personages,
such as Royal or noble infants, it is evident that cradles were provided
fully as splendid as the richly-upholstered beds of the parents.
Accounts speak of luxurious fabrics, scarlet bordered with ermine, or
cloth of gold and blue. These may well have furnished a cradle which
was no more than a plain rectangular box, swinging between two
carved posts like the one to be seen in the London Museum. Henry
VIII's infant daughter, Mary, apparently had what was almost a
miniature state bed, complete with canopy and curtains, of yellow
cloth of gold and crimson velvet, fringed with gold thread mixed with
red and blue silks. Such cradles, whether the costly one for the child
of rich parents, or the humbler one of osier used by lesser folk, stood
inside the bed-curtains at night within reach of the hand of mother
or nurse.

In early Tudor times fashions were changing, and beds were
beginning to be made with the wood framework no longer decorated
with fabric which was reserved for the hangings. Two carved posts
stood at the bottom of the bed, to help to support the top or canopy
which was made up of panels. The headboard consisted of two similar
posts connected by a row of narrow panels, four or five in number, all
fixed to the bed-frame. The panels were usually carved with ornament, especially with the contemporary linenfold design found on
other framed pieces of furniture such as the chest. Some pieces, made
of oak and dating from the early sixteenth century, still exist and
show these features. One, for example, has the headboard fitted with
five linenfold panels, whilst the posts are square in plan for the
first third of their height, carved with a kind of Gothic tracery. The
remaining two-thirds become octagonal, cut up into tiny geometrical
divisions, rather like honeycombing, giving an effect of richness. In
another bed, the upper part of the posts is octagonal and carved with
a diamond or lozenge pattern. Another piece of the period has four
long linen-fold panels in the back, and the carved posts are shaped
more like balusters. Even if the complete bed has not survived bedposts have been preserved, and some of these show the transitional
character which arose from the gradual introduction of Italian
Renaissance motifs of ornament which are seen combined with types
of design still distinctly Gothic in feeling. Another bed, of mid-
sixteenth-century date, has two rows of panels forming the headboard,

the lower carved with linenfold, but the upper row which reaches to the wooden canopy or top, has panels each containing a profile head in a shaped compartment formed by a flattish band from which spring carved fleurs-de-lys at intervals. The cornice now becomes important, and conceals the rod from which the curtains hang.

During the Elizabethan period and the early Stuart period following, the carved wooden bedstead appeared in considerable numbers, as England prospered and more people of the middle classes found themselves in easy circumstances. There was no longer any need for the bed to be ready for dismantling, and the pieces now made were almost monumental in character and richly decorated, the panelled and carved headboard at one end and the great posts at the other together supporting a framed top which was edged with elaborate cornice mouldings. The Italian Renaissance influence showed clearly, even if the original was misunderstood, in the column-like design of the posts, and the arrangement of the cornice mouldings, which displayed a version of the full classical entablature, with architrave, frieze, and cornice. Elaborate carving ornamented such pieces, at every point, and there was a certain amount of inlaid work as well in some cases. The design of the details, the ornament especially, as in other branches of the decorative and applied arts, depended on ideas taken from printed pattern books imported from Germany or the Low Countries, with their curious repertory of grotesque pilasters, arabesque ornament, strapwork patterns and the like. The characteristic bulbous feature, carved with acanthus leaves and gadrooning, constantly appeared in the design of the bedposts. These stood at the bottom of the bed, very often not attached to the bed-frame, but standing clear of it, thus allowing the curtains to be drawn round within them.

A notable development, which distinguished Elizabethan and Jacobean beds from early Tudor ones, was the elimination of bedposts as such from the structure of the bedhead or headboard. This was composed of two tiers of panels, the lower row fairly plain, since they would be hidden for the most part by the pillows, but the upper part divided into two large panels on which ornament was lavished in profusion. These panels were divided from one another by a short carved pilaster, or a scrolled terminal figure, somewhat grotesque, repeated at each side of the headboard. The panel itself was usually filled with a carved arcaded motif, perhaps also with some design inlaid in contrasting woods in the centre. Numbers of beds in this style survive, some made of oak, others of solid walnut. One such bed was made of walnut, and inlaid with holly and bog oak. It has an inlaid headboard, with dumpy carved pilasters separating the two inlaid sunk arcaded panels. The panelled top has an elaborate cornice, carved with gadrooning, and the mouldings carved with small leaves. The top is supported by two bulbous gadrooned and fluted bedposts with squarish bases and large Ionic capitals. These stand free of the bed-frame. Another bed is made of solid walnut, with a headboard of two rows of three panels each. These are inlaid with strapwork designs and are separated by eight stiles formed of terminal figures. The two detached bedposts have Corinthian-type capitals, on fluted shafts with carved vase-shaped bases. In another example, the oak headboard consists of two panels each inlaid in lighter woods with a flowering plant, and surrounded by mouldings carved with dentil and guilloche ornament. The panels are framed between three short pilasters each carved with an Ionic capital, and decorated with leafy, fluted and reeded ornament. At either end there is a short terminal figure shaped like a grotesque bird.

The most famous of all Elizabethan beds, the Great Bed of Ware, was of really gigantic width and breadth, and a whole family might well have slept in it. Now on exhibition at the Victoria and Albert Museum, this piece has elaborately carved posts and a headboard with panels each inlaid with a design of a building and garnished with fantastic carved and painted grotesques. This bed was renowned in Shakespeare's day, for Sir Toby Belch in *Twelfth Night* (Act I, Scene II), urging his timid friend Sir Andrew Aguecheek to challenge Malvolio to a duel, bids him write:

> 'as many lies as will lie in thy sheet of paper although the sheet were big enough for the bed of Ware in England'.

To realize what these wooden beds looked like originally, it is necessary to visualize the hangings and coverings with which they were furnished. The curtains and valance, perhaps of red damask or embroidered linen, hung from rods concealed within the cornice, whilst the bed itself was spread with a counterpane embroidered all over with twisted stems, enclosing all kinds of flowers, small animals and birds, in many-coloured silks and gold thread. There might be as well display pillows in bright covers embroidered in the same manner.

These great carved beds were in vogue for many years, but during the early Stuart period some great state beds were made after the old style, using much upholstery and hiding the simple wooden structure from view. A famous example still stands in one of the state

Cradle 1691

apartments at Knole, near Sevenoaks in Kent. This piece is very high, nearly reaching to the ceiling, and the entire framework, consisting of a low shaped headboard and posts supporting a canopy, is covered with red taffetas enriched with a bold strapwork appliqué design in buff-coloured silk. The canopy is covered outside and lined inside with fabric, and from it hangs a rich valance and curtains all about. Spangles, and luxurious fringes of gold and silver thread, were used to enhance the effect yet further. The bedcover and the great pillow-case match this upholstery in splendour.

Although cradles continued to be made of wickerwork many of the early Stuart period were of wood, usually oak. They resembled a simple panelled box on flattish rockers, with a kind of head at one end formed of a low back with short sides. The whole piece was framed up in simple panelling with knob-shaped finials at the ends and on the head, which were used to rock the cradle.

After the Restoration, great upholstered beds continued to be fashionable, especially for state bedrooms in Royal palaces and the houses of the rich aristocracy. It was the fashion, introduced from the Continent, for Royal personages to hold audiences and for great ladies to hold receptions, while in bed, and for these occasions what could be more fitting than such tall and luxurious pieces? In the main the general lines were simple, except for the low headboard with its more elaborate shaping. This like the cornice was upholstered, perhaps in velvet, and very fully decorated with rich tasselled fringes. Again a fine example at Knole may be mentioned. Here the bed-hangings are of cloth of gold, lined with coral satin, and are embroidered with coloured silks and gold and silver threads. Fringes enrich the curtains and valance. The feet to this bed take the form of couchant lions, a motif associated with Royalty.

The lavish use of rich upholstery was an outstanding characteristic of English furniture of the Restoration period. The inventory taken at Ham House in Surrey, in 1679, contains many descriptions of sets of hangings for beds, from which it is evident that in wealthy houses there might well be at least two sets, one for summer, one for winter, for each important bed. For example, there was at Ham House a bed which was hung with yellow damask, edged with a blue and yellow silk fringe with four sets of great yellow plumes, one set at each corner above the cornice. For this bed there was a summer set of hangings of green and white damask, embroidered with gold, silver, scarlet and black. A bed in another room at Ham was furnished with hangings of cloth of gold decorated with raised flowers of blue velvet, lined with blue satin and edged with gold fringe, the plumes being white. The second set of hangings was made of 'sad-coloured tabby' lined with 'pink satten' and edged with gold fringe. With these went plumes of pink feathers with white at the centre. The plumes which were such a charming addition to the tester or canopy (and called 'sprigges' at the time) continued to be a decorative feature of fine upholstered beds until well into the eighteenth century.

As the seventeenth century neared its close, fine beds grew taller and taller, in keeping with the exaggerated height of the state apartments of the period with their coved ceilings. The bed cornices began to show strongly-carved mouldings which gave vigour to the design. For these, damask was preferred as a covering, since its relative plainness did not interfere with the profile, crimson being the colour most in fashion. All these beds had the typical low headboard, more or less elaborately carved, with the covering fabric closely glued on. Sometimes the owner's cipher and arms or coronet, in raised work, appeared on the headboard, and perhaps on the cornice as well. The curtains hung down straight from below the valance and included, besides those close to the sides, other narrow ones about the posts at the foot, thus enclosing the bed entirely when required. Besides crimson damask, velvet might be used, figured in large repeating patterns, in red, green and gold, but less sumptuous hangings were made of needlework, done in coloured wools in bold designs on linen. A state bed of enormous height was made for the Prince and Princess of Wales (later King George II and Queen Caroline) for their state apartments at Hampton Court Palace, where it may still be seen. This measures nineteen feet to the top, which has the four typical 'carved cuppes' or vases, from which the ever-popular ostrich plumes spray out like flowering plants from a stone garden vase. Fringes, it may be noted, became less elaborate as time went on.

By mid-eighteenth century, since mahogany was gaining in popularity as the fashionable wood for furniture, the four posts supporting the traditional canopy or tester were designed to show. These slender mahogany posts stand on a small support, e.g. a diminutive cabriole leg, or a very small plinth, their tapered shafts each rising from a vase shape. The column forming the post is often fluted or may be reeded, or otherwise ornamented. The influence of the French rococo and the 'Chinese Taste' was naturally reflected to some extent in the design of beds during this period. For instance, one bed has a cornice of typical rococo curved outline, with scrolling foliage swirling freely upward, delicately carved, pierced to some extent, and gilded; the whole effect is very light and elegant. The mahogany posts are reeded, with a garland of small leaves and berries twining up the shaft.

In Chippendale's *Director* the designs for beds are generally graceful in shape and elegant in proportion, with special attention given to the bedposts, for which many ideas are drawn. Indeed, it is clear that the day of the huge bed, expressive of pomp and power, was now over, and a period of increasing refinement had set in. As an expression of the Chinese Taste, the tester could be designed like a pagoda roof, with a curly-tailed dragon perched at each corner. The back, instead of the traditional low headboard backed by a curtain, would be filled in with Chinese-style latticework, and the posts be designed to imitate bamboo. The whole would be painted (or japanned) in black, red and green, and the important details picked out in gold.

Robert Adam in due course was to design fine beds for his aristocratic clients. One Adam example, an early piece, made for Kedleston in Derbyshire, still had something of the carefree rococo feeling about it. The two posts were carved like palm-trees, with scaly bark and waving fronds, and the gilded cornice was designed in keeping, with flourishing foliage and bunches of plumes. His more characteristic neo-classical style showed itself in designs of more restraint, with simpler posts and cornice, and draperies of elegant embroidered satin or velvet. At Osterley Park House in Middlesex there may be seen the state bed made to Adam's design for the rich banker Robert Child. Here the raised dome is a prominent feature, an idea borrowed from France. The narrow posts are of satinwood, according well with the gilded canopy and its typical Adam ornament of anthemion, etc.

59

Adam was also responsible for the design of the draperies of soft olive-green velvet which, like the coverlet of oyster-colour satin, are embroidered in pinks, greens and yellows. Queen Charlotte's bed, once at Windsor Castle and now at Hampton Court Palace, shows strong evidence of Adam influence with its elegant gilded cornice and posts. Delicately embroidered satin furnishings of various colours on a golden ground complete this piece.

It will be inferred that most important beds of the later eighteenth century were gilded, but there was also a vogue for painted furniture which was of course less expensive. The famous actor David Garrick had a bedstead (c. 1775) made for his villa at Hampton in Middlesex, which later found its way to the Victoria and Albert Museum. This bed has a wooden coved tester supported in front on two reeded columns which have lotus capitals. The whole piece is painted green and yellow. For a long time this bed retained its contemporary hangings. These were of cotton (chintz) painted in colours with the so-called 'Tree of Life' designs, and comprised a deep valance under the wooden canopy, curtains at the head and sides, and a lesser valance about the feet. Such painted cotton hangings came mainly from a warehouse of the English East India Company at Masulipatam, and like similar Indian fabrics embroidered in coloured silks, enjoyed a considerable success in the eighteenth century. English people found they matched very agreeably with furniture in the Chinese Taste and in rooms hung with Chinese wallpaper, since all combined together to create the desired exotic atmosphere.

During the eighteenth century many cradles were made of wicker-work, which may have been preferred for reasons of health. If a baby had an infectious illness, a cheap wickerwork cradle could be burnt afterwards without regret. It is noticeable that when mahogany came into fashion in the middle years of the century it is in inventories seldom mentioned for cradles. Whatever the framework was made of, the fine upholstery materials and the coverlet could be relied on to give any touch of luxury that might be desired. Towards the end of the century the cradle was superseded in the fashionable world by the swinging cot. This was slung between two simple posts which were connected by one or maybe two stretchers to give stability. The sides of the cot might be of panelled wood or of canework; in some cases the sides consisted of a row of small balusters making open sides. A hood at one end might be part of the structure or be contrived of some fabric draped over a light frame. These cots swung gently at a touch of the nurse's hand, but some were fitted with a clockwork spring which could be set to swing the baby mechanically for a short time.

During the Regency period, although the four-poster bed continued in favour, there was an attempt to introduce the new 'Empire' design of bedstead from France, which was smaller in size and was often without a tester and posts attached to the framework. Some designers, e.g. Sheraton and George Smith, showed extravagant draperies which, almost independent of the bed, flowed down freely from a small dome, and were spread in lavish style to either side, often looped up again to fall once more. The bed itself was intended to stand alongside the wall, not at right angles to it. It was fitted with a low straight headboard and footboard, perhaps veneered in rosewood and ornamented sparely with brass motifs, such as the contemporary anthemion, and narrow brass lines. Some of the designs published show curious eagle-headed supports as posts to the framework, others again the cat-headed animal leg used for Regency chairs and sofas. These ornate pieces were intended to be gilded, and the draperies are coloured in strong blues, crimsons or apple greens, edged with heavy straight gold fringe. The 'Empire' style of bed and its counterpart in the 'antique' or 'Grecian' mode (i.e. with the eagles, etc.) cannot be said to have had a great appeal to ordinary English taste, which as Victoria's reign began was firmly adhering to the traditional closely-curtained four-poster. It would be many years before the English would prefer to sleep in really airy surroundings. Dickens in his *Pickwick Papers* (1836/7) describes the predicament of his hero, wandering into the wrong bedroom by mistake at the Great White Horse Inn at Ipswich. Here Mr Pickwick found himself in a double-bedded room, and for a short while concealed himself within the curtains of one of the four-posters when the rightful occupant suddenly entered. Examples may be seen represented in contemporary pictures, either the full four-poster, or the half-tester type with the curtains kept to the head of the bed only. In this latter the draperies, possibly of some dark material, e.g. red figured damask, were merely ornamental, though perhaps they kept off a certain amount of draught from the head of the sleeper. Such a piece is depicted in the bedroom scene of 'Past and Present' painted by Augustus Egg (1848).

During the Victorian period a notable innovation was the introduction of metal for bedsteads, produced by the foundries of Birmingham, especially from the 1840s onward. This was consonant with the gradual increase in mass-production of furniture. The metal tubing employed could be adapted for a variety of forms, curving or straight, freely used for the bedhead and foot, whilst it was an easy matter to have in addition a metal frame to support drapery about the whole or part only of the bed. Meanwhile wooden bedsteads of both tester and half-tester continued to be made, with a low, solid footboard of plain mahogany, and a headboard, either entirely of mahogany, or of padded upholstery. By the 1870s the *Furniture Gazette* was pointing out the advantages of 'metallic' bedsteads which it claimed were 'easily cleaned, relatively moderate in price and practically ever-lasting'. The solid iron bars or welded iron tubes, it says, are quickly bent to any combination of curves that may be desired, bound together at the junctions with a number of paterae, or other ornaments of cast-iron. These frames were then japanned or painted black, six coats being applied. The best goods were further embellished with painting: 'Filagree or floral, in gold or colours, or a combination of the two, is obtained by transfer from papers prepared with the designs.' The garments of the women workers in the factory were witnesses to the colours in use: black, green, bronze, chocolate, blue and violet.

Papier-mâché, another material in use for Victorian furniture, might be employed for the head- and footboards of a bedstead. One of mid-nineteenth-century date has such panels, cut in an eccentric wavy outline, and decorated with polychrome ornament. At the head is a half-tester with a deep valance and back and side curtains. As the nineteenth century went on even wood bedsteads became less massive in appearance. Instead of having a solid panel the ends began to be constructed of narrow wooden bars topped with a wooden rail, horizontal or curved. This was perhaps due to the influence of the metal bedstead design, but it was also in line with the development of furniture design in general, inspired by the current so-called 'Sheraton style'.

The manufacturer was now making 'bedroom suites', shown in trade magazines as including dressing table (i.e. a chest of drawers with a swing toilet mirror fixed above), wash-hand stand and wardrobe. These were made in woods of varying quality, sometimes in a cheap wood stained to imitate the dearer satinwood or mahogany. A bedstead of wood might be bought to go with this suite, or a metal one independent of it. By the end of the century at least one design for a bedroom shows furniture of mahogany, with what looks like some satinwood marquetry decoration, the bedstead having a head and foot of narrow vertical brass bars with a half-tester lightly draped with

Metal bedstead. c. 1875

pale green hangings. The whole scene has an air of spaciousness and light, with light colours for the wallpaper and the carpet.

Meanwhile, in the nineteenth-century nursery world, some impressive cradles and swinging cots had been made for certain important little people. A very notable example is to be seen in the London Museum, a royal loan. This is a swing cot, shaped like a boat and cosily padded inside, mounted on a mahogany framework decorated with gold leaf. Overhead is a semicircular frame from which hang curtains of green satin, which can either be looped back or drawn closely together. This piece (1840) was made for the birth of Queen Victoria's first child, the Princess Royal (later Empress of Germany), and was used for others of Victoria's children, then passed to Alexandra, Princess of Wales, and eventually to Mary, Duchess of York, later Queen Mary.

Some designs for wooden cradles on rockers appeared in the catalogue of the Great Exhibition (1851); the curved and bulging sides are shown entirely covered with ornament, doubtless intended to be carved. Elaborate pieces of this type can hardly be taken as characteristic examples of the Victorian period, when many quite simple cots and cradles were in use, as can easily be seen in the illustrations in children's books of the time. Occasionally a more remarkable cradle was made, such as the one designed by the architect Norman Shaw (1831–1912) for the baby son of another architect, Alfred Waterhouse. This cradle is mounted on a fairly substantial

63

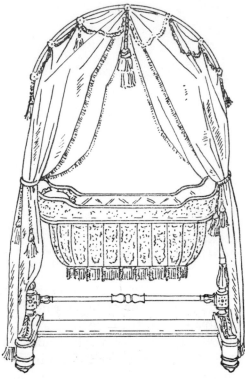

Swing cot. Early Victorian

wooden framework, and has panelled sides and hood with a painted and gilded decoration including floral sprays and signs of the Zodiac. By the time of the Edwardian period, it was common enough to have the type of cot (which did not swing) known as a bassinet. This had a very light framework, all entirely hidden by the frilly muslin draperies, decorated with bows of ribbon, which covered the sides and made a canopy at one end.

By the beginning of the twentieth century beds had, generally speaking, assumed a modern appearance, and after the First World War became much as they are today. In the 1920s single beds, which had made a rare appearance earlier, became more common, and bedsteads were mainly lower than formerly, the mattress being placed on a much lower framework. Four-posters were abandoned, except by people with romantic inclinations, who either bought them secondhand as 'antiques' or from shops which stocked reproductions of old furniture. The divan type of bed (i.e. without the conventional head and foot) both single and double size became very popular. Sometimes the divan bed was associated with the fitments which in some houses or flats, in order to save space, were fashionable instead of traditional furniture. In such a case the divan might be placed against a designed fitment, consisting of a large shaped piece of wood supporting a shelf or shelves for a reading lamp, combined with a bedside cupboard. These developments reflected changes in domestic planning. Houses for most classes were now smaller in size, and with lower ceilings than those of the Victorian period.

Some manufacturers, however, produced rather luxurious furniture with an eye to the extravagant purchaser, such as some famous film star, for whom a richly-furnished home which could be illustrated in the current periodicals was excellent publicity. These pieces might be made in rich veneers, and in the case of the beds might have much heavy padding to the headboard and foot, covered with expensive-looking fabric, either a real silk or printed glazed chintz, or one of the new artificial textiles. Chromium-plated tubing which had a short success in the 1930s was chiefly used for chairs and light tables, and was less happy for bedsteads.

Children's cots during these years chiefly took the form of a small bed, mounted fairly high off the floor on stick-like legs fitted with castors, and surrounded on all four sides by a 'railing' of simple turned spindles. This railing was high enough to prevent the baby, or even the small child when it could stand, from falling out. One long side could usually be adjusted to drop down when mother or nurse was attending to the baby or making up the little bed. The open nature of the design allowed for plenty of fresh air, but other cots of the bassinet type were occasionally in use with the frilly curtains forming a sheltering canopy. In the mid-twentieth century, a novelty was the introduction of bunks for children; these were modelled on ship's bunks with two beds arranged one above the other in one structure, but as a movable piece of furniture. These bunks may be delightful fun for the young occupants, but the difficulties of changing the linen and of daily bed-making are obvious. The declared object is the saving of space.

After the Second World War, with its years of austerity and extremely limited production, bedsteads were once again manufactured in every conceivable design, the four-poster excepted. This can be seen in shop windows any day when strolling down the chief shopping streets of any city or town.

CHAPTER SEVEN

Chests

In the Middle Ages and until the design of cupboards and chests of
drawers began to be developed during the seventeenth century, the
chest was a most important piece of furniture for storage. Indeed, in
medieval times it was the principal article of furniture in the home
where it served various purposes, as table, seat and travelling trunk.
It was above all a necessity for the safe keeping of clothing and
household gear, besides any documents, jewellery, money and other
articles of value. His most prized possessions were usually kept by
the master of the household in a chest in his own bedroom, and might
include silver cups for drinking wine, silver-gilt ceremonial salt for
dining in the hall, the spoons and his wife's best household linen.
These early chests were made of solid oak, perhaps ornamented with a
little carving, such as Gothic tracery, and were notable for their
great iron hinges and the fearsome nature of the locks by which the
owner tried to secure his goods from theft. Early names for these
pieces of furniture included ark, coffer, hutch and standard. The term
hutch appears to have been interchangeable with chest, but was also
apparently applied to a chest-like sort of cupboard. The coffer was no
more than a small chest and the term standard might refer to a very
large one, perhaps used for travelling.

All early types of chest fall into three categories, the primitive
kind which were hollowed out of the tree trunk and then bound with
iron to keep the shape, and secondly those with the solid front and
back rebated into the ends which were arranged as feet, thus keeping
the body of the piece off the ground. This latter type may be designated 'boarded', and continued to be made until the early seventeenth
century. The third type, consisting of framed panels joined together,
dates from the thirteenth century, and was made in various styles
until chests were finally superseded by chests of drawers, cabinets
and other furniture for the storage of clothes.

Chests made from hollowed tree trunks hardly permitted of ornamentation, but the boarded type was often decorated on the front.
Chests which survive from the fifteenth century show decoration

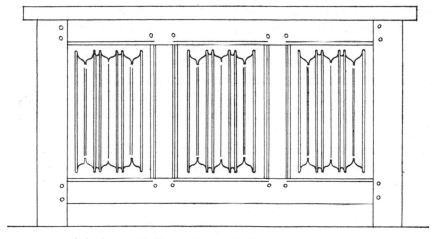

Oak chest with linenfold panels. Early sixteenth century

gouged out of the solid, and representing Gothic tracery. This ornament may be simple and perhaps associated with geometrical roundels,
or may very faithfully copy full tracery designs with all the details
of cusping seen in contemporary masonry or woodwork. By the early
sixteenth century, framed chests often had the long front divided
into two, and later three, panels. For these the carved linenfold
ornament so popular in interior decoration was the obvious choice.
By 1500 the framed chest consisted of four posts which acted as legs,
connected by horizontal rails which, with the vertical stiles, were all
joined together by mortise-and-tenon construction. This was further
secured by small oak pegs, or dowels, which show on the surface, and
which indicate the position of the tenons. Into these structural members which frequently bore scratched mouldings the panels themselves
were slotted. The top might be formed of one piece of timber, or of
planks tongued and grooved together. These chests which were of a
skilled type of construction were the work of the joiner, so were
frequently referred to in contemporary documents as 'joyned chests'.
Another term was 'wainscot chest', an allusion to the panelled front
no doubt, since the panelled walls of rooms were very often called
wainscoted. At this time it was the front panels which received the
ornamentation. This might take the form of linenfold carving, but
some examples show the contemporary influence of Italian Renaissance motifs. The profile bust, perhaps in a lozenge shape or roundel,
which appeared in interior decoration was occasionally carved on the
panels.

During the sixteenth century, and the early seventeenth, wealthy

67

people owned more impressive pieces of furniture, mostly imported from Flanders. These foreign pieces were made of such woods as spruce, cedar or cypress, which were thought to protect from moth the furred gowns and woollen clothes they contained. It is more rare to find mention in inventories of chests from Italy, although it seems that the Earl of Leicester, favourite of Queen Elizabeth I, had at Kenilworth one from Venice, which was of 'walnut tree carved and gilt'.

In Shakespeare's play *The Taming of the Shrew*, the old wooer Gremio, anxious to secure the young Bianca as his wife, boasts of his possessions:

'My house within the city
Is richly furnished with plate and gold:
Basins and ewers to lave her dainty hands;
My hangings all of Tyrian tapestry;
In ivory coffers I have stuff'd my crowns;
In cypress chests my arras counterpoints,
Costly apparel, tents, and canopies,
Fine linen, Turkey cushions boss'd with pearl. . . .'

The ivory coffer Shakespeare envisaged would be more like a small box, but the cypress chests he speaks of would have kept company with the English ones of oak, which stood in the parlour and bed-chamber. One such piece, still to be seen today with several others in the Victoria and Albert Museum, is of oak, richly carved. The two front posts are partly fluted, matching the two stiles which divide the front into three panels. The panels themselves are decorated with applied carving in the form of arcading surrounded by mouldings carved with egg-and-dart. The top and bottom rails are carved with a sunk 'thumb' motif, repeated like fluting. The side and back panels are plain, like the top.

In a class by itself is the so-called 'Nonsuch' type of chest, popular during the late sixteenth century. These were distinguished for the use of elaborate inlay to the front which was normally divided into two panels. Each panel was decorated with a fanciful representation of a building, with battlements, towers, turrets and cupolas, and with weather vanes and flags flying from the roof at various points. These might be set in an applied architectural frame, rather like a triumphal arch complete with pediment. The whole design was divided, in lieu of the conventional stiles, by very narrow panels of inlay, decorated with a little turret crowned with a steeple flying a pennant. This

architectural scene resembled the inlaid decoration sometimes seen
on the panels of Elizabethan bedheads, for example on the Great
Bed of Ware. The building represented did not necessarily bear a
factual resemblance to Henry VIII's luxurious Palace of Nonsuch in
Surrey, celebrated for the extravagant richness of its appointments,
which was dismantled and destroyed in the Restoration period. The
design in fact owed its origin to the pattern books of the Low Countries, but the term 'Nonsuch' is accepted as a convenient one descriptive of this unusual type of chest.

An oak chest, a characteristic piece of the early seventeenth
century, has four panels in the front, tenoned and mortised into the
stiles, rails and posts. The panels are inlaid with holly and bog oak
in a formalized design of tulips and leaves, the effect enhanced by the
contrasting light and dark tones of the inlay. Applied mouldings surround the panels, and the stiles and front posts are simply treated.
The bottom rail has the 'thumb' type of carving, but the frieze rail
is more elaborate with formal flower rosettes alternating with lozenge
shapes. The top is made of three long pieces of wood, and inside there
is a small lidded box suspended at one end. These boxes are presumed
to have been used for the rather large gauntlet gloves of the period.
An interesting entry may be noted in the very full inventory taken
of the contents of Tart Hall (1641), the London home of the Earl of
Arundel. This records a wooden chest containing some 'Joyners
Tooles', which had 'a little Box therein' which also had some tools in
it. A number of other chests listed include 'a great Dutch Chest'
which was covered with leather, six of which were painted (though no
details are given) and another 'of Mother of Pearle' which is described
as a trunk but cannot have been very large.

Some surviving examples of the early seventeenth century show
quite elaborate ornamentation. For instance, the posts and stiles may
be carved with wavy leafy stems, enclosing rosettes, or with scrolling
and interlacing bands forming alternate square and round compartments. The top and bottom rails may be carved with repeating
lunettes formed of floral scrolls. The guilloche repeating pattern may
also appear as ornamentation. An oak chest, dated 1637, which still
survives, is said to have been made for the Hobson family, tenant
farmers on Lord Yarborough's estate in Lincolnshire. The front has
had a great deal of carving lavished on it, but in very low relief. The
front has four panels, each end one having a formal symmetrical
design of narrow leaves and a pomegranate, the other two carved with
a stem bearing formal rose-petalled flowers and leaves like those of

the tongue fern. The three stiles are carved with a scrolling vine pattern, and the front posts with a formal design of rosettes in circles, with foliage. The bottom rail is carved with lunettes, but the frieze rail has scrolling foliage and grapes. An incised inscription spread about either side of the key escutcheon reads: THIS · IS · ESTHER · HOBSONNE · CHIST. 1637.

Inscriptions recording the name of the owner and a date were not uncommon during this period, not only on chests but on other pieces of furniture.

Not all chests of the early Stuart era were panelled, for some might have the sides made up of boards. An example made of elm has a lengthy inscription on it, including the name James Griffin and the date 1639, running around the base, the lower edge of which is cut about in a shaping which raises it a little from the ground, there being no posts to perform this function. All the carving is in very flat shallow relief, consisting of bands of gryphons and scrollwork enclosing lozenges filled with foliage. The ends are carved in similar taste. Traces of red and green paint are just discernible. In a chest of mid-seventeenth-century date the general framework is simple, the posts, rails and stiles merely being decorated with grooved mouldings, but the three front panels have been painted in colours on a white ground. The design consists of a two-handled vase with a small neck, in which sprays of flowers, roses, tulips and carnations are arranged in a flat and formal manner.

A new development was on the way, however, which was to cause striking changes, and was eventually to remove the chest from the important position it had held in the household for so many centuries. This was the introduction of the drawer which, pulling in and out, was not only much easier to manage than the heavy chest lid, but also allowed more convenient arrangement of the contents. At first the drawer appeared below the lidded chest proper forming one piece with it. This is noticeable particularly after the Restoration. One or two examples, veneered in walnut in the prevailing style, show a light piece of furniture perhaps only about three feet wide, the upper part having a lid like a chest, the lower fitted with a drawer and the whole mounted on four curved supports connected by flat, curved stretchers forming a light stand. According to the Royal Wardrobe accounts (1700/1) a small clothes chest of this kind was provided for William III by the cabinet-maker Gerrit Jensen (or Garret Johnson), which was veneered with walnut and given a quilted lining, 'For H.M.'s little Bedchamber'.

Chest veneered with walnut and decorated with marquetry, with drawer in base. Restoration period c. 1675

It is true that some oak chests continued to be made, perhaps decorated with split-baluster turned ornament applied to the stiles, but the taste for huge pieces of furniture was being superseded everywhere by the liking for furniture of more elegance in size and proportion. Furthermore, the chest of drawers was quite adequate for storing articles of clothing, the graduated size of the drawers allowing for what might be called in modern language a kind of filing system. There remained, however, the question of storage of blankets and other bulky household stuff. Such things might either be kept in chests inherited from earlier times, or be placed in chests which had more of an air of fashion, being finished in lacquerwork of black and gold in contemporary style. One of this type may still be seen at Hampton Court Palace.

During the 1730s William Kent, who essayed the design of important furniture and was inspired by Venetian styles, was responsible for a limited revival of the chest as a fashionable piece of furniture. These pieces resembled closely the Italian cassone, shaped like a sarcophagus with its bulging curved sides, and were decorated profusely with suitable carved ornament, finely gilded. They were intended to stand in the great rooms of state in the houses of grandees, and stood, moreover, quite apart from the general run of furniture in use during the first half of the eighteenth century. Like other pieces by Kent, they were in fact part of the whole interior decoration

71

scheme. Such chests, from their size and weight, may well remind one of the legendary fate of Ginevra, the young Italian bride who for a frolic hid herself in a great chest or cassone and perished there, for the lid was too heavy to raise from inside. The Italian marriage coffer, intended to contain the bride's dower, thus became on one tragic occasion her tomb.

The commode, introduced from France and fashionable during the later years of the eighteenth century, took the place of the chest as an imposing piece of furniture in reception rooms, with the chest of drawers firmly established as primarily a useful object about the house. Although Chippendale describes one of his designs as being for a 'Dressing Chest and Bookcase', it is in fact a chest of drawers and not a chest which forms the lower part of the piece. The chest therefore ceased to be a notable piece of furniture for many years. A humble version was used, made often of deal boards (not panelled) and painted and grained to resemble mahogany, during the Victorian period. This type, placed in remote parts of the house, served for the storage of blankets and travelling rugs, or for the hoarding of objects which no one liked to throw away, and has in more modern times yielded up some astonishing treasures.

Some revival of the chest as a respectable piece of furniture took place during the twentieth century, due no doubt to the current interest in 'antiques'. Some were made as bedroom or hall furniture during the 1930s, perhaps in limed oak. Framed up in panels, they presented a much smaller and very simplified version of the traditional Elizabethan or Jacobean chest. The craze for 'antiques' also encouraged, to a limited extent, the making of somewhat larger examples in carved oak or plain mahogany, which had something of a 'period' look about them. These could often take up a dignified position in the hall of the suburban house, where they were perhaps useful for storing a miscellaneous collection of articles, e.g. tennis racquets, croquet mallets and so on. Some perhaps fulfilled the traditional function of storing blankets but as households diminished in size the amount of household gear was likewise reduced, until by the mid-twentieth century with the provision wherever possible of built-in storage accommodation to save space, the chest became once again but a rare survival, and its honourable history seems to have come finally to an end except in large institutions.

CHAPTER EIGHT

Tables

The history of the table began with the forthright piece of furniture used for meals in the medieval hall and even used by retainers for sleeping on at night, and as time went on it included tables of all shapes and sizes with many ingenious ideas being incorporated in their design. From artists' tables to writing tables, from console tables to tripod tables, a range of furniture was devised, especially in the centuries after the Restoration, which was based on the simple principle of a flat board mounted on a number of legs or some kind of central support. The changing styles which gave character to furniture at different periods were expressed in the design of the table whatever its purpose, chiefly in the shape of its supports and in the decorative motifs introduced in the treatment of the costly pieces.

The table was one of the very few pieces of furniture in use in the Middle Ages. In the great hall of the castle or manor house, where the company assembled for meals, a number of long tables were needed to accommodate everyone. Whilst the hall continued to be the main living-room for most of the household, it was convenient for these early dining tables to be of the trestle type, so that when required, the loose tops which rested by their sheer weight on their supports could together with these be dismantled and removed. Such pieces, usually made of solid oak, were severely practical and no pains were taken with their embellishment. The trestle was in effect a solid baulk of timber resting on four flat crosspieces which served as feet and steadied it on the floor. A little crude crocketing was sometimes used in the shaping of the upright. The top was long and relatively narrow, made of immense planks of timber forming a continuous board. The table on the dais, reserved for the master of the house, his wife and children and special guests, appears to have been a modest affair, also probably of the trestle type.

An advance was made as times became more settled, and with more refined ways of living a special parlour was set aside for dining in the early Tudor period. This encouraged the gradual establishment of a table made with fixed supports, as the need for clearing the floor from

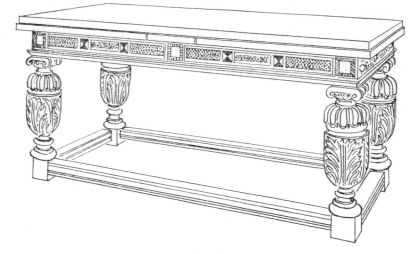

Draw table inlaid with holly and bog oak. c. 1600

time to time ceased to be a necessity. A fixed or framed table, i.e. a rectangular top supported on four or more legs connected by stretchers all 'joined' together, came into common use by the mid-sixteenth century, although it is evident that it was some time before the trestle table was finally superseded.

In the late Tudor and early Stuart periods the dining table was often a magnificent piece of furniture, and the draw table variety with its extending top was a great favourite for the dining parlour. The legs were usually of baluster or bulbous form; the bulbous shape was often richly carved with gadrooning and acanthus leaves. They were united by solid stretchers which, being close to the floor, served as foot rests. The frieze was usually enriched with ornament, for example carved with lunettes, or, which was rarer, inlaid with light and dark woods. In most cases oak was employed for all parts, except the top which was often made of elm boards. One table, of c. 1600 date, has a draw or extending top, with the frieze rail inlaid in chequer pattern in sycamore and bog oak. The heavy baluster legs have a type of Ionic capital over a bulbous-shaped body which is carved with acanthus and gadrooning. The low straight connecting stretchers are slightly moulded. The top can be extended in the usual manner by pulling out an extra leaf at each end. In well-to-do households these long dining tables were covered between meals either with a Turkey carpet imported from abroad, or with a long 'table carpet' of English needle-work in tent stitch closely resembling tapestry, or with a velvet fabric

74

finished with a fringe, all of which can be seen in many portraits of the period.

The longer framed tables which might be used in the hall, naturally required six or possibly more legs, in proportion to their length and the need for stability. Some of these longer tables were called shuffle or shovel boards, and in fact were used for a game which seems to have been the ancestor (a giant one) of the modern shove ha'penny. These shovel boards were marked at one end with a number of transverse lines, and might be fitted with a tiny till or box at the end edge. A fine example, thirty feet long, can at present be seen at Littlecote in Wiltshire. Sometimes these shovel boards were placed in the long gallery of Elizabethan and Jacobean houses. A dining table of mid-seventeenth-century date which still survives, is of oak and is just over nine feet in length. The front frieze rail is carved in flat relief with lunettes enclosing acanthus, and the six legs are of turned baluster form connected by stretchers.

Some small tables were also in use, chiefly in parlours, on which boxes, books or other objects could be placed. These occasional tables might have round, oval or octagonal tops which were supported on bulbous legs of a slender type, perhaps fluted. Folding tables, fitted with a flap supported on the gate-leg principle, were in use at the end of the sixteenth century. One example of the early Stuart period has an octagonal top when the flap is raised on a gate-leg support; the main framework consists of four neat bulbous legs connected by a shelf near the ground, almost a half-octagon in plan and obviously designed to stand against the wall most of the time. Another small table with a hinged folding top is semi-circular when closed, and is supported on three turned baluster legs, like plain columns, connected by stretchers. The deep frieze, containing a compartment, is decorated with a strapwork pattern carved in shallow relief. At this time the court cupboard with its open shelves fulfilled the function of a side table, or sideboard table, in most houses.

By the middle of the seventeenth century the gate-leg table with its round or oval top had become established. One such piece has an oval top when extended, the narrow centre portion being fixed at each end to a broad upright support which rests on a trestle-type foot. A broad flat stretcher connects these two feet and into it swings the 'gate' on each side, which consists of slender turned baluster legs and stretchers.

During the later Stuart period the fashion came in for the company to dine at a number of small tables instead of at the traditional long rectangular one. For this purpose the folding table, with its round or oval top supported on a single 'gate' or double 'gates' at each side, was very suitable. The legs were now mostly of the spiral-turned type connected by spiral-turned stretchers, not so close to the floor as formerly. The frieze rail was mostly plain without carving, and a drawer was occasionally fitted into it at the 'end' (in the closed position). These tables were made of oak or solid walnut.

The increased refinement in ways of living introduced after the Restoration was reflected in the provision of many more tables, small rectangular ones being found useful or decorative, either for the centre of a room or at the sides. The most fashionable pieces were made of walnut and decorated with floral marquetry. A typical example of the Restoration period would have a rectangular top with two drawers fitted into the frieze, and would be supported on four spirally-turned legs with bun feet connected by flat curved stretchers. Each drawer front would be ornamented with two small panels of floral marquetry and the top might either be entirely covered in this manner, or be divided by bands of oyster-piece veneer into a central oval and four corner panels.

More costly tables were decorated with silver, either wholly covered or decorated with plaques, ornamented with repoussé work. Sometimes these very decorative tables were made *en suite* with a pair of stands matching a looking-glass and two sconces on the wall behind. A very notable set of silver furniture of this kind is to be seen at Knole, in Kent. John Evelyn remarked in his diary (1683) on the elaborate silver furniture in the apartments of the Duchess of Portsmouth at Whitehall. At Ham House near Richmond there are various decorative tables, including a fine piece described in the 1675 inventory as 'one ebony table garnished with silver'. Various ornamental plaques of silver ornament the top; the design of the central plaque incorporates the initials 'E. D.' with a countess's coronet. The motif signifies Elizabeth Dysart, Countess of Dysart in her own right, and dates therefore from before her marriage with the Duke of Lauderdale in 1672. The table is mounted on four caryatid supports, partly gilded, and has carved and gilded apronwork under the frieze rail on each side. The treatment of the caryatid legs bears a strong resemblance to contemporary French design.

Plainer tables fitted with drawers, and obviously intended for use rather than show, were also made; those of the seventeenth century were supported on the tapered baluster leg which had now superseded the spirally-turned support. The legs were connected by shaped

76

stretchers, and a finial was placed at the crossing or other salient point. Some small plain tables were made with folding tops and might be of solid oak or veneered with walnut. One example of the period is half-oval in plan, the hinged top resting when extended on two gates at the back. The framework, or frieze, is deep and fitted with three small drawers and two small sliding trays. Five turned tapered legs support the piece, the three front ones being united by flat shaped stretchers, and the feet are hoof-shaped. Another, of oak, has a very narrow rectangular folding top supported when extended on two hinged legs. These fit into the framework when closed, and all six legs are of baluster shape ending in ball feet. The two drawers have each a brass drop handle.

Towards the end of the century some fine, even if small, tables appeared, which were carved and gilded in the contemporary Louis XIV style, including the use of the S-scroll shape for the legs. One such can be seen in the State Apartments of William of Orange at Hampton Court Palace, and is said to have been the work of John Pelletier, refugee Huguenot craftsman, in 1690. A typical example in this style, of late seventeenth-century date, has a top with a finely-moulded edge and an elaborate carved and pierced apron below the frieze rail. The legs are of elaborated baluster form, the caps being carved with light gadrooning and delicate foliage introduced else-where. The vase-shaped finial is similarly treated and is placed where the foliated scrolled cross stretchers rise to the centre.

From this time onward most decorative tables were usually gilded, and the fashion of adding a marble or scagliola top was introduced. The material for this was generally imported from Italy. Those gilded tables which were intended, as the majority were, to stand between the tall windows of some important reception room, were, for the next hundred years or so, to be referred to as pier tables. The accompanying mirror placed on the wall above was known as a pier glass. As the cabriole leg gradually became fashionable it was used for supports to tables. A walnut piece, characteristic of the transitional period, has eight legs of the pied-de-biche type, and the size of the octagonal top suggests it was intended as a dining table. It has no stretchers.

During the Queen Anne and early Georgian period card tables were made in increasing numbers, specially for playing at cards. Formerly any folding table served the purpose. These newer card tables had folding rectangular tops, with circular corners where doubtless a candle could stand at one's elbow, by which to examine one's hand at play. The cabriole legs were simple and there might be

77

some shell or acanthus motif carved on the knee, or none at all; they were usually finished with a plain spade or club foot. Fine walnut veneer decorated the flat surfaces, whilst the inner sides of the top were normally lined with a fabric to prevent the cards from slipping in play. This inner surface also usually had a small 'dished' oval well for money or counters, since gambling was much indulged in by English-men, and by women too for that matter. No stretchers were used, and the two back legs were hinged on the back frieze rail to move out and support the table when the top was fully extended. When closed, this card table stood back against the wall and served as a side table. As mahogany came more into use the card table top had squared corners, and the cabriole leg was sometimes more elaborately carved and ended in the fashionable claw-and-ball foot. Card tables do not appear to have been made in such quantities after the middle of the eigh-teenth century as in the first half.

Small tables for tea or to show off porcelain were made from c. 1730 onward. The top was circular, supported on a central column with tripod feet of cabriole form ending in one of the current shapes, claw-and-ball, club or paw. In old accounts this type of table was usually referred to as a 'claw' table, or a 'pillar and claw'. A certain type of small rectangular table is thought to have been used as a lady's dressing table. The piece was mounted on four cabriole legs, and it had three drawers, the central one being shallow to allow the framework to be shaped to rise a little, thus accommodating the knees of the person seated at the table. In eighteenth-century pictures showing a lady seated at her 'toilet' (the old name for this furniture) it is impossible to see the shape of the dressing table, as it is depicted fully draped with a frilled 'skirt' of some light material which also ornaments, and partly obscures, the easel-type toilet glass standing on the table top.

In the early eighteenth century some decorative tables were of the 'console' type, i.e. the small top, often of marble, was supported on a carved and gilded bracket which might take the form of a dolphin or of a winged eagle mounted on a small plinth. These console tables were mostly used as pier tables. In the 1730s William Kent sponsored the design of some very elaborate side tables, the design of the sup-ports for the front 'legs' often being derived from heraldic animals with an intricate mass of carved apronwork between. Sphinxes, dogs, wolves and the copious use of carved swags, forming supports and underframing, made these pieces not only impressive to look at but also practically impossible to move, especially if the whole table was mounted on a plinth. Some of these tables might be painted to suggest

Console table in the style of William
Kent. c. 1730

white marble, but fine gilding was usually preferred by makers
working in this style; a gorgeously-coloured top of red marble, or in
a brilliant design of mosaic or scagliola, completed the effect of splendour.

Some gilded tables of the early eighteenth century were enriched
with gesso work where the carved ornament required specially delicate treatment. Furniture supplied in 1714–1715 for Hampton Court
Palace for 'the Prince & Princess of Wales' Privy Chamber' included
a small table finished in this way, the top decorated with a strapwork
design incorporating the Garter, royal crown and the double cipher
'G. R.' This piece was signed by Moore, partner in the firm of Gumley
and Moore. Another table supplied by them 'for dittos Bedchamber'
was described in their bill as having an 'Indian' top. Today this top can
be seen to be an incised lacquer panel in polychrome of green, blue,
red and white, with touches of gold. The square legs are ornamented
with scrolled motifs in gesso, and have lion paw feet. Both tables were
supplied along with a pair of matching stands, the bill in the first
case being £45 for the set, whilst for the set 'with Indian tops' the
charge was £50.

Needless to say many people had to be satisfied with less decorative
furniture. Walnut or mahogany side tables with cabriole legs, with
or without the carved apronwork, were made; by the Chippendale
period they were becoming less imposing in style than Kent's pieces.
The construction became lighter, and if the top was of marble this was
thinner than before.

The name library table is given to the piece which consisted of a
top laid over two pedestals of drawers. The mahogany was often
enlivened by the gilding of the carved enrichments.

The effervescent nature of the styles prevailing during the mid-
Georgian or rococo period brought a charming variety into the design

of tables—breakfast tables, china tables, pier tables, side tables and tea tables. The exception was the dining table which was once again rectangular in plan but was given a very plain framework. Perhaps the fact that the tablecloth would hide so much of the table discouraged cabinet-makers and the carvers, who lavished such pains on other work, from paying much attention to this piece of furniture. The dining table was usually designed to be used for different numbers of people in company, but the draw principle so popular at an earlier period was not revived. Two side tables, each with a folding leaf, could be placed end to end with these leaves meeting in the middle. Another device was to put together three portions, i.e. a centre table with folding leaves would be placed between two plain ones which might be nearly semicircular in plan. These last two tables could, again, be used as side tables when not required for dining. The 'sideboard table' for which designs appeared in Chippendale's *Director* (1754) had a plain rectangular top supported on square legs, or might be more fanciful with rococo details such as a fretwork frieze rail, introduced into the design. More elaborate than the foregoing were the console tables and pier tables in the full rococo manner. Here the top was often shaped, and the supports shaped in double C-scroll outline linked by a short elaborate rococo stretcher, the whole piece being charged with rocaille, foliated C-scrolls and other rococo motifs. These tables had none of the monumental massiveness characteristic of the Kent manner. Nearly all were finely gilded.

Designs for china or tea tables had rectangular tops (sometimes of the tray-top type which had appeared a little earlier) on elegant cabriole legs ending in French scroll feet. Sometimes a delicate gallery of fretwork edged the veneered mahogany top. In some tables the plan of the top might be serpentine, or broken-front. The circular tripod table, also used as a tea table, often had a 'pie-crust' edge to the top, reminiscent of the rich borders of the contemporary silver salver, and the pillar rose from a vase carved with acanthus foliage which sometimes was also used on the feet, now ending in a French scroll or volute. These tables looked very handsome when the top was tipped into the vertical position and the piece was put against the wall. One mahogany table of this type has a circular top in which the edges are scalloped, and carved lightly with flowers, fruit and foliage, and C-scrolls, spaced at intervals. The baluster support is decorated with floral motifs in low relief and the feet still have the original leather castors.

Elizabethan and early Stuart period: buffet of carved oak with two griffin supports and two bulbous supports, and the middle shelf carved with nulling. Early seventeenth century.

Late Stuart period: cabinet on stand, with marquetry of walnut and other woods. c. 1680.

Queen Anne and early Georgian period: bureau-cabinet of red and gold lacquer. Early eighteenth century.

Mid-Georgian period: Chippendale design for two pier glasses. 1754.

Regency period: secretaire, of rosewood inlaid with satinwood, and furnished with mounts of gilt brass. c. 1810.

Victorian period: corner of the Victorian Room at the Geffrye Museum,
London. 1850.

Twentieth century: unit furniture, usable as space divider in modern
'open-plan' type of house.

Bedstead of carved oak. 1590.

Bedstead with crimson and white draperies. c. 1695.

Bedstead, of wood painted green and yellow with contemporary Indian hangings of painted cotton, from David Garrick's villa at Hampton, Middlesex. c. 1775.

Bedstead with papier-mâché panels. c. 1850.

92

Above: chest of carved and gilt gesso. c. 1720.

Above left: chest of oak, carved with linenfold decoration. Early sixteenth century.

Left: chest of oak, inlaid with holly and bog oak in a floral design. Early seventeenth century.

Above: gate leg table of oak. Later
seventeenth century.

Above right: table of mahogany. Early
eighteenth century.

Right: folding card table, veneered with
walnut. Early eighteenth century.

94

Tripod table of mahogany. Mid-eighteenth century.

Table of carved mahogany with scagliola top. c. 1740.

Dining table of mahogany carved with fluting. c. 1775.

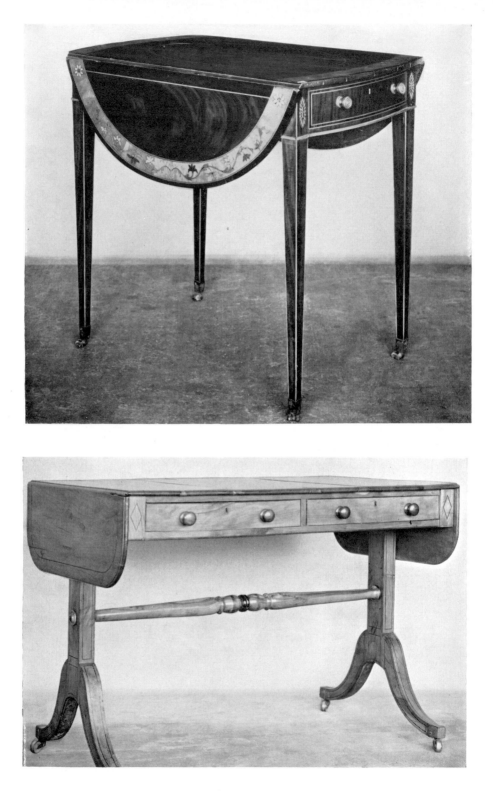

Above: chair of 'thrown' or turned oak, archaic type. Possibly c. 1600.

Above left: Pembroke table of painted satinwood. Later eighteenth century.

Left: sofa table of yew, inlaid with dark lines. Early nineteenth century.

Armchair of oak inlaid with cherry, holly and bog oak. c. 1600.

Armchair of carved walnut with caned back and seat. c. 1685.

Armchair of carved beechwood with needlework cover. c. 1675.

Chair of walnut with caned seat and back. Later seventeenth century.

Above: chair of mahogany with interlacing splat. Mid-eighteenth century.

Above right: settee of mahogany, in the
'Chinese' taste. c. 1760.

Right: settee design (called a sofa) by
Chippendale. c. 1760.

Armchair of carved mahogany with needlework cover. c. 1760.

Above left: chair of walnut, with cabriole legs and paw feet. Early eighteenth century.

Above right: Windsor chair in 'Gothic' taste. c. 1770.

Left: armchair of walnut with Prince-of-Wales feathers in the back. Late eighteenth century.

Left: chair. c. 1795.

Below left: armchair of beech painted black and partly gilt. c. 1810.

Right: chair of rosewood inlaid with brass. Early nineteenth century.

Below: armchair. Early Victorian.

Below right: chair of oak designed by C. R. Macintosh. c. 1899.

Left: occasional chair, black metal frame and latex foam upholstery, designed by Robin Day, RDI, FSIA. c. 1959.

Below: four-seater settee and tub chair with beech frame and foam cushions, designed by Robert Heritage. 1958.

Right: stool of oak with turned legs. Mid-seventeenth century.

Below: stool of carved walnut. c. 1685.

Above: stool of carved walnut. c. 1730.

Left: stool of mahogany. c. 1800.

112

Breakfast tables were commonly small in size, apparently for the use of one person, the top extended by a narrow flap on each side, supported on brackets, making the whole nearly square when fully open. Two sides and one end were filled with open trellis or lattice work of mahogany enclosing a shelf, and there was usually a drawer opening from each end. In such pieces the legs were generally plain and square, and mounted on castors. The 'Gothick Taste' occasionally appeared in the design of the legs of some china tables, carved to imitate slender columns of the Early English period in architecture, whilst the 'Chinese Taste' might be expressed in the typical Chinese lattice or fretwork ornament, solid or pierced, used on frieze rails and stretchers of tables, or as open trellis elsewhere. Sometimes a hint of 'bamboo' was given to the legs of china or side tables. All this work was usually carried out in mahogany, but some pieces were finished with japanning in black and gold.

With the coming of Robert Adam upon the scene, and the beginning of the later Georgian or neo-classical period, the design of tables showed a change in the shape of the legs as happened in chairs and other furniture. The curved cabriole legs were now discarded for the straight lines of the square tapered support. Tables such as the console, pier and side table, for the public rooms of a large mansion, continued to be gilded and the tops to be of marble to some extent. The general lines were now more severe, lacking the freedom of the rococo and its fantasies. The plain rectangular side table sometimes became a sideboard table (without drawers) placed between two pedestals with urns on them in the dining-room. The frieze rail was usually fluted, and the tapered legs also. The dining table of mahogany also had square tapered fluted legs and could be extended in the same manner as in the preceding period. Adam's typical ornamental motifs of paterae, swags of husks and sometimes the ram's head, were used in the decoration of the framework as in his other furniture. Pier tables semi-oval in plan, in this style, stood under looking-glasses and might be gilded, or painted in colours to harmonize with the decoration of the room. Sometimes the tapered legs to these pieces were of light baluster form, turned and delicately fluted.

As satinwood became fashionable, it was much used for the elegant furniture supplied for drawing-rooms where the semi-oval side table with its slender tapered legs was finely veneered and usually enriched with simple marquetry of cross-banding, perhaps with an oval patera in the centre of the top filled with a fan motif. Sometimes the satinwood had floral designs painted on it. The Pembroke table, its folding flaps raised on small brackets to make an oval or rectangular top (with rounded corners), was a very useful piece for various purposes. In a portrait by Sir Joshua Reynolds, three fashionable ladies are seated closely about such a table with book or embroidery frame at hand. The two brass ring handles of a drawer can be seen at one end of the table. Decoration was now by means of painting or marquetry, carving being less employed than during the mid-Georgian period. Designs were very light and delicate, sometimes being in the style of Pompeian arabesques. Occasionally a narrow cross-banding and some light and dark stringing kept a satinwood table simple in character. The tapered leg became more and more slender, with a small square foot or no foot at all. A dark stringing finished the vertical edges of the tapered leg.

Some small tables of satinwood were fitted as dressing tables; the box-like top hinged to open as two lids to form a tray or wing on either side. The centre portion thus revealed was fitted with tiny compartments for combs, make-up, etc., besides a small toilet glass rising on a ratchet frame in the middle. Below was a long shallow drawer fitted with ring handles. An example of this type, made c. 1790, is of satinwood, decorated with marquetry of narrow cross-banding and light and dark stringing; the slender tapered legs are inlaid with fluting and are shod with brass castors. The hinged lid opens on an interior lined with green baize and fitted in this instance with a centre slope for writing on, flanked by small compartments each having a hinged lid. The upper of the two shallow drawers in this table is also fitted with compartments, these having sliding lids. This is an elegant example of a lady's writing table, small in scale (it is only two feet wide when closed) and dainty in appearance.

Sheraton, whose designs in his *Drawing Book* (1791) showed much ingenuity, includes among them what he calls a 'Harlequin Pembroke Table', a type which he says was invented by a friend. This plate shows a rectangular table with the usual flaps, mounted on square tapered legs on castors. The body is deep enough to contain a 'till' (here a secretaire fitting of pigeonholes and tiny drawers). This till, concealed when not in use, takes up the whole length and half the width of the table top, and was to be raised bodily by some mechanism so that a person might sit to write on one extended flap of the table with the secretaire conveniently erect before him.

A more spacious type of writing table, popular during the last years of the eighteenth century, was the 'Carlton House Table'. Although the name is contemporary the reason for it has not been traced, no connection with the Prince of Wales' London residence, or with the Regent himself, having been established. This table, mounted on four tapered legs, had a wide straight front fitted with three shallow drawers in the frieze, the back being rounded with the sides. The top was surrounded with a low fitting containing small drawers and a small cupboard or two.

During the Regency period the most important development in design included the circular parlour table, the sofa table and the trio or quartetto (i.e. a nest of three or four small tables diminishing in size). The circular table was derived by nineteenth-century designers from classical sources and owed its popularity to the current fashion for the 'antique'. Thomas Hope of Deepdene designed and had made a piece which he called a 'monopodium', in reference to the solid central support or pedestal which widens out at the base to rest on claw feet. Other circular-topped tables had central pillar supports with four short shaped legs which resembled the curved sabre leg of the contemporary chair. These fairly simple tables were the parents of the Victorian parlour table. Sheraton in his *Cabinet Dictionary* (1802) showed designs for circular library tables with shallow drawers in the frieze; he suggests three winged chimaeras for the supports of one of these pieces. The sofa table enjoyed great popularity, either as an occasional table at which ladies wrote, read or did a little painting in water colours, or else as a useful small table for serving tea and coffee after dinner, or even for a modest meal. Its top was rectangular, with a folding flap raised at each end to extend it. The supports at each end were often designed in the lyre shape or an adaptation of it, or as a rectangular support finishing in two feet of sabre curve. A long horizontal stretcher, often turned, connected the end supports of the sofa table, and it was usual to find two shallow drawers fitted into the frieze. Occasionally the sofa table was mounted on a central pedestal with four feet. Card tables were designed with either four turned legs fairly straight in outline, or on a central pedestal with claw feet after the manner of some sofa tables. The hinged top was D-shaped when closed and swivelled through a quarter or half turn to allow access to the storage compartment in the frieze, whereupon the top was fully opened to its rectangular plan to rest crossways upon the frame.

Some small tables were designed for both games and work, a drawer with a workbag (or 'pouch') being fitted under the top which was inlaid with squares for the game of chess or draughts. In the dining-room long tables were provided on the sectional principle, the individual parts mounted on a central support with four curved feet (sabre type usually), a nineteenth-century version of the 'pillar and claw'. A spare leaf could be fixed, 'by means of iron straps & buttons' says Sheraton (1803), between two such tables to form a long one, and the idea could be repeated and extended to any length required. How long a Regency dining table could be on occasions may be seen at Apsley House in London. The advantage of the 'claw' support was that no diner was inconvenienced by finding himself obstructed by the presence of an ordinary table leg.

Among the various occasional tables, the trio and quartetto both proved very fashionable and popular. In a characteristic Regency set the design of the little table was light, a narrow rectangular top being supported on very slender turned baluster legs, two grouped together at each end on a curved trestle type of foot, whilst a thin shallow curved piece of wood joined the supports. This was not in fact a stretcher as it did little to strengthen the piece; it did however serve to steady each little table and controlled the trio or quartetto when the nest was formed.

During the Victorian era tables, like the rest of furniture, were increasingly mass-produced. In the early Victorian period they were solid in design and mostly made of mahogany rather bright in colour. The long rectangular table for the dining-room was usually supported on four substantial turned and tapered legs, perhaps decorated with some carved gadrooning or fluting. The top could be enlarged by unwinding it, so to speak, by means of a handle inserted at one end. This half of the table then drew apart from the other leaving a space to be filled with one or more (portable) leaves to choice. A neat fit was secured by the use of the tiny wooden pegs which slotted into

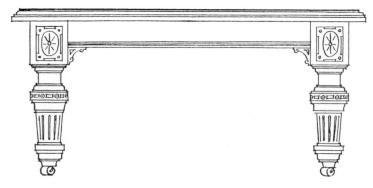

Dining table, design dated 1875

holes in the edges of the different portions of the top; a sliding part of the framework inside the frieze rail gave support to the leaves which had been added. In the parlour, family and guests often gathered round a circular table supported on a central column with four feet, the latter curved in shape, but the whole design much more solid and coarser in character than the Regency table of this type. Early Victorian tables were made of solid mahogany and there was little or no use of veneer; indeed the table top which might have been ornamented in some way was often entirely covered with a cloth. In the case of the parlour table this might be of red velvet or some less expensive material, sometimes decorated with a fringe. The parlour table was of course immensely popular in the middle-class home, and the gasolier placed centrally overhead gave light to the evening's occupation. Even in wealthier households the company might gather in this way, for sometimes pictures show Queen Victoria and her ladies grouped about a round table, some of them with their crewel work in their hands, whilst one of the gentlemen reads aloud from a book. In drawing-rooms an occasional table or two were placed. These had small oblong or oval tops, perhaps finished in burr walnut or maple, mounted on end supports which might or might not be connected by a stretcher. Some small tables could almost qualify to be called stands, consisting as they did of an oval or circular top mounted on a tripod. When japanning came into fashion these small pieces were often given this finish, in black enriched with mother-of-pearl or painted decoration and enhanced by touches of gold or bronze paint.

In the bedroom, the dressing table consisted of a simple piece of furniture, oblong in shape, with two shallow drawers with wood knob handles fitted into the frieze. Since the Victorian lady's complexion was her own and did not, like that of her forebears, depend a great deal on artificial aids, she did not require a dressing table fitted with numerous compartments, such as had been the case in Georgian times. The table was mounted on four straight turned legs, or, very often, on curved supports at each end which were connected by a low shelf. A swing toilet mirror mounted on a shallow stand containing a drawer was placed on the table top.

With the increasing variety offered in design from the mid-nineteenth century onward, the dressing table became more important and was part of the suite of bedroom furniture supplied by the manufacturer, who now gave more attention to it. To obviate the need for adding a separate chest of drawers in some suites, the dressing table took on the now familiar role of chest of drawers with toilet mirror attached. The design varied in the number and disposition of the drawers, and it is doubtful if the manufacturer cared much whether the lady sat or stood whilst at her toilet (in the modern sense of the word). Quite obviously, if she had no lady's maid to dress her hair while she sat at ease, the Victorian woman must often have stood at her dressing table mirror, since the dressing table top was fairly high and the swing toilet glass was mounted above this. In some cases the chest of drawers was lower with an extra drawer and recess rising above on each side, between which a vertical mirror was fixed which allowed more of the person to be reflected. The tops of these toilet glasses were often finished with a plain or broken pediment which gave its character to the whole suite, being repeated on the wardrobe and the back of the wash-stand. The suite of bedroom furniture was obtainable in different woods according to price.

The round parlour table tended to disappear from the scene as time went on, especially if the house no longer had extra sitting-rooms. In the drawing-room many more occasional tables were introduced, usually with very slender straight or curved supports, the latter sometimes vaguely suggesting the cabriole outline, whilst the top was rounded or shaped and a shelf might be inserted below. Ebonized wood was much used for drawing-room pieces but other small tables might be rectangular and made of oak, varnished or highly polished. Some had the frieze rail formed of a row of tiny spindles which also made a rail to the shelf below, a decorative feature popular in other pieces of furniture, e.g. the sideboard. A writing table might appear in the drawing-room, consisting of a flat top covered with leather with a gold-tooled or blind-tooled ornamental border; this top was mounted on two legs at one end and a narrow pedestal of drawers at the other. The placing of the pedestal allowed the writer's knees to go comfortably under the table top proper which would have a shallow drawer in the frieze to accommodate the blotting book or pad.

Some very cheap small tables had bamboo legs and rattan tops, rectangular or sometimes octagonal. Other tables, for the garden, were designed in 'rustic' work. A romantic notion was the very small table indeed, which consisted of a circular brass tray of 'Benares ware' (perhaps mass-produced in Birmingham) which was placed on an accompanying wooden framework. This framework was composed of two 'gates' hinged at their centres to open out to give a four-legged support. The legs and stretchers which formed the framing were of knobbed turning, suggesting Oriental design. These tables were in keeping with the limited fashion for having interior decoration in mock-Oriental or Near East style, which included much use of pierced carved woodwork of the type known as meshrebiyeh work.

During the first half of the twentieth century tables were made in all kinds of designs and sizes, reflecting current fashions for the continued revival of past styles; this was particularly so between the two World Wars. In the dining-room, the oak table might have bulbous legs recalling the Elizabethan and Jacobean period, or be of walnut or mahogany with cabriole supports. The oak gate-leg table of the later seventeenth century was also revived, with an oval or rectangular top on spiral-turned legs and stretchers. In the sitting-room, as the fashion for displaying a multitude of ornaments and bric-à-brac declined, only one or two useful small tables were left. Nests of three with slender supports were popular, perhaps in mahogany with cabriole legs or of walnut or oak with straight legs. These nests of tables were much appreciated for the after-dinner coffee cup, and the necessary ash-trays since so many people were smoking cigarettes. Replicas of the early Georgian and Chippendale tripod tables, mainly small in size with plain tops or pie-crust edges, were useful to carry reading lamps and books. The dressing table followed the variety of styles and woods found in the bedroom suite.

During the 1930s, when fitments became fashionable, even the dressing table might be incorporated into the bedroom interior fittings. Again, one or two designs for tables appeared in which the top was mounted on the chromium-plated tubular legs which were being used to a limited extent for stools and other seats. Some larger tables with rectangular tops were also supported in this way; others had supports of bent laminated wood. In general, the dining table was made much smaller in size than formerly, to suit the smaller rooms (and families) of the time, and not all were made to extend. In the garden, a green-painted folding table of metal had a circular top on a folding frame, the top pierced to allow a garden umbrella to stand in it.

After the Second World War, whilst the furniture trade returned again to making adaptations of past styles, the design of dining tables was less elaborate than before, the supports in particular being simpler in shape. New fashions from abroad brought a tapered support coming almost to a point at ground level, and the metal 'stick leg' also appeared. Tops, usually rectangular, might be veneered with some exotic wood, but were usually now treated to resist damage from heat and damp. Tables for kitchen use and the preparation of food were covered with a special plastic material for this purpose, often in a gay colour to be in keeping with the bright colour schemes for this part of the house which had become so popular. Some dining tables had circular tops supported on four legs. In the living-room, nests of small tables of wood continued to be very popular; they now tended to be lower in height along with the low seats of chairs and settees. The nest might be arranged differently, for example a rectangular table might have two small square ones under it placed side by side. Other nests were of rectangular or square tables, diminishing in size and placed one above the other in the traditional way. Some small tables for the living rooms had tops painted to simulate dark rich marble (a fashion from Italy) and were mounted on metal legs of brass or painted black. There was also a fashion for supports of wrought ironwork painted black or white, and here sometimes the tops were of thick transparent glass. These last were chiefly intended for the sophisticated town 'patio' or the roof terrace, although naturally they could be used anywhere.

The vogue introduced from the United States for having barbecue parties encouraged rather exotic designs for garden furniture in general, with great use of lively colours. More sober designs included tables of plain wood, usually square, the tops formed of open spars (this discouraged rain water from collecting and spoiling the piece) on four plain rectangular legs, whilst the metal folding table associated with the sun or garden umbrella continued to be popular. As sun umbrellas became shaped like canopies, supported on a single metal pole, they became divorced from the table.

Today the retailer can offer tables of every size, shape and material, suitable to the taste and purse of his customers.

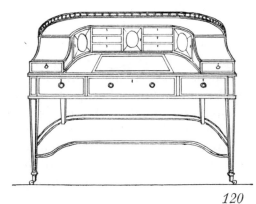

A 'Carlton House Table'. c. 1800

CHAPTER NINE

Chairs and Other Seats

The history of chair design is the longest and most varied in the whole story of English furniture. Although basically the chair consists of a seat with legs and back, with or without arms, changes in its structure, material and ornamentation, have occurred more frequently than in any other class of furniture. This is interesting, since its proportions have to be related to the shape and size of the human figure and thus have to conform to certain basic requirements. The back especially has offered scope for variety in design, whilst the legs and their connecting stretchers, if any, are continually in sympathy with stylistic changes seen in other pieces of furniture. The change from one kind of wood to another has to some extent played a part in design, not to mention the startling innovations when metal has been adopted for the construction of the frame. The use of upholstery, too, especially where the piece is 'over-stuffed', has a notable effect on its appearance.

The chair today is such a commonplace object wherever seats are required, that it is perhaps necessary to recall that it was originally almost as important as a throne, and its use reserved for only the most important of personages. This was so during the greater part of the Middle Ages, when chairs with arms were provided for the lord of the household and some of his chief guests. For everyone else a stool or a chest must suffice, with a long form or settle when eating at table. None of this suggests much comfort compared with modern standards, but again it must be recalled that today the great mass of people lead very sedentary lives, in work which mainly keeps them indoors on the office chair or factory stool. Medieval people on the other hand lived of necessity a much more active physical life, and much of their time was spent in outdoor occupations, hunting, riding, sports and the cultivation of the land. Lack of effective artificial light indoors also to some extent limited the hours of activity. The chair, then, was of special importance and may be seen in illuminated manuscripts as an almost isolated piece of furniture, occupied by the king or noble at meals on the dais of the great hall of his castle or manor house, or portrayed standing in a more private dining parlour before the winter fire which conveniently warms the back of the diner. In pictures which show people (lords and ladies usually) talking at ease, or in representations of Biblical scenes such as the birth of Christ, men and women in contemporary medieval dress seem either to sit on the edge of the great bed or to be accommodated with stools, or even only with great stuffed bolster-like cushions arranged on the floor. Sometimes one of the ladies, in a birth scene for example, may be shown seated before the fire on a small chest. Where chairs did exist, they seem to have been somewhat crude in design, box-like in appearance with enclosed arms and panelled back. The chair of state for the great personage had a wooden canopy fixed to the back.

By the early years of the sixteenth century when English life was beginning to take on some semblance of refinement, the design of chairs falls into three categories. This may be judged both from contemporary pictures and from the rare survivals. These categories may be designated respectively as the X-framed chair, the turned chair and the enclosed chair. In the X-frame type the front supports crossed over to meet the seat frame at the corners and continue to the arms. This was echoed at the back, but was modified so that the back uprights could rise vertically from the seat to support the rectangular back which was upholstered. Portraits of the early Tudor period show personages in such chairs, and it is noticeable that all the parts appear to be covered with fabric, often a red velvet, with a good deal of fringe to enhance the effect of luxury. These pieces were only for the very wealthy. The frames were of practically no value in themselves, the cost lying in the rich upholstery. Very costly examples might well have been imported from abroad, e.g. from Flanders or Spain. One which is described as being of walnut, covered with crimson velvet embroidered with initials and scallop shells and fringed with gold, might have been of foreign workmanship.

The turned chair is so named because it was made up of turned members, knobbed and ringed, which fitted together into sockets. The piece could thus easily be dismantled for removal. Many of these turned chairs had a triangular-shaped seat, with the back upright in one length from the floor to the top rail of the back, the back itself being formed of slender turned vertical spars. Elaborate examples might have extra pieces added for effect, in the form of turned bobbins and pendants. The enclosed chair was panelled throughout, with solid back and sides, and the seat very often hinged like a lid over the lower part which thus formed a coffer. The whole outline is very rigid and severe with a fairly tall narrow back, quite vertical, and flat horizontal arms. Some enclosed chairs are quite plain, but others may have some carved linenfold decoration on the panels, or perhaps a profile head carved in a medallion. Some Italian Renaissance ornament, e.g. arabesque, may be introduced. Less severe in appearance is the contemporary type of armchair sometimes called 'caqueteuse' or 'caquetoire' (chatterbox), which has an open structure. The back usually consisted of a very narrow panel, sometimes almost wedge-shaped, attached to the solid wood seat. Light straight arms spread out from the back to be supported on the front uprights which were prolonged to meet them. In these chairs the design allowed little room for ornament which could only be used on the back. Here a profile head in a medallion is characteristic. English chairs of the medieval and early Tudor period, like most furniture of native manufacture, were made of oak, although walnut is also mentioned in inventories from time to time.

During the Elizabethan period the enclosed box type of armchair disappeared. Instead the chair had a solid back and seat, with open arms sloping gently downward to be supported on the front uprights which were extended above the seat to meet them. The legs were connected by four horizontal stretchers, plain and stout, tenoned into the legs a bare inch or two above the floor. A noticeable refinement was the slight rake or slope now given to the back, which meant some increase of comfort. The back legs were plain, but the front legs were turned. In one example of the late sixteenth century, the sides are filled in between the arms and seat with turned spindles which are repeated along the back under the horizontal back panel. This latter is ornamented with flat carving in very low relief.

The turned chair, more or less extravagantly embellished with knobs, pendants and rings, continued to be made into the early years of the seventeenth century, with the characteristic triangular seat. Tradition connects this type with the West Country, the borders of Wales, Herefordshire, Cheshire and Lancashire. Horace Walpole, on the look-out for anything 'Gothic' which would be an addition to his house of Strawberry Hill, was anxious for a friend to investigate this area on his behalf when on a visit there. He speaks (1761) in a letter of another friend who had collected a number of chairs, one by one from various farmhouses, and says they were of wood, 'the seats triangular, the back, arms and legs loaded with turnery'. For comfort, all these wooden armchairs required the addition of a loose cushion or two, since padded upholstery was hardly known.

123

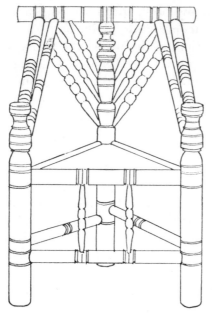

Chair of 'thrown' or turned oak. Early
seventeenth century

An armchair c. 1600, now in the Victoria and Albert Museum,
shows the raked panelled back with the new cresting added to the top
rail, and the small earpieces added at the sides. Both these features
are carved in shallow relief, with volutes and acanthus foliage. The
back is formed of a large main panel with a narrower one above, and
both are inlaid with floral scrollwork and birds, done in holly, cherry,
bog-oak and stained woods. The two uprights, and the crosspiece
between the panels, are inlaid with flowers growing from a stiff
leafy stem. The narrow arms slope down in a curve, to scroll over
just beyond the junction with the front upright. The front legs which
also form the arm supports, are turned in short baluster form and
fluted. The seat rail is decorated with an inlaid band of lozenge or
chequer ornament, and the flat part of each front leg is inlaid with a
short floral spray. The four connecting stretchers are plain, and the
pegs which secure the mortise-and-tenon joints show clearly on the
surface of the legs. This type, with some individual variations, continued during the first part of the seventeenth century, or early
Stuart period. An occasional example of mid-seventeenth century may
perhaps show considerable elaboration of carved ornament instead of
inlaid work, the carving being flattish and depending mainly on
scrolled foliage for its effect. Small versions of the wooden armchairs
were made for children, but with longish legs. It is assumed that this

124

was to enable the child to be fed at table at a height convenient for the nurse. These heavy and somewhat immovable armchairs were to be superseded in due course by the Restoration type of chair with its open carved back.

Stools continued to be made during the Elizabethan and early Stuart period. They had rectangular seats supported on four legs, usually canted, and united by stretchers placed very low. The legs varied in shape, those dating from the late sixteenth century often being of a modified bulbous form, fluted and more slender than the bulbous supports used elsewhere in furniture. Other examples may be seen carved with concave gadrooning. As the seventeenth century advanced, however, the bulbous support was superseded by a turned one, e.g. in ring and ball design, or turned baluster form. In all these wooden 'joint' (i.e. joined) stools the seat or top had moulded edges. In some cases the top was hinged, the stool then being fitted with a box under the seat, the four legs being consequently much shorter but still connected by plain stretchers.

Other seats were made in the shape of forms and settles. The oak form, intended to accompany the long dining table, had a very long narrow wooden seat supported on four legs, or, if the length was excessive, on six. These legs were simple in character and were connected by plain stretchers, usually fixed near the ground. The seat rail might be carved. One example, of early seventeenth-century date, has the seat rail carved with lunette ornament continued along all four rails; the legs are of baluster form, and in this instance are connected by a single broad stretcher from end to end. When the gate-leg table with its folding circular or oval top became fashionable for dining after the Restoration, there was no need to continue to make the form, since it could not be accommodated to tables of this plan. Chairs, too, were to be made in sufficient quantity for the eating parlour in due course. The long form therefore would only survive in the servants' quarters, and ceased to be a fashionable piece of furniture until it was revived for a very short time in the last years of the seventeenth century.

The settle was distinguished from the form in having a tall wooden back. It, too, was long enough in the seat to accommodate a number of persons and usually had an open arm at each end. One dating from the early seventeenth century is supported on four rectangular legs united by plain stretchers, and has arms which are slightly curved. The upright back is divided into four panels, each being carved with a rosette within a guilloche design, whilst the seat rail is carved with

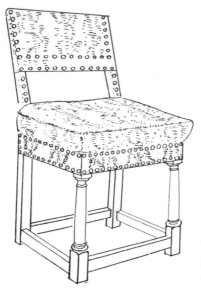

'Farthingale' chair in walnut, covered with figured blue cloth decorated with applied embroidery. Early seventeenth century

circular and oblong strapwork. The settle can hardly be called a fashionable piece of furniture. Sturdy in appearance, it was suited to the requirements of people of modest social position, and was in a way the humble ancestor of the more elaborate settees with wooden or upholstered backs, which established themselves in favour after the Restoration. The solid wooden settle thereafter found a more humble place in farms and cottages where its back, fitted with a version in wood of the wing or earpiece seen on upholstered chairs and settees, provided excellent protection from draughts during the eighteenth century.

Meanwhile, in the early Stuart period, some attempt was being made to introduce a more comfortable kind of seat with a little up-holstery. A notable type of chair, without arms, had a lightly-padded seat and a small back panel. The modern term 'farthingale' has been applied to this design, on the assumption that, being without arms and having a relatively wide seat, it showed off to full advantage and in comfort, the circular 'French' farthingale. The great width of this dress spread out almost like a circular shelf at hip level, and the skirt depended from it like a curtain. The framework of the so-called farthingale chairs may consist of quite plain legs united by four low stretchers, with a back formed by a narrow upholstered panel having a space between it and the seat. In one example surviving, the front legs are shaped like very slender columns. This particular piece was made of walnut, and the covering fabric is a woollen cloth enriched with appliqué embroidery of coloured silks on canvas, resembling bands entwined with lilies. Brass-headed nails, set close together, secure the cloth to the frame, making a decorative border. At Knole near Sevenoaks, there is a set of five chairs of this farthingale type, of a date c. 1610. The framework is of birch, painted, the front legs are shaped like simple columns and the stuffed seat and back are covered with plain crimson velvet garnished with a deep fringe, again with gilt nails securing the fabric to the frame. Another example, in the Victoria and Albert Museum, is dated 1649 on the back, and its design reflects some new developments. The front legs have spiral turning, and so has the front stretcher which connects them half-way up. The covering to the seat and back is of 'Turkey work' in a brightly-coloured floral design.

Another upholstered piece was the X-frame, or cross-framed, armchair which was revived during the early Stuart period. The arms now sloped gently downward, and the wide rectangular back usually had egg-shaped finials at the corners. The lower structure, of X-form, was strengthened with stretchers from back to front, and there was a circular medallion at the intersection of the legs. There was often an additional cushion (squab) to the seat, increasing the height, and another for the back. The whole piece, intended for the rooms of some great house, was covered with fabric stuck down closely to every inch of the framework including the finials, and strained over the stuffed upholstery; lavish trimming with a deep fringe completed the effect of luxury. Some fine examples survive at Knole, one being covered with red and buff silk decorated with spangles. Besides plain crimson velvets, the patterned fabrics used for these luxurious pieces included crimson and silver damask, and silver and cream brocade. Stools, also cross-framed, with the circular medallion at the centre, were upholstered in equally sumptuous style and some survive *en suite* with the armchair.

Although upholstered settees did not come into general use until the late seventeenth century, one or two examples of unique interest may be seen at Knole. One has a plain open framework, including straight arms and a wide rectangular back. A curious side piece, quarter-ellipse in shape, makes a vertical fixed 'wing' at each end between the back and the arm. This feature is seen later as part of the design of a Restoration armchair called a 'sleeping-chayer' in the Ham House inventory of 1679. In an even more refined form it became the 'ear-piece' of the late seventeenth-century upholstered wing armchair.

127

During the Commonwealth taste inclined, in keeping with Puritan morality, to favour furniture of a much less luxurious nature. An upholstered chair therefore was more likely to be covered with leather which might be either plain, or stamped and gilded with some pattern; the framework began to show a lighter type of construction. Canework for the seat and back was introduced a few years before the Restoration, being set in plain framing and supported by spiral-turned members, i.e. the legs, back uprights and stretchers.

A distinctive type of chair, with an open back and no arms, appears to have been made c. 1660, and is commonly thought to have been of regional origin, chiefly Yorkshire and Derbyshire. In such examples, the front legs with their connecting stretcher were usually turned, the side and back stretchers being plain. The wooden seat was sunk (dished) for a squab or loose cushion. The back, however, gave the chair its special character. This might be of arcaded design, between two plain back uprights ending in scroll finials. In one surviving example the arcaded back consisted of an upper rail carved with three arches which rested on two small baluster columns supported on the carved lower rail; both rails were surmounted by acorn knobs. The lower rail might be plain or have a shaped lower edge, and both rails might have a small amount of low relief carving. Another distinctive type of back in these regional chairs might consist of two hooped and scalloped cross rails, each carved with scrolls and garnished with three tiny turned drops. Here again the wooden seat would be sunk for a loose cushion, the legs and front stretcher perhaps having ball turning, the side and back stretchers being left plain.

After the Restoration there was more variety in seats. Single chairs, i.e. without arms, became increasingly more common and there was much more use of upholstery. Beech or solid walnut was used for the framework, as well as the traditional oak. The distinctive type associated with the Restoration period was derived from Dutch designs. In this the back became taller than formerly, with a vertical panel of canework flanked by carving in it, cane also being used for the seat. There was much use of spiral turning for the back uprights and stretchers. The front stretcher, however, was broad and elaborately carved in a style similar to the top rail of the back, whilst the front legs frequently assumed a scrolled form. The carving of these pieces might be fairly simple or very elaborate, but was open, i.e. pierced, in contra-distinction to the carved work on the solid characteristic of earlier periods. Motifs used included opposed S-scrolls, and cherubs supporting a crown or coronet were almost a stock ornamen-

128

tation for the back top rail and the front stretcher. The seat rail was lighter than before, and the top surface sometimes had a thin running pattern carved upon it. A small knob or finial topped the back uprights which now rose above the top rail. One typical surviving example is of walnut, with openwork carving. The back consists of a rectangular panel of canework framed by floral scrollwork, with two cherubs holding a coronet forming the top rail. The turned back uprights are enriched with carving and crowned by knobs. The scroll front legs are joined by a broad stretcher carved with a coronet and cherubs.

Armchairs closely followed the style of the single chairs. The arm itself continued to have the downward curve but was now moulded (instead of being plain and flat) and finished in a scroll over the arm support. An armchair of this type which is traditionally said to have belonged to Nell Gwyn, and which is now in the Victoria and Albert Museum, is very elaborately and richly carved. The sides of the canework panel to the back are carved with vine branches and roses springing from a basket and supporting cherubs and birds, whilst the lower rail is carved with two cherubs and a basket of flowers. The upper rail is carved with cherubs crowning a woman amongst scroll-work, and the front stretcher echoes this treatment. The spiral back uprights are each surmounted by a crowned female head. The curved and moulded arms each have a lion couchant carved above the scrolling end where the hand of the person seated would rest.

Two-back or three-back settees with arms came into fashion about the 1680s. These resembled closely the contemporary carved armchair, some pieces with a two-back chair design having an arm at each end and another in the centre. Instead of a caned panel to the back an open splat formed of split balusters, flat side outward, might be used.

The upholstered chair of the Restoration period might be a single chair with a plain rectangular body, but many were made with arms. The legs, stretchers and the arm itself followed the prevailing style. A splendid example, one of a pair at Knole, is thus carved and gilded, the seat and back being covered with a bluish-green Genoa velvet boldly patterned and richly trimmed with a ball fringe. Upholstered stools might be made *en suite* with these upholstered pieces. At Ham House, near Richmond, a great number of pieces of Restoration furniture have been preserved, of which a quantity can be identified with the entries in the inventories taken in 1679 and 1683. Many chairs are listed, including some described as 'back friends'. This eloquent term seems applicable to those chairs in which the design resembles a stool (since the back and front legs are identical), with which a tall open back has been incorporated. Such were the '12 back stooles with cane bottoms, japaned' mentioned in the inventories. There are listed besides numerous armchairs and single chairs in which rich upholstery figures, and which, like the hangings and bed-furnishings, bear witness to the luxurious taste of the then owners, the Duke and Duchess of Lauderdale.

Another set of twelve, including six single and six armchairs, can be traced. These have frameworks of most striking design, based on carved dolphins which appear as legs, stretchers and arms. These pieces are fully gilded, and the ample seats and square backs are stuffed and covered with the original brocade, edged with fine silk fringe. According to the inventory they had protective covers of 'shot sarsnet'. Yet another set of twelve, with the framework painted black and partly gilded, are designed with typical Restoration scroll-work. The seats and the tallish rectangular backs are covered with the contemporary red velvet. The colours given for upholstery fabrics at Ham show much variety, some chairs being listed as covered with green and gold velvet, others with blue or yellow damask, others again with black and gold or crimson and gold. In the most important bedrooms, it is evident that the same materials were specially chosen for bed-hangings and chair covers, thus presenting a rich and beautiful colour scheme. Mention of 'fringe' is frequent, and it is interesting to note the provision of protective 'cases', i.e. outer covers, such as those of shot sarsnet already referred to; others seem to have been of crimson taffety.

The period of William and Mary saw some changes in chair design which give the years from c. 1685 to the beginning of Queen Anne's reign something of the nature of a transitional style. Chair backs became noticeably taller, and the rich, rather overloaded look given by the typical Restoration carving disappeared from many chairs. A distinctive feature was the half-hoop cresting which topped the back, and which also appeared in the design of the front stretcher. This cresting of course added yet further height to the piece, and this was enhanced in many cases by the back being actually narrower in width than before. The canework panel was worked in a fine mesh and sometimes spread across the uprights, instead of being designed like a splat as in the Restoration chair. Spiral turning went out, a slender upright column frequently taking its place for the back supports. The legs varied somewhat in design but were almost always straight, usually square in section, the front ones tapering from a broad nulled cap to end in a small bun foot. From c. 1685, back and

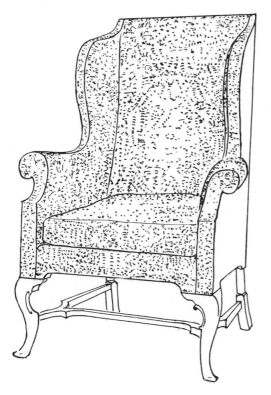

Winged armchair covered with embroidery in coloured wools. c. 1700

front legs began to be connected by shaped and moulded stretchers arranged crosswise, with a small turned finial placed at the intersection or crossing. Stools of the William and Mary era usually had upholstered seats and followed in their construction the same styles of stretchers already described. Examples may be seen of both the earlier type (c. 1685) in which the curved cresting formed the basis for the front and back stretchers (i.e. the longer sides), and of the later type in which the two stretchers are placed diagonally.

Upholstered chairs and settees were supported on a framework conforming in design to the other chairs. Both single and armchairs had the typical tall back of the late seventeenth century, sometimes rectangular, but also at times with the top of the back shaped, an echo of the hooped or curved cresting seen in open chair backs. For the double settee, the top of the back was divided by two or three curved outlines. Where armchairs and settees had open arms (i.e. not upholstered) gently curved and moulded, the front leg was continued up to form the arm support and was carved in the same style as the lower part of the leg. The upholstery material covered the seat rail completely and was brought round the junction with the legs. The fully-upholstered armchair (and the companion settee) was made with or without the winged ear-piece and the arm itself, formed on C-scroll lines, was now designed to take a sharp downward sweep before reaching the front rail of the seat. This shaping initiated a style of long duration, due possibly to the greater convenience thus afforded to people when seated, both to the women in their great panniered gowns and to the gentlemen in their wide-skirted coats. A loose cushion for the armchair and two or perhaps three for the settee were usually provided. The upholstery materials used included both original Italian velvet and its English imitation, with cut-pile patterns of bold design and colouring. There was also an increased use of needlework for this purpose consisting of coloured wools worked on canvas in gros or petit point or the two together, entirely covering the surface. This embroidery was a very fashionable pursuit, Madame de Maintenon in France and Queen Mary II in England being expert and industrious needlewomen and setting an example eagerly followed. The cross-stitch and tent-stitch designs used for furniture were various, including figure groups, the armorial bearings of the family, a vase of flowers or an all-over decoration of branching leaves and flowers. Sometimes, e.g. for the seat and back of a chair, a centrepiece was formed, perhaps the figures of a lady or gentleman surrounded by scrollwork with flowers and foliage outside this. Petit point might be used for the finer work of the centre, gros point for that outside. The use of elaborate fringes continued, but was presently to be abandoned and brass-headed nails likewise, due to structural changes in the design of seats as time went on.

In the last years of the seventeenth century, solid walnut chairs of very decorative aspect may be noted, with the carved pierced cresting associated with a splat to the back consisting of carved pierced motifs. These were usually compounded of small foliated scrolls involved with lambrequins showing French influence. Some surviving examples of this type of chair have upholstered seats. The curved cresting of the back gradually combined with a curved frame for the back as a whole, and the front legs began to take on the cabriole form but were still connected by stretchers, the two side ones being reinforced by a central one. The back might be filled with upholstery or canework but there was an increasing tendency to upholster the seat, a practice which once fully established was to be the accepted treatment with few exceptions all through the centuries to follow. These transitional pieces serve to bridge the gap, or to fill in the sequence in design between the tall narrow-backed type of chair most typical of the William and Mary period and that with the curvilinear character which today is popularly termed 'Queen Anne'.

Among the pieces of furniture made or provided for Hampton Court Palace at the close of the century were a number of seats. It is especially interesting to see the mention of '4 long formes of walnuttree carvd rich' for which Thomas Roberts 'Joyner to His Mats' was asking payment of ten pounds (accounts 1699–1701). These long forms, of a type sometimes referred to as 'long stools', were intended for William's Privy Chamber, doubtless for the use of persons in close attendance upon the King. They were the alternative to having a large number of ordinary stools arranged along the walls for this purpose. Such pieces were in fact an extension of the stool design, with four front and four back legs connected by carved stretchers in the prevailing style and thus having some affinity with the contemporary day-bed. A year later Thomas Roberts was sending in a bill for 'an elbow chaire of walnuttree carvd feet and cross stretchers and pollishd' for which he asked one pound ten shillings. At the same time Richard Bealing, Upholsterer, who had supplied two stools, presented an itemized account for them which included charges of fifteen shillings 'For curld hair to stuff them and linnen to stuff in', ten shillings 'For guilte nailes and sewing silk', and smaller sums for making the covers. John Johnson, Mercer, was asking payment for rich damask, and Thomas Carr, 'Fringmaker', for lengths of fringe 'all crimson ingraines spect with gold colour' (*sic*) for which he charged by weight at two shillings and sixpence the ounce. It is not indicated for what particular work the damask and the fringe were supplied.

As the eighteenth century opened, some very significant developments began to take place in chair design. Among the last of the accounts of William III's reign (1700–1), there is mention of a set of chairs made by Richard Roberts 'of walnuttree ye foreparts Carvd horsebone, french feet & four rails' (*sic*). These chairs were covered 'in crimson genoa velvet fringed with crimson ingraine silk twisted fringe & finished with gilt nails'. The description 'carved horsebone' suggests the new type of front leg, curved like a cabriole leg in embryo and finishing in a plain paw or hoof foot. This early type of curved leg is usually termed 'pied-de-biche', and may be seen connected with the back leg by a moulded and shaped stretcher in addition to a centre one. The former straight lines of the back itself were transformed into the curved pattern, sometimes called hoop-back,

133

with a shaped splat, mainly solid, between the curving uprights. The outline of the back was curved vertically in sympathy with the lines of the human spine which was to rest against it. The seat still for a time kept straight sides but soon took on a curving plan; as the cabriole leg became fully established the use of stretchers was abandoned. They were awkward to fit to the rounded section of the cabriole leg, and furthermore the chair had become so beautifully balanced that they were not necessary to the structure.

The new type of chair (c. 1700) is sometimes specified in contemporary accounts as having a 'bended back'. At first such pieces continued to be made entirely in the solid walnut, but as the lines of the back took on a curve in plan and the seat frame became rounded at front and sides in a continuous sweep, fine walnut veneer came into use. This veneer was applied to the vertical front surfaces of the walnut back uprights and the splat, and also to the outer surface of the curved seat rail which was now adapted to receive a drop-in upholstered seat. The cabriole legs and the arms in armchairs and settees were made of solid walnut, with only a minimum of carved enrichments, e.g. on the 'knee' of the front leg. The motif used here might take the form of an escallop, husk ornament, a lion mask or a small cartouche. Even a human mask may sometimes be found carved on the knee. The escallop shell, for example, may be found ornamenting the centre of the seat rail as well. The cabriole leg itself might finish in a club foot, a lion's paw or the claw-and-ball foot. A noticeable development is the general change in the proportion of the back which gradually lost the tall character prevailing during the William and Mary period.

A typical walnut chair of the early eighteenth century was partly finished with veneer and fitted with a seat covered with needlework. The rounded or hoop-shaped back was a solid vase-shaped splat veneered with fine-figure walnut, and ornamented with a little light carving consisting of a shell between scrolls or volutes at the top where it combined with the top rail. The cabriole front legs were carved with escallop shells on the knees and had claw-and-ball feet. The seat rail was rounded to the front and veneered. Another surviving example of walnut has a rounded back with curved side uprights and a solid vase-shaped splat. The cabriole legs have paw feet and the knees are carved with leaf ornament and flowers.

Armchairs were similarly designed, but the arm was no longer supported on an extension of the front leg since this was unsuitable with the new cabriole shape. Instead, there was a short support fixed to the seat rail somewhat behind the front leg. The arm itself either appeared to merge with this or simply rested upon it. The arm was now round in section, but was flattened at the part where the sitter's elbow might be expected to rest. This exacted more skill from the chair-maker than heretofore, but was an advance in comfort and refinement. Sometimes the arm terminated in a lion's head but an eagle's head was very common. The double-chair-back settee followed this general pattern, but an alternative type was the upholstered settee which often had a plain rectangular back. This might be combined with the C-scroll over-stuffed arms, or with plain wooden arms.

Chairs and settees were often made *en suite* but there were two outsiders, namely the upholstered winged armchair and the so-called writing chair. The first continued with little change from the previous period, except for some stylistic modifications in the design of the legs as might be expected. The second took a particular form, the design being such that the seat might be round or triangular. The rounded back rail took up two of the sides as it were, being supported on two splats between three of the uprights. The front portion of the seat rail was usually curved in outline over the fourth, or front leg. A surviving example is of walnut, with a rounded back rail terminating in eagles' heads supported on two solid vase-shaped splats and three baluster-shaped columns. The seat is curved in front and is supported on four cabriole legs, carved on the knees with shells. The seat is upholstered in plain velvet. Another type of seat, usually provided with arms, has been given in recent times the name of 'love seat'. This piece had a seat which was too wide for one person alone but hardly wide enough for two people, and thus could not qualify to be called a settee. The back and seat were usually upholstered, the arms likewise, or made of plain walnut.

Stools, except for the State apartments of Royal palaces, were much less used than formerly; a typical specimen would have a rectangular upholstered seat, perhaps with an escallop shell carved on each long side. The four cabriole legs might be carved with escallops on the knees and terminate in hoof or club feet.

The fabrics used for upholstery during the Queen Anne and early Georgian period included needlework embroidery in coloured wools in gros and petit point as before, and damasks, silks, velvets, serge and leather. Boldly-figured velvets were reserved for the more monumental pieces, e.g. those designed by William Kent in the 1730s, being too large in scale for the simpler pieces in general use. Fringes went out of fashion, their use being incompatible with the new drop-in type of seat, whilst brassheaded nails also seldom appear. In some pieces, for example a large set of stools at Hampton Court Palace, a fretwork band in wave pattern is carried round the seat rail over the fabric. This had a charming effect but meant that it had to be re-moved every time the piece had to be re-covered.

Although mahogany began to be fashionable c. 1725, its use did not at first influence the design of chairs. William Kent (1684–1748), however, introduced some variety into the scene. His pieces were especially designed for the great rooms of important houses, and had a magnificent and opulent character quite distinct from the furniture supplied by cabinet-makers to less pretentious homes. In that furni-ture the frame, of walnut or mahogany, might have the carved en-richments gilded, a fashion which had first been evident c. 1720 and lasted for about twenty years. Much of Kent's furniture (1730–1745) and similar pieces showing his influence was entirely gilded, chairs and settees included. His chairs tended to have very wide seats, mostly with straight sides, supported on variants of the cabriole leg which was often used for the back as well as the front legs. The cabriole form was sometimes clumsily handled, assuming almost a tortured shape. In surviving examples it may be seen to end in a dolphin head or a scroll for the foot, and the knee may be carved with heavy shell ornament, or foliage or with acanthus and scaling. Sometimes carved and gilded garlands are swung between the front legs of chair or settee, like an openwork apron-piece. One settee indeed appears to be supported not only on legs but on a composition including sphinxes and other motifs, surely somewhat uncomfortable to the person sitting on it. Backs to his armchairs are low and wide, the top being straight or curved, and the wooden arms have the tops padded and upholstered. Sometimes the framework of the back is more curved in form with a wavy top rail ending in scrolls. Many of Kent's pieces may be seen covered with large-patterned damasks, or else with cut-pile velvets in bold designs, the red and gold colours on the white ground being in keeping with the gilding of the exposed frame. Occasionally the seat rail is seen carved with a wave pattern, plain or combined with rosettes. Another type of chair associated with Kent's style is of X-frame construction, again a design remote from the prevailing styles.

Some account must now be given of the well-known Windsor chair which came into use in the early eighteenth century and has continued to be a favourite ever since. The name is rather misleading since there is no connection with Windsor, but it would be pointless to try to change it now. These useful chairs consist of a wooden seat, saddle-shaped, the back being formed of turned spindles or stick uprights, set in a shaped top rail and fixed directly into the seat. In examples dating from the early eighteenth century, the front legs usually took a simple cabriole form with no refinements of carving, and were sometimes connected with the turned back legs by simple turned stretchers. Occasionally the back might have a simple solid or pierced splat inserted centrally between the spindles. In Windsor armchairs of the period an extra horizontal rail was added at the appropriate height, running right across the back and prolonged to form the arms. The arm portion had turned spindles of shorter length, of course, to support it. This characteristic use of spindles in the Windsor chair has caused it to be referred to sometimes as a 'stick-back chair'. A very simple version of the Windsor chair had turned, instead of cabriole, legs.

The extended version of the armchair may perhaps be termed a settle because of its solid seat. Surviving examples may be seen made with a long top rail supported on a suitable number of sticks. These are slotted through the horizontal member which runs through and is prolonged to form the arms in the usual way. In one such piece the six cabriole legs are connected by three simple turned side stretchers united with a long central one. The long solid seat is shaped in saddle style to indicate the number of people who can be accommodated.

These Windsor chairs were all a truly English product hardly touched by changes in fashion, and were made in London and various parts of the countryside, e.g. Lancashire, Somerset and elsewhere. The chief activity was however carried on around High Wycombe, in the beechwoods of the Chiltern hills. Until quite recent times the 'bodgers', as they were called, worked in the woods cutting and shaping the turned spindles used for the legs, the stretchers and the 'stick' back. Eventually, the various parts, including the saddle seat, were assembled by other craftsmen in the villages round about or in Wycombe itself. This practice continued until recently, and was hardly disturbed by Victorian mass-production methods. The local museum at High Wycombe shows the sequence of making up the parts, as well as examples of Windsor chairs made up at different periods.

Another simple type of chair which was not in the fashionable class, but which may be seen in 'conversation pictures' of the 1740s and thereabouts, had legs and back uprights simply turned usually connected by slender turned stretchers. The back was fairly tall and formed of a number of flat shaped splats arranged horizontally in the manner known as 'ladder-back'. These unsophisticated pieces had rush-bottom seats.

About the middle of the eighteenth century or mid-Georgian period, the design of chairs began to be influenced by the changes in style characteristic of the rococo. At the same time, mahogany super-seded walnut as the chief wood for furniture, which also permitted some changes in craftsmanship. Effects were now to be gained by the skilful use of carefully-designed carving instead of depending mainly on the figure of a veneer. The most notable development in chair design was in the shape of the back which took on the form now popularly associated with the name of Chippendale. The splat was formed of a series of interlacing straps or loops giving a yet lighter and more elegant appearance than formerly, whilst the top rail lost its hooped shape and took on a serpentine line, undulating like a bow, which might finish in a slight volute at each end. A slight use of carving, e.g. foliage, may be seen on the back. The cabriole leg continued to form the front support to the seat, but with some modi-fications. It would seem that the claw-and-ball foot went out of fashion in favour of the small French scroll or volute, whilst the motifs most often carved on the knee included the cabochon, and leaf or ribbon ornament. Stretchers were not used in these cabriole-leg chairs. The plan of the seat was changed, the back and sides reverting to straight lines but the front seat rail was often gently curved. The framework was usually, though not always, rebated as before, to receive a drop-in removable seat. The arms had the usual flattened place for the elbow and ended in a volute which turned over the curved arm support. In some cases the arm is seen turned over to continue in the sweep of the support instead of appearing to rest upon it. The arm support itself was fixed to the side seat rail, a little behind the position of the front leg.

Although the chair back of the mid-Georgian or Chippendale period has the general characteristics given above, within these limits there was plenty of variation in design, from the simple interlaced splat to the elaborate complicated designs known from Chippendale's *Director* as 'ribband back'. Further diversity was given by the in-spiration afforded by the fashionable Gothic and Chinese Tastes. In chairs of the Gothic Taste, the interlacing of the splat held some hint of Gothic tracery and crockets. This so-called Gothic type of chair back usually had straight front legs, square in section, perhaps carved to suggest Gothic piers. Yet another variation is seen in the response to the Chinese Taste which was in fact much more fashionable than the Gothic and combined well with the rococo. The chair back, rather square in proportion, was filled in with latticework in Chinese style, and sometimes the top rail suggested a pagoda roof appearing rather like a cresting. The legs again were square in section, perhaps with a little fretwork bracket where they met the seat rail. Sometimes the legs were pierced with fretwork or carved to suggest bamboo canes. Card-cut latticework frequently decorated square solid legs and ran along the seat rail. It is usually seen that chairs of this period which have straight legs are made with connecting side and centre stretchers. These are slight, being very narrow in proportion to their depth. Stretchers fitted to chairs in Chinese Taste may be pierced to give an effect of latticework or fretwork.

Chair-back settees were made *en suite* with single chairs or armchairs, especially in the rococo style, and to some extent in Chinese Taste also. The settees follow the usual practice as regards the design of the back with an arm added at each end. Chippendale's trade catalogue (first published in 1754), which he called *The Gentleman and Cabinet-Maker's Director*, was described by him as containing 'a large collection of the most elegant and useful designs of household furniture in the Gothick, Chinese and modern taste'. By the third edition (1762) this had become 'household furniture, in the most fashionable taste'. Among the varied types of object dealt with in the *Director*, chairs took a prominent place. Among the most elaborate designs are three for 'Ribband back' chairs, with graceful lightly-carved cabriole legs. Chippendale said himself that these 'if I may speak without vanity, are the best I have ever seen'. A set of chairs and a double-back settee can be seen in the Victoria and Albert Museum, which closely resemble these designs. They are of carved mahogany with seats covered in needlework. Nearly all the designs for chairs show alternative treatments for the front legs.

Among the designs published in 1762 are six chair backs (no seat or legs) showing interlacing strapwork or carved openwork splats which it must have been a simple matter for chair-makers to copy. Numerous chairs c. 1760 with backs of this kind have survived, often with plain straight front legs and simple stretchers which may well have been made by provincial craftsmen, for whom the task of copying a decorative cabriole leg, from a drawing only, might have been too difficult. A simple alternative to the splat-back chair was the so-called 'ladder-back' chair. This term adequately described the piece, for the back is filled in with three curved horizontal rails, usually pierced for lightness and lightly touched with carving which echoes the design of the shaped top rail. This back was used for chairs with either straight or cabriole legs, all of mahogany.

Chippendale provided various designs for armchairs with upholstered seats and backs. In parenthesis it may be noted here that the traditional winged armchair with its high back had now gone out of fashion. Those armchairs which contemporary mid-Georgian taste labelled as 'French' chairs usually show much use of foliated rococo scrolls in the design of the framework, i.e. for the arm support, the shaped back and the elegantly-carved seat rail with the lines of the elaborate apron-piece merging gracefully into the delicate cabriole legs. Existing armchairs of this character are found either of solid mahogany or of wood finely gilded.

The design of the upholstered settee of the rococo or mid-Georgian period took on flowing lines, the upholstered back tending to be lower than formerly and continuing on to form the ends or sides. In one example (c. 1740) which is made in mahogany, the long seat is supported on short elegant cabriole legs with carved apron between, whilst the narrow frame to the back and sides is shaped in flowing curves. In another (c. 1745) the back and sides are over-stuffed with no framework showing, the sides, or arms, being scrolled over. During the 1760s several versions were produced, with the continuous shaped upholstered back and scrolled arms. A design in the 1762 *Director* shows one of these, very elegant in line, with a circular bolster lying at each end. The upholstery fabrics chiefly used during this period included damask, woven tapestry, dyed leather, printed chintz and only a small amount of needlework, for embroidered coverings were going out of fashion. Where the chair does not have a drop-in seat, the fabric is brought over the rail, sometimes covering it entirely and secured to it with a row of brass-headed nails closely set together.

Some freakish designs for garden chairs were published in the mid-eighteenth century. The backs, square in proportion, were intended to be carved to resemble the rough branches of trees, 'growing' naturally and filling the open back with a kind of rustic trellis. The legs were to be carved as if made of knotty branches. A set of chairs made in this rustic style are preserved in the Victoria and Albert Museum. One of Darly's designs appears almost macabre, the back formed of twisting 'roots' while the legs appear to writhe out of the ground in a most unattractive manner.

By the late 1770s, or late Georgian period, fresh developments in chair design began to show themselves. The cabriole leg was superseded by the straight tapered leg, plain or fluted, and by the tapered balustered leg. This not only afforded a change in style but also allowed much more economy in the use of wood. The back too showed changes and more variety in outline. In all chairs, whether open-back or upholstered, the actual size is noticeably less with the seats smaller, the backs lower and the general scale even more refined and elegant, with the details more delicately designed and handled. It may be noted, in passing, that ladies' dresses were becoming less bulky, the enormously wide hooped gown being only worn when appearing at Court.

Robert Adam (1728–1792) actively concerned himself with the design of chairs, of which many actual examples survive at Osterley Park House and elsewhere. Chair designs are notable too in Hepple-white's *Guide* (1788, 1789, 1794) and in Sheraton's *Drawing Book* (1791, 1793, 1802). Besides variety in design there was also more variety in material, although naturally the fine pieces intended for the most important rooms continued to be gilded. Solid walnut and solid mahogany were used but for some pieces the authors recom-mend satinwood, perhaps combined with a little marquetry decoration or painted ornament. For others painting or japanning is advised. This new departure introduced more colourful effects than had been pos-sible during the mid-Georgian period with its almost universal use of mahogany with its dark, even if rich, tones. The use of satinwood and of paint allowed the furniture to blend with or to match the soft colours fashionable for interior decoration schemes and for window-curtains and bed-hangings. An interesting instance of this occurred in the set of five chairs formerly the property of the famous actor David Garrick, where they were part of the furnishings of the 'left-hand Back Bed Chamber' in his villa at Hampton. These chairs were painted yellow with green spots and had open-work backs formed of interlacing bands, and the rush seats were supported on slightly tapered legs joined with stretchers. These chairs (c. 1770) are amongst a number of pieces (wardrobe, wash-stand, etc.) all painted in this green and yellow colour scheme.

As for the design of chair backs these now included the last version of the Chippendale style, perhaps with the lyre-shaped splat which Adam first introduced, but other and more characteristic designs superseded it. These were the square, shield and oval shapes, with an interlaced heart-shape developing naturally from the shield in open-back chairs. Another type, in one continuous curve and open like a hoop, may be seen with a wheel centre. The square back might be filled with a lyre-shaped splat (c. 1775) or with four upright bars (c. 1790) or with a plain trellis design. The shield shape may be seen with an open-work splat filled with a carved urn, rosette and festoons (c. 1775) or with upright bars. This shield-back type with vertical bars seems to have been the chief, if not the only, kind of design used for open-back settees. A Hepplewhite design (engraved 1787) shows a four-back piece supported on tapered cylindrical legs. This is entitled a 'Bar Back Sofa'. Whilst the shield-back chair showed to best advantage when made with the open back, the square-backed chair was occasionally upholstered. One example made of mahogany has the back, seat and sides padded and covered with silk. The top rail is slightly curved and from it the arms curve downwards. Beyond the padded elbow rests they finish in scrolls carved with foliage. The supports form a continuation of this curve, and the front legs are fluted and tapered. Such chairs with padded sides were sometimes labelled 'burjair' or 'barjier' by English designers, both the shape and the term being derived from the French *bergère*.

Both the square and the shield backs were flattish with no curve in plan. The oval-shaped back, on the other hand, was concave, curved in section both horizontally and vertically. Sometimes of open form, it might be filled in with a design of ostrich feathers and festoons of drapery (c. 1780). Seats for oval-backed chairs are usually rounded in plan, either circular or with a serpentine front rail, but for the square and shield-back types straight sides are most usual. Here too a square tapered leg, plain or ending in a spade foot, suits with the general character of the design and is chiefly seen in such pieces. For the oval-back chair the cylindrical or baluster tapered leg was generally chosen, used for both back and front legs; again this was in keeping with the nature of the design which was French in origin. Stretchers were not used with the latter type of leg, but plain ones may be found sometimes associated with square tapered legs.

In armchairs the arm and the arm support usually followed one continuous sweep, perhaps in two curves. The support now, instead of ending on the seat rail behind the front leg as in the first half of the eighteenth century, had a tendency to coincide with the front leg itself. Some of Sheraton's designs (1790s) show armchairs with square backs in which the arm rests on a prolongation of the front leg, an arrangement hardly seen since the late seventeenth century. The front leg in Sheraton's drawings is shown as a tapered cylindrical type, for the arm support itself and again for the leg below the square junction with the seat rail. Throughout the late eighteenth century where the chair back was upholstered, a small padded elbow rest was placed on the open arm.

Motifs used on chairs of the late Georgian period include wheat-ears, the crinkled water-leaf and urns with drapery festoons, besides medallions, paterae and the Prince-of-Wales feathers. In the more elegant chairs there was a delicate use of fluting or guilloche pattern, carved along seat rails and frames to backs.

Surviving examples of all the types described are many, notably at Osterley Park House, near Gunnersbury in Middlesex. Here the original furniture chiefly made to Adam's own designs includes more than one type of lyre-back chair. In the Eating Room there is a set made in mahogany, and in the Library another set veneered with satinwood. There are also some fine oval-back pieces. A set in the State Bedroom have upholstered backs and padded arms, the curved seats having serpentine front rails. The legs are cylindrical and tapered, fluted and carved near the top with leaves. The encircling rail to the back has a patera, and is carved with a tiny guilloche pattern which is repeated along the seat rail. An unusual feature is the introduction of two winged female sphinxes as supports to the back above the seat rail. In the Tapestry Room the set of oval-back chairs have pads on the curved arms, with round seats supported on tapered fluted legs. French tapestry from the Gobelins works (like the wall hangings) was used to cover these chairs and the settee *en suite* with them. The colour scheme is brilliant with flowers and pastoral figures on the seats and backs respectively, in pinks, blues, yellows and greens, set off by a bright rose-coloured ground. The upholstered settee here was designed in rather a severe manner following, like the chairs, the Louis Seize influence. There is a long uninterrupted curve to the back curving round and down very gently to the arm, being stuffed and covered in one continuous sweep. Both sets of furniture (State Bedroom and Tapestry Room) are gilded, as befits their important position in the chief apartments.

During the late Georgian period, fully-upholstered pieces included not only the 'burjair' chair type already referred to and the simply-designed settee of which the Osterley example is typical, but also other seats which were planned on more elaborate lines. Designs for these, at any rate, appear in Hepplewhite's *Guide* where the 'confidante', the 'duchesse' and the window stool are featured. In Sheraton's *Drawing Book* the 'chaise longue' is introduced. Both the duchesse and the chaise longue, of French inspiration, seem designed for one person only and therefore are included in the chapter devoted to day-beds and couches. The confidante was a curious composite piece, consisting of a long upholstered settee to which a triangular seat with arms was added at each end, being placed there at an angle and fully upholstered. These end seats, designed for one person, resembled the upholstered bergère or burjair and were intended to be a fixed part of the settee but might also be detachable. The lines of the Hepplewhite confidante show a more flowing or undulating curve to the back, and the piece presents altogether a less severe appearance than the Adam settee at Osterley.

The necessity for providing window stools arose from developments in interior design. Embrasures to sash windows with their hinged shutters had been, when Sir Christopher Wren built the new wings at Hampton Court Palace, filled in with solid window seats, the wall skirting running continuous across them. In other houses c. 1700 the embrasure was filled with a wooden window-sill and the space beneath often accommodated small cupboards with panelled doors. A movable piece of furniture for the window embrasures of later eighteenth-century interiors, particularly the reception rooms, was a useful innovation. It was designed without a back, and its length was governed by the space available which was unlikely to exceed four feet or thereabouts, i.e. the width of the sash window and its frame. The narrow seat was given raised ends, or arms, usually scrolled over but delicate in proportion, the seat and ends alike being upholstered. Designs in Hepplewhite's *Guide* (1794) show an elegant framework; the narrow seat rail perhaps ornamented with fluting and a central patera connects square or cylindrical tapered legs, whilst the scroll ends are decorated with some leafy motif and finish in a rosette. Ordinary stools were not much required in houses of the later eighteenth century. In shape they were usually rectangular, the rails being plain or shaped (i.e. serpentine, bowed, etc.) and supported on legs of elegant proportion often tapered or even of a delicate cabriole form. They might be made of mahogany or japanned, and would be covered with a fabric to match other upholstered pieces in the same room.

Upholstery fabrics used for the finest pieces of furniture included tapestry (often specially imported from France), damask, brocade and silk, but covers of woollen embroidery had gone completely out of fashion. So too had the boldly-figured design in woven fabrics, which were now enriched with small-scale patterns. Designs might show a distinctive stripe, either plain or alternating with a floral stripe, which was in key with the patterns of contemporary wallpapers. Colours were in the main refined and delicate rather than robust, especially for pieces intended for the drawing-room, the best bedrooms and the lady's boudoir. There was also some use of dyed leather and of woven horse-hair cloth as in the previous period.

During the early years of the nineteenth century or Regency period, the antiquarian or archaeological trend which influenced fashionable furniture showed itself with some vigour in the design of chairs and other seats. There was a decided and conscious reaction from the shapes which had been so much in vogue during the late Georgian period. The shield and oval back pieces were completely outmoded and new lines took their place. The new designs included many which were proclaimed to be in the true Greek, Roman or Egyptian styles. The chief enthusiast to herald new ideas in the 'antique' vein was Thomas Hope, whose *Household Furniture and Decoration* (1807) includes designs for chairs and stools. George Smith's book, with an almost identical title (1808) but with a less precise knowledge than Hope displayed, helped to spread the latest changes in style. Both men were indebted to France for a lead. Meanwhile Sheraton had already sensed the developments in style which were imminent, and in his *Cabinet Dictionary* (1803, but not completed) had produced some designs for chairs, two of which he styled 'Herculaneums'.

The chairs of this Regency period may be divided into two categories: those which still kept something of the elegance of line and proportion which had so thoroughly imbued late eighteenth-century work, and those, slightly later, which had become much more solid and massive incorporating such features as the animal leg and Egyptian sphinx in their design. The materials used were also chosen in a reaction from the light-toned colour schemes of the immediate past. Mahogany, rosewood and zebra wood were esteemed for their rich and sombre hues and these were echoed in the painted furniture, black being used to a great extent. A noticeable feature was the return of canework for the seat and back; it was also sometimes used to enclose the armchair at the sides. The main lines of the Regency chair back were rectilinear, with a certain emphasis on the horizontal in the design. One type, more popular in France than in England, was distinguished by the broad flat panel which formed the top rail and ran right across the uprights projecting beyond them. The back was normally open (i.e. not filled with upholstery), and two straight or curved cross-bars usually formed the splat. This type certainly had a

K

true classical origin, whence also were derived the narrow front legs sharply curving in sabre form. Contemporary illustrations show this chair in fashionable Regency interiors, together with armchairs in similar style; two scrolling curves formed the arm and its support. Sometimes the front legs of chairs were cylindrical, fluted and tapering, but so stout in proportion that they hardly resembled the eighteenth-century tapered leg at all. This Regency type of chair leg foreshadowed the rather clumsy support used later for mid-Victorian dining tables, and occasionally for dining-room chairs.

In a second type of Regency chair the back uprights curved over backward at the top, the horizontal back top rail being contained between them. This top rail was usually flat, perhaps itself curled over in sympathy with the uprights. The open back was filled in in a variety of ways, but generally the horizontal rail which either took the place of a splat, or supported a canework panel, was placed quite high above the seat rail leaving a considerable open space. This treatment helped to emphasize the horizontal nature of the design. In some chairs this horizontal splat might consist of a central plaque between pierced curves, or it might be entirely solid. Again, the horizontal rail might support a splat formed of interlacing straps small in scale. An oval panel of canework might be set horizontally between the top and bottom rails of the back. The seats of these Regency chairs often appear narrow in proportion to their depth, even in the case of armchairs. This is a reminder that after the French Revolution (1792 onward) a radical change took place in dress, new fashions being set by the French and copied in England. The ladies began to wear gowns *à la grècque*, without hoop or pannier, and their thin muslin draperies were scarcely crushed in these smaller chairs. Gentlemen too were wearing frock coats less ample in cut, whilst the wearing of swords had gone out of fashion.

In some Regency chairs the back upright, the side rail of the seat and the front sabre leg were designed to unite in a continuous flowing line. In the armchair the arms were designed to flow down from the back upright, beginning at a fairly high point (it will be noted that backs were low in themselves in comparison with earlier styles), and continued forward to scroll over, resting on a scroll-shaped or simple baluster support placed well forward on the seat. The backs of armchairs were similar to those of single chairs, and the sides might be filled in with canework or some carved motif. Legs usually did not terminate in feet at this time, except in those special types where an animal leg formed part of the design. An alternative to the sabre leg was a cylindrical tapered one, splayed slightly outward and carved at intervals with two or three rings. Stretchers were usually absent from these Regency chairs.

Whilst most of these pieces were made of mahogany, perhaps carved with some reeded decoration or inlaid with narrow brass lines for the spare ornamentation characteristic of the time, beech was used for painted furniture. The black ground was painted with narrow lines of gold, although sometimes a Greek key pattern decorated the seat rail. Occasionally a little polychrome decoration was used, often in the form of floral designs, small in size, and perhaps limited to the centre of the back rail. An occasional settee was made of painted beech with a long horizontal back rail, simple open arms and short tapered legs. The back and the seat (and sometimes the sides) were filled with canework and a long upholstered squab cushion was usually supplied. The traditional settee for several people was to some extent rivalled by the new 'Grecian' sofa, but this was intended for one person to recline on and was not strictly speaking to be regarded as a seat at this time.

Distinct from the foregoing types of chairs was the piece to which the designer attempted to give the true 'antique' character. Massive in their proportions, sometimes completely gilded, these chairs amongst which armchairs predominated often achieved a somewhat bizarre appearance. This was chiefly due to the use of animal legs as supports, and of the cat or lioness head as terminal to the back uprights, to the end of the arm and so on. Sometimes the front legs were crossed in the curve X-frame style designated 'curule' in the Regency period, and these appear in some designs ending in lions' heads for feet. In some mahogany examples the back and seat were padded and upholstered, in others canework was employed. Designs for stools were also made incorporating the cat-headed leg, or the curule type of support. Stools of this period, and in this manner, usually had a wooden seat, for example of veneered mahogany or rosewood.

Throughout the Victorian era the design of chairs and other seats went through a variety of phases. This was more or less a direct outcome of the increasing part played by mass-production in the making of furniture with its concomitant conditions, i.e. the decline in informed taste on the one hand, and on the other the necessity for making furniture (cheaply and in competition) to appeal to a variety of customers. Some influence on design was also felt when materials other than wood were used for chairs; this included wickerwork, bamboo and cast-iron. This latter was used to only a limited extent.

147

'Balloon' back chair, a type made throughout most of the Victorian period

Otherwise mahogany and walnut were mainly used in the earlier part of the period, but a great variety of woods in the later part.

During the early Victorian period the design of chairs fell into two classes, those which were used for sitting up (at table, etc.) and those for sitting down (e.g. the easy chair, which became increasingly important from now on). New styles of upholstered seating were also introduced with great emphasis on the thickness and comfort of the padding. The chair provided for the dining-room was sturdy, while its counterpart in the drawing-room, parlour, or bedroom was distinguished by its treatment, for instance by the introduction of a small amount of carved ornament. The design of the open back followed a development from the Regency chair which had a deep horizontal top rail, and gradually took the form known as 'balloon-back'. Here the framework of the back became continuous in outline; the top rail merged with the sides of the frame in a swollen kind of shape which can certainly not be described as oval. A horizontal-shaped bar formed a kind of splat where the sides of the back began to form the back legs. This strengthened the chair besides giving some support to the sitter. This curvilinear form lacked a true feeling for structure, the wood being treated as if it were a flexible material such as rubber. The seat of these early Victorian chairs began by being straight-sided; gradually the front rail became curved in plan and the back and sides rounded. With the earlier type of chair went a circular tapered front leg, carved with fluting or gadrooning, but the curved form developed a seat rail merging with the front leg into a modified cabriole shape. These later chairs, with perhaps a small amount of carved foliage ornament, had a curious rococo appearance. Sometimes the back was filled in with padding and covered to match the seat.

As the Victorian woman's skirts became more and more voluminous culminating in the large circular crinoline, the design of chairs had to be adapted to make sitting down convenient for her. The absence of arms from so many chairs of the period may be attributed to this cause which doubtless also accounts for the popularity of ottomans and 'sociables'. The easy chair for sitting down by the fireside soon assumed the same curved form of structure as other chairs. The back was given a modified version of the 'balloon' shape, extending down to meet the seat which was low in height and curved in plan. Here the legs were therefore shorter than on the single chairs. Back and seat were well upholstered. Some easy chairs were covered in Berlin wool-work, a coarse tent-stitch or cross-stitch embroidery on canvas often referred to as crewel work, and a favourite leisure occupation for ladies in the early and middle years of the nineteenth century. This embroidery was often used to cover another type of chair, the 'prie-dieu', a curious anachronism encouraged by the current romantic interest in the Middle Ages. This chair if it can be called such, for it was intended for use when at one's private devotions, had a low 'seat' to kneel upon and a fairly high rectangular back finished with a broad top rail on which to rest the hands or prayer book. The patterns

Upholstered 'spoon' back easy chair of rosewood. Mid-Victorian

149

worked by the ladies were of course not their own design but were often imported from Germany. They usually consisted of large motifs in rather strong colours, sometimes discordant to the modern eye. Large red roses, or enormous water-lilies with their appropriate leaves, were embroidered with great realism.

Mahogany used for chairs at this time was of the same bright hue as that used for other furniture; walnut was sometimes used for the rococo-type parlour chairs with the cabriole legs. An exception was the type of chair made of oak and termed 'Elizabethan' by its designers, although this was a misnomer. The tall back was usually of openwork carving finished with a high cresting of William and Mary type repeated for the front stretcher. The back uprights were usually spirally turned (a Restoration feature), so altogether this chair was an ill-informed combination of late Stuart styles. The seat might be of solid wood or upholstered; the back sometimes had a narrow upholstered panel inserted in it, on which Berlin woolwork might again appear. One of these chairs might stand in the hall for the use of a caller but sets were made for the dining-room.

The sofa, recalling the elegant Regency society lady, was transformed into a piece more suitable for the middle-class Victorian home. It might continue to have a half-back and one roll-over end throughout the entire Victorian period, the frame being mounted on short turned feet, but the typical Regency motifs were quickly discarded. The Victorian lady might like to recline in her bedroom or boudoir on a sofa after luncheon or before dressing for dinner, but furniture-makers soon found there was a demand for a piece to seat two or three persons. Although by tradition a settee, there was a tendency to call this piece of furniture by the name of sofa, a confusion which continued into the twentieth century. In this Victorian sofa the long back rail had a continuous curve, and the roll-over sides provided some support for the figure at each end. Sometimes the padded upholstery entirely overwhelmed the framework, a very clumsy and amorphous appearance being the result, swollen, bulging and lacking any grace of line.

In fashionable circles, for use during parties, balls and receptions, other types of upholstered seats for several people were designed. These included the ottoman which had neither back nor sides, and the 'sociable' which took more than one form. The ottoman was merely a bench covered with well-padded upholstery. The sociable on the other hand had more character. One type was designed as two armchairs (the arms set very low indeed near the seat) joined together but facing in opposite directions, so that the occupants sat side by side and face to face. Another type was circular in plan, people sitting all round it with their backs to the centre, which was often designed to support a potted plant. Here the idea was that the ladies could sit gracefully whilst the gentlemen stood by conversing or handing light refreshments.

For all heavily-upholstered furniture the covering fabric was 'buttoned' down, the buttons being covered in the same material. This ranged from rich silk damasks to the more homely leather (chiefly popular for rooms sacred to the menfolk, the gun room, estate room, den and so on), and the well-known woven horsehair cloth. Heavy fringes decorated the more expensive pieces.

When the Gothic Revival was affecting furniture it had much less effect on chair design than on other pieces. Some armchairs appear to have been made with wooden seats and sloping backs supported on legs of the folding type. On other examples the chair back might have the top rail treated with Gothic cresting or pinnacles, and the designer might resort to Gothic tracery for other ornament. Legs to chairs might be carved to suggest Early English piers (i.e. of clustered columns).

In the later Victorian period manufacturers competing for business began to produce chairs in styles reminiscent of the past, chiefly invoking the magic names of Sheraton and Chippendale. This usually meant adaptation rather than factual reproduction, and it is not possible to summarize satisfactorily all the variations that appeared. Traces of the source of inspiration can be noted in the shape of the top rail of the back, perhaps in the typical Chippendale 'line'. Chairs throughout the house became lighter in appearance whatever 'style' they followed, and whether they were made of 'ebonized' wood, oak or other timber. The custom of having loose covers for chairs and settees became popular.

The Windsor chair continued to be made during the nineteenth century, the back perhaps finished with a flat vertical top rail. The legs were made either in the traditional turned spindle shape or in a simple version of a more up-to-date turned leg. Some Windsor and other types of armchair were mounted on rockers. Other unfashionable chairs included those made of wickerwork, bentwood or bamboo. The last hardly calls for comment. Armchairs of wickerwork were rather like cages, the seat enclosed by back and sides above and below. A loose cushion covered the seat and the back was often lined with upholstery. More stylish chairs with sloping backs, and with arms in which a receptacle for a glass tumbler was arranged, are advertised in

Bentwood chair

the 1870s onward, but may have been intended for use on liners travelling to and from the Far East. A modified version of these was acceptable at home for the verandah or the garden summerhouse. The frames of bentwood were simple, the 'bent' support being round in section and forming an open back and legs. The seat of plywood might be perforated with a pattern of small holes. A feature which formed part of the design of other furniture, i.e. the rows of tiny spindles, sometimes appeared in the construction of the arm-support in chairs or for the low half-back of the sofa or settee. Canvas folding deck-chairs, with or without adjustable head-canopies and foot-rests, were popular on board ship and could also be bought for the garden where croquet parties and tennis parties were becoming more and more part of country house or suburban villa life. Chairs of a more permanent type were made of 'rustic' work, the structure being of roughly-treated wood matching the simple garden table. Long seats, painted white, were made with an open arm at each end and had open backs filled with thin narrow vertical splats.

As the twentieth century began late Victorian styles continued, chairs looking rather thin and spindly; the open back might be narrow and tall, slightly influenced by Art Nouveau. The chairs made to the design of Charles Rennie Mackintosh were eccentric in appearance, the tall spindle back uprights soaring some way above the top rail. Upholstered chairs and settees became extremely large and clumsy in shape in the 1920s and 1930s, with immensely thick backs and roll-over arms. Other chairs and settees had lightweight wood framing filled with canework for back and sides; these required the addition of loose cushions. At this time there was a certain amount of 'reproduc-tion' furniture being made for sale, the tendency being to have

'Chippendale' chairs for the dining-room and 'Queen Anne' for the sitting-room, but the Queen Anne type was used in all rooms. Its appearance was somewhat marred by a high polish which was quite out of character. This style was very popular for the mass-furnishing of hotels and restaurants of the more pretentious class. A 'cottage-y' type of chair, besides the eternal Windsor chair, was made with ladder back and rushwork seat, another revival. There was a large variety of choice in upholstery fabrics of all sorts and kinds including leather, and these were neatly and closely fitted to the piece; 'buttoning' was sometimes used but was not a general practice. Loose covers to protect the permanent upholstery fabric were usually bought or made independently of the furniture, and were carefully tailored for the bulky overstuffed armchairs and settees. For these loose covers printed chintzes and cretonnes in summery colour schemes were often chosen to match or blend with the window curtains.

During the 1930s some chairs were made of chromium-plated tubing. A continuous length of tubing was ingeniously bent to form the back of the chair and the front legs, whence it was bent along backward again at floor level to balance the chair, obviating the necessity for back legs. A padded panel was added to the back and another formed the seat. An arm with padded elbow rest was sometimes incorporated. These chairs were very small in size and could be stacked one above the other without difficulty when not in use. A few matching settees, but with solid backs, were attempted with tubing supports. Another type of stacking chair was made of laminated wood, the supports being of a simple, straight design; most of these were imported from Scandinavia.

A certain number of stools were made during the 1920s and 1930s, the most popular being those supplied as a 'nest' of three of diminishing size, stacked one over the other. These were rectangular with plain straight legs. They were distinguished from the contemporary nest of small tables by having a sturdier framework and an upholstered top for seat. Some stools were made of chromium-plated tubing. 'Stacking' stools with round seats mounted on three legs were made of laminated wood. This fashion for having stacking furniture reflected the post-war size of rooms and the anxiety not to clutter the floor space with unnecessary furniture. The making of folding 'bridge' chairs to accompany the folding card table was another example of this desire to economize in space. A more striking manifestation was in the convertible piece, either a settee which could be folded down for use as a double bed, or the armchair for use as a single bed.

Most houses, even quite small ones of the semi-detached type, now had direct communication with the garden by a glazed French door from one of the living rooms; the love of fresh air and the passion for sunbathing were becoming ever more popular, so too was the buying of special garden furniture. Variants of the earlier canvas deck chair continued to be made; there was also the very luxurious swinging seat supported on a metal frame. This latter was a two-seat or three-seat settee with arms, the back and seat being neatly upholstered. A generous canopy was adjustable overhead, and the gayest and brightest colours were chosen for the printed upholstery coverings.

After the Second World War some elegant garden chairs to recline on at full length were made of lightweight metal, a loose padded cushion being flung over the frame which took a gentle curve flowing in line with the human spine and also allowing a slight bend at the position of the human knee, all making for extra comfort and encouraging relaxation. This garden 'lounge' chair usually had two small wheels at one end and a pair of handles at the other, so that it could be moved about like a wheelbarrow.

In the 1950s some notable developments took place in the design of chairs and other seats. Instead of clumsy internal springing, upholstery padding could be made of 'foam-rubber' or a synthetic, rubbery, springy material by which the thickness of the upholstery could be reduced to a minimum without loss of comfort. This enabled the design of chairs and settees to be much less clumsy in style.

The fact that television viewing has become the rage in nearly every home means seats are needed with low backs, either as a continuous settee or as chairs which can be placed close together appearing like a settee if required. In either case the shape may be rectangular or gently curved in plan. Such furniture has very low comfortable seats, the backs being very slightly tilted and the framework mainly over-stuffed, supported on short legs which may be of the 'stick' type. Some lounging chairs are made of a light tubular framework on which a shaped piece of strong brightly-coloured canvas forms the seat-cum-back. Since many women now wear the fashionable slacks or tights they can relax agreeably in this unconventional chair in very modern style, perhaps adding a small cushion or two of contrasting colour for more comfort. Another type of this so-called 'dog-basket' chair is a more literal expression of the name, the 'seat' being made of wicker-work cunningly woven to achieve the rather basin-like shape. Other fashionable chairs include those of laminated wood with a broad horizontal back panel on a centre support only (no back uprights), the

Easy chair with metal underframe (chromium-plated or stove-enamelled dark grey), preformed laminated wood frame, rubber foam cushion, modern upholstery covering. Design by S. Hille c. 1956

wood seat being mounted on legs of laminated wood bent to form a back and front leg together, each side. These chairs are used at table and can be stacked. Others, usually with very small seats and the minimum of back, are supported on slender metal frames with 'stick' legs, the frame usually painted black. Gayer paint is occasionally used.

The easy chair may be a modern version of the traditional winged armchair but usually with the arms placed lower, perhaps open rather than upholstered; sometimes the piece is carefully designed with the back sloping at two angles to follow the bend of the human body at rest. The seat level in this latest period in the history of furniture is lower than ever before, partly for comfort when viewing television so that the eyes are not forced to look up or the head be held too high; it is also in line with the current fashion for keeping all furniture at as low a height as possible in houses and flats with low ceilings (an economic necessity in building). Convertible armchairs and settees for beds are perennially popular, merely following in design any convenient style.

Chairs for small children had been made, as already noted, in the early seventeenth century, on the principle of having a small seat and back mounted on long legs. This practice continued, following stylistic changes in fashion in the grown-up world during the eighteenth and nineteenth centuries. Occasionally in the Victorian period children's chairs were made with short legs, to 'child size', but it was not until the twentieth century that the cult of having children's furniture suited to the use of a small person really arose. Small chairs of simple design are now made of wood and painted in light and attractive colours. The high chair is now simply a baby-chair, separate from the other nursery furniture and often convertible into a low chair with low table attached.

Bath chairs, invalid chairs, dentists' chairs and others of the kind hardly come into this story, but reference may be made to those small lightweight pieces designed as camping equipment, or to be carried by the motorist to be used with its companion table for wayside picnics. This picnic furniture is made of metal and brightly painted, with a gaily-coloured fabric woven of some test-tube fibre with all the qualities now demanded (non-creasing, easily cleaned and so forth), for upholstery where needed.

The chair which began, centuries back in history, by having the rarity, dignity and importance of a throne, has thus progressively become more and more of a common necessity, designed in a variety of ways to meet the need for every kind of usage.

CHAPTER TEN

Sideboards and Dressers

The terms cupboard, buffet, dresser and sideboard are all names used at different times for a piece of furniture whose chief function, from medieval times to the present day, has been the display and storage of plate, dishes and other objects connected with the service of meals. The first term in use was cupboard, i.e. cup-board which literally signified a board or shelf on which metal cups were set and from which they were taken to table when the diner called for wine or ale. In illuminated manuscripts of the medieval period such furniture is clearly shown, standing on or near the dais in the great hall. It seems to have consisted of a number of shelves ranged one above the other in graduated tiers, with or without a cupboard enclosed with doors below. Linen cloths were spread on the shelves, on which stood various ewers, jugs and cups, and perhaps some ornamental pieces of gold plate. The actual number of tiers or shelves were in proportion to the status of the owner, increasing in number according to rank, or so it would appear from these contemporary illustrations. The shape of the piece was usually plain and rectangular, with the introduction of some carved Gothic tracery as decoration. As linenfold ornament came into use, that too might appear on any panelling to the front. When Catherine of Aragon came to marry Prince Arthur, eldest son of Henry VII, it is recorded that at the celebrations there was a great cup-board standing five tiers high, whilst at the coronation of Anne Boleyn there was one standing ten tiers high, on which was displayed a great quantity of splendid gold plate 'most marvellous to behold'.

During the second half of the sixteenth century and the early Stuart period, when the great hall was left more for the use of the servants and as a general assembly room, the cupboard for plate was set up in the dining parlour where it had now become an established custom for the family and guests to take their meals. This piece of furniture was usually designed in one of two ways. Either it consisted of three shelves, open on all sides, with specially decorative carved supports at the front corners, or it took the form of a cupboard (in the modern sense) enclosed with doors. This latter was a natural development arising from changes in social customs. Although it might still be thought well to display fine possessions in gold plate, especially when important guests were present, a piece of furniture in which useful articles could be temporarily stored became more necessary. This was even more likely in the houses of the middle classes rising to new prosperity.

The first or open type, sometimes called a buffet, sometimes a court cupboard, was usually just over four feet wide and about four feet high. Of the three open shelves the lowest, like a kind of platform, stood on short feet almost like blocks, and was generally plain, covered with a table carpet. The middle and top shelves may occasionally be seen with an inlaid design. The back uprights or supports were normally plainly designed, being narrow and flat; it is assumed that the gold or silver vessels on display, or the pewter or pottery, hid them from view. In many pieces, however, great care was lavished on the design of the front supports usually richly carved. For these the bulbous shape fashionable for the legs of dining tables and as posts to great beds was often employed. This vase-shaped bulb was generally carved in the contemporary manner with gadrooning and acanthus leaves. The edges of the shelves, front and side, were carved and the frieze rails were often inlaid with light and dark checker or geometrical ornament. The rail to the middle shelf might be carved with interlacing strapwork. Both top and middle shelves might be fitted with a drawer underneath, the central drawer being conspicuously deeper. Oak or solid walnut was employed to make these pieces, with such woods as holly or bog oak for the inlaid decoration.

A typical buffet or sideboard of late sixteenth-century date is one in two tiers, each supported in front by a pair of bulbous columns carved with nulling and acanthus, and behind by rectangular uprights carved with chevrons; the frieze of the top is decorated in front and on the sides with inlay of checker design in holly and bog oak, the front opening as a drawer. The middle shelf is inlaid with a geometrical design, its front is carved with strapwork and opens as a drawer. Below the bottom shelf is a band of checker inlay. More unusual and highly decorative, were buffets in which heraldic beasts were introduced as supports, for example, the Royal (Tudor) supporters, the greyhound and the dragon, or some fabulous eagle-headed monster. One buffet still in existence has carved busts in high relief for the front supports, but is otherwise very plain.

The second type, i.e. the enclosed cupboard, popular during the late sixteenth century and early seventeenth century, was mostly constructed in two stages. The characteristic piece had an upper stage, perhaps half-hexagonal and partly recessed forming a shelf in front. At the front corners separate bulbous supports or baluster shapes helped to carry the top. In some very late examples these supports might be omitted, a pendant at each corner of the top taking their place and giving the effect almost of a canopy. The lower stage was enclosed with very plain panelled doors. During the early Stuart period a number of enclosed cupboards were made of great width. Some of these pieces were lightly carved in low relief with flat patterns, and many which survive have a date carved on them.

Yet another type of cupboard or sideboard was made, which cannot be classed either as an open buffet or as an enclosed cupboard, since in design it was intermediate between the two. In such a piece the lower stage alone was open, the frieze being fitted with a drawer. The upper stage was enclosed, being three-sided in plan and fitted with a central inlaid door, whilst the top was carried at each corner by the contemporary bulbous or vase-shaped support.

In addition to the buffets and court cupboards of the Tudor and early Stuart periods, which stood in the dining parlours and perhaps in the hall, there was another piece called the livery cupboard. This was not for the display of plate but was strictly for use, since it was mainly intended for the sleeping chambers and to contain refreshments which might be required after retiring to rest. This was an old custom dating from medieval times when rations of bread and wine or ale were provided. For these refreshments an enclosed piece of furniture was designed which yet allowed for some ventilation. These cupboards might stand on the floor, but quite often were hung on the wall. The front and sides might be made of solid wood, but pierced to resemble window openings in the form of tracery, or in some kind of diaper pattern. A standing livery cupboard of oak, representative of this type, is four feet wide and five feet four inches high. It dates from about 1500, and the corner posts are prolonged to form legs. The central upper door is pierced and filled with a kind of crocketed ornament, with the panel on either side pierced with Gothic tracery. The central lower door is also pierced with Gothic tracery, and the panel each side is pierced and filled with a motif resembling a feather, giving rise to the theory that the piece had had some connection with Arthur, Prince of Wales, son of Henry VII. The depth of such a piece might be as much as two feet, but for the hanging livery cupboard it was usually much less. One example of the late sixteenth century is only about eight inches deep, another of early seventeenth-century date is ten and a half inches deep. This is practical, in view of their hanging on the wall. In the first piece which is about two and a half feet high, there are two doors filled with two tiers of short turned balusters between three stiles boldly carved with a trailing vine pattern. The solid sides are carved with a guilloche design enclosing a rosette. In the second piece, the front entirely consists of two rows of turned slender spindles of which the central seven of each row in reality form a door, hingeing on one of the spindles. This gives a very light and airy effect to the piece. The ends are formed as two panels.

After the Restoration, the medieval custom of making a show of wealth by the display of articles of gold plate was more or less abandoned. Not only had much gold plate been melted down during the Civil Wars, but also silver had superseded it to a great extent for fine articles of domestic use. Besides this, with greater refinement in the way of living, there was a greater variety of things on which wealth could be expended for the gratification of the owner, not least the fine new furniture of marquetry, splendid looking-glasses for the walls and so on. The buffet and the court cupboard of earlier times was therefore superseded by a kind of sideboard which became part of the furnishing of the dining parlour, and was designed to a height suitable for the carving of joints or for the setting out of dishes before they were brought to the table. A typical example would in consequence be lower than its predecessors, about three feet high, the whole piece tending to be long and narrow and consisting of drawers, three or four in number, mounted on turned legs united by simple stretchers. The drawer fronts were usually ornamented with applied mouldings forming geometrically shaped panels, and were fitted with pear-drop or knob handles of brass. The turned supports were often of simple baluster form. Split balusters might be used as applied ornament on the stiles between the drawers. These sideboards were mostly made of oak.

During the late Stuart period another piece of furniture related to the earlier court cupboard was developed. This was the dresser which was destined to be for a long time a favourite and useful piece of furniture in kitchens in the countryside and in provincial towns. The dresser was designed in two parts, the lower consisting of enclosed cupboards with a row of drawers above, under a wide long top which again was at a height convenient for carving. The upper part, with a high back, supported long and extremely narrow shelves on which dishes could be arranged in rows. Such dressers were most often made of solid oak, very plain in design in keeping with their purpose and

160

position in the house, and brightened by the brass lock-plates and handles on the drawer fronts and cupboard doors. Their chief ornamentation, of course, derived from the great dishes, in graduated sizes, of pewter or brightly-painted earthenware which stood upright along the shelves. The kitchen dresser never followed fashionable styles, but kept a traditional simplicity throughout the eighteenth century, and later took the form of a fixture rather than a movable piece of furniture. As such, the dresser might be made of painted deal.

Meanwhile, in fashionable circles, changes had been taking place. As the eighteenth century began, the passion for display took a new form. The wealthy were making collections of Oriental porcelain, a vogue chiefly introduced into England from Holland by Queen Mary II. These fragile objects, at first placed about rooms on the chimney-piece and elsewhere, were soon to be put behind glass for safety, and cabinets (q.v.) with glazed doors were designed for this purpose, but had no place in the dining-room where the furniture now tended to become limited to the necessary tables and chairs, with sideboard tables instead of the late Stuart sideboard. These tables were placed against the walls and were useful adjuncts for the serving of meals. Such pieces might be of carved walnut with a marble top supported on fairly stout cabriole legs. In the more elaborate examples the legs might be connected by a carved apron in which acanthus foliage might be the chief motif.

By the mid-Georgian period, the sideboard table was being made of mahogany with a wood or marble top on cabriole legs of more or less decorative form, judiciously carved with a certain amount of rococo ornament and ending on claw-and-ball or rococo scroll feet. The frieze rail in special pieces might be carved with a key fret in very low relief and the top, if of marble, would be variegated in colour. In Chippendale's *Director* (1754) they appear as side tables. Sideboard tables for the dining-room were on the whole a simple version of the similar, more decorative tables intended for the hall or the great saloon. (See Tables.)

Further developments took place during the later Georgian period, when Robert Adam appears to have been the first to make acceptable a new arrangement for the dining-room. This consisted in having a sideboard table as before, without drawers, but placed between a pair of low pedestal cupboards each with an urn on it. The urn was either separate from the pedestal or attached to it. The central table was rectangular in shape, or had a slight serpentine curve to the front. It was not unduly long, and was supported on four or six tapered fluted legs without connecting stretchers. It was frequently found convenient to keep a cellaret, a separate piece of furniture for wine bottles, under this table. The frieze rail to the table might be fluted, or carved with swags of husks or festoons of drapery, with paterae above the legs in Adam's typical style. The top might be plain or of light-coloured marble, and was sometimes fitted at the back with a light rail of brass against which articles of gold plate or of silver, such as salvers, might rest. The pedestal was square or sometimes bombé, in shape, and had a door opening on a cupboard for the storage of dishes, or was fitted as a cellaret. These pedestals were made of mahogany with the flat surfaces veneered; a little applied carving might be added for decoration. The urn above, following the classical shape made fashionable by Adam, was made of metal or of carved mahogany. The urn was intended for the butler's use, perhaps being lined with lead to hold iced water. Alternatively, it could hold hot water for washing cutlery. The top of the urn was raised on a central rod designed to keep it steady in position as required. These urns were sometimes fitted inside as knife cases padded with coloured velvet, perhaps crimson, to receive knives and forks, the handles uppermost. Some examples made of mahogany were delicately carved with ornament, e.g. drapery swags and satyr masks. Where Adam designed furniture for special interiors, such as certain dining-rooms in which the end wall or walls might be curved or apsidal in plan, the sideboard table was curved in plan to fit the lines of the recess. For example, at Kedleston in Derbyshire, he designed three sideboard tables in this manner. In each the top was of marble and the supporting framework was painted white with the carved enrichments gilded.

In some cases, this group of furniture serving the purpose of a sideboard was painted in harmony with the interior decoration of a particular room. For instance, in the Eating Room at Osterley Park House in Middlesex, there are pedestals, circular in plan this time, painted white and soft pink and pale green, matching the prevailing colour scheme. Delicate fluting swirls about the body, and above it is a particularly magnificent urn with a pair of swan-neck handles. These urns are fitted with spigot and tap for drawing off water. At Ken Wood, in North London, a single sideboard table with a mahogany top supported on a framework painted white, stood between a pair of white circular pedestals each with a mahogany urn on top. At Saltram in Devon, Adam's designs (1781) for sideboard table and pedestals were carried out in wood painted green to match the walls of the dining-room, and the enrichments were coloured buff. During the later eighteenth century additional side tables might be placed in the dining-room. These were similar in design to the sideboard table, and gave extra facilities for the servants when a meal was being served.

From this association of table and separate pedestals it was a short step to the sideboard as a composite piece, in the form which the modern use of the term connotes. By the later years of the eighteenth century this piece was being made in a typical design, consisting of a shallow central drawer flanked by a pair of lateral cupboards or deep wine drawers, the whole supported on four front and two back legs of square tapered form ending in a plain foot. The flanking cupboards replaced the separate pedestals in purpose. In some cases there may be on one side a cupboard, on the other two drawers, a shallow one over a deeper one. If so, it will be seen that the cupboard door has been designed to resemble the drawer fronts, including the position of the handles. The deep drawer found in many pieces was intended as a cellaret and was divided into six compartments for wine bottles, and sometimes lined with lead. These late eighteenth-century sideboards might be rectangular in plan, but very frequently were bow-fronted or serpentine, or hollow-fronted, with the curve of the top following the same outline. The sides might be straight or partly curved. Mahogany veneer was much used for these pieces, with a narrow cross-banding of tulipwood between a narrow light and dark stringing used as a border on the top and to the drawer fronts and doors. Certain motifs were often used in addition, e.g. a shell in a small oval panel of marquetry on the top, and fans in the spandrels of the segmental arch under the centre drawer. Sometimes a patera of marquetry decorated the stiles, or again these might have a narrow panel of satinwood edged with light and dark stringing, a treatment sometimes repeated on the square tapered legs. A brass rail, the uprights perhaps ending in a tiny urn finial, was fitted as a 'stay', as Sheraton called it, against which salvers or trays or dishes might be propped. Sideboards of this period were mostly fitted with plain ring handles mounted on circular or oval plates. Sometimes the lion mask mount with ring handle might be used.

In the main the sideboard of the late eighteenth century was supported on legs, but in the Regency period extra provision was made. The shallow centre drawer, straight or slightly bow-fronted, connected the two pedestals which were now designed with extra capacity, since each stood on four short feet only, and were not raised up on legs. They therefore presented much more the appearance of full pedestals than the late eighteenth-century piece had done. The sides and front of the pedestal might be straight but were often tapered, and the door opened to disclose two drawers, the lower one arranged as a cellaret. The feet might be of animal paw design or simple spade shape. Each pedestal might well be continued to a height above that of the main centre drawer to contain yet another drawer. This limited the space on the top of the sideboard, giving less room for carving. In some pieces there will be seen, in addition, a box with tapered sides on each pedestal, mounted on four ball feet and acting as the equivalent of the Adam case or urn. The centre portion of the sideboard might have a brass rail across the back, or have a wooden back shaped to a low curve which connected with the two pedestals. Regency sideboards were mahogany or rosewood, the flat surface being veneered, but very few mouldings were employed. There was some use of inlaid lines for decoration, of ebony or brass which, with the brass of the handles, followed the limited repertory of ornament characteristic of the period. Very occasionally a sideboard table might be made in addition to the sideboard proper. In view of the more limited space for carving on the Regency sideboard this might well have been a necessity for larger households. One sideboard table made c. 1800 has a break-front top supported on six legs, the two back ones being plain, tapered and fluted, whilst the four at the front are lion-headed ending in a paw foot. All six legs rest on a shelf, recessed at the centre front and supported on short feet, cylindrical, tapered and fluted.

During the early Victorian period numerous sideboards were made for the new prosperous middle-class homes. These were more massive than the Regency pieces and in some cases were of truly monumental proportions. Yet more accommodation was provided than formerly by filling in the centre portion with cupboards. The arrangement of meals was taking on the pattern in use today. The Victorian family met at the dining table for four large meals a day, for which the manufacturer of china was supplying large services. In some houses the butler's pantry might accommodate much of the silver, i.e. the pieces required for formal dinner or luncheon parties, but for people leading a more homely kind of existence the dining-room sideboard had to store rather a miscellaneous collection of objects. There was perhaps less emphasis on the provision of wine, although a 'tantalus' for spirits might stand on the sideboard.

A typical early Victorian sideboard would be made of mahogany, rather brighter in colour than before, or of deal stained to imitate it. It was designed as one long carcase, placed directly on the narrow base or plinth and was divided into shelved central and side cupboards, one of the latter being fitted with a cellaret drawer. A range of shallow drawers, possibly four in number, were arranged under the top which might be rounded at the front corners. Mouldings were not conspicuous, and wood knob handles were fitted to drawers and doors. Knife-boxes went out of fashion for these middle-class homes, the cutlery being supplied by the maker in large flat boxes specially designed to contain it. These new cases for cutlery cannot be regarded as furniture, and were utilitarian objects of little decorative value. The carving was done by the head of the household or his wife seated at table, which left the sideboard free for display. Compositions of wax fruits realistically coloured, and protected by a tall glass dome, were a favourite ornament and appeared in pairs on the sideboard. These indeed had pride of place, but were rivalled by other ornaments also under glass domes, such as large pieces of branching white coral, or small stuffed birds on little trees.

During the later Victorian period, sideboards, like most other

Sideboard design for mass-production in wood, with mirror panels in the back. From crude drawing in trade journal of later Victorian date

furniture, were largely being mass-produced and their design was affected by the prevailing fashions and desire for variety. In appearance many tended to be less massive, although a superstructure of small cupboards and a shelf or two under a long cornice was now usually added. The general effect, due to the introduction of finicky details with narrow rails and stiles fluted to decrease their apparent size, became less ponderous. The search for new ideas sometimes produced a design which was large in size and heavy in treatment, and enriched by the copious application of ornamental motifs considered to be in keeping with the period style which was said to have inspired it. In this class are those designs given high-sounding labels such as 'Gothic style', 'Henri Deux style' and 'Elizabethan style'. Those declared to be 'in the Sheraton style' were less ponderous.

The sideboard continued to be made at the traditional height convenient for carving, although the top was now used chiefly for trays and other accessories for meals required by the servants, besides being crowded wherever possible with ornaments such as vases, or the epergne for fruit and flowers when it was not actually on the dining table, and even in some houses supporting a pair of bronze figures, fashionable importations from France. A typical piece, whatever the 'style' claimed for it, generally consisted of a row of drawers at a convenient height with cupboards below, but in many cases the cupboards were varied with open shelves. The upper part, recessed from the front by about a foot, was usually open in the centre with a small cupboard and an open shelf, or a tier of open shelves at each side. The whole of this high back was frequently panelled with mirror plate, and a small cornice ran round the top at front and sides. A certain amount of relief might be introduced on drawer and door fronts, with little to distinguish its style. The labels of style already mentioned, used to suggest derivation from one or another style of the past, often denote little more than slight differences in ornamentation. This furniture was often made in some cheap wood stained to counterfeit satinwood, or perhaps was made of solid oak. Cheap cast-brass handles, drop-shape for the cupboard doors, and various forms of ring to the drawer fronts, were fitted to these pieces.

When William Morris and his friends, for example the architect Philip Webb, began to take an interest in the design of furniture, the results were much less complicated and some pieces made by careful craftsmen still survive. These were however special pieces of furniture, and their advent had no effect on what was being produced in the factories. Nor had the work of the architect Charles Rennie Mackintosh and other exponents of the Art Nouveau style towards the turn of the nineteenth century.

Confused designs combining various ideas derived from the past continued to be made during the early twentieth century. By the 1920s a romantic attachment to the so-called 'Jacobean' style was in full swing where dining-room furniture was concerned. This was very popular and involved the use of solid oak which (mistakenly) was treated to give it an 'old-world' appearance, and known as 'fumed oak'. The result was rather unpleasant, destroying the quality of the wood and creating an effect resembling dark brown leather. A dining-room suite in fumed oak included, besides table and chairs, a smallish-sized sideboard containing cupboards and drawers, and supported on some kind of bulbous leg which was usually plain and uncarved. A form of dresser was an alternative to this piece. The popularity of Queen Anne reproduction dining-room suites allowed the inclusion of a simpler type of sideboard, all the pieces being carried out in walnut and incorporating the cabriole leg as support wherever possible. All these pieces, like most mass-produced furniture of the time, were treated with a high polish which tended to give a somewhat unpleasant effect.

An outstanding exception to these two 'period' styles was seen in the furniture produced in limed oak by a limited number of firms. Here the sideboard was small in size, simple in its lines and nicely-proportioned. The design was limited to the provision of a drawer or two with perhaps two cupboards, forming a clear rectangular shape, supported on straight square legs. The drawer and door fronts might have simple moulded edges. There was no upper structure.

Some attempt was made during the 1930s to produce furniture with supports of tubular chromium-plated metal. This idea was applied with limited effect to a simple rectangular sideboard fitted with drawers and cupboards in the usual way. During the 1930s the fashion for fitments extended to the dining-room, especially in small houses or flats. In such cases the sideboard fitment was usually painted to accord with the colour scheme, particularly with the walls, and occasionally the top was covered with mirror-plate or clear glass. This was an extravagant and not very practical measure, but as the wheeled trolley had come into use for the conveyance of hot dishes and other things directly to the table, the sideboard was beginning to lose some of its traditional functions.

During the Second World War, shortages of all kinds were so severe that there was a temporary lull in furniture design and

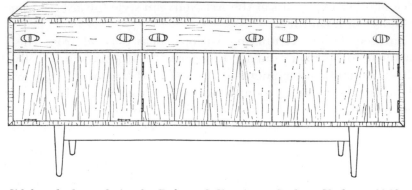

Sideboard after a design by Dalescraft Furniture, Pudsey, Yorks. c. 1962

production. 'Utility' pieces only were made, designed with the bare essentials, but this austerity was discarded afterwards as soon as possible. This was a natural reaction to some extent, and once again the furniture industry has shown a great deal of variety. At one end of the scale is the piece produced on 'contemporary' lines, owing a good deal to the inspiration of furniture imported from Denmark and later from Italy. The sideboard in this category tends to be much lower than before, being in effect a shelf on which the minimum is placed, e.g. a bowl of fruit, or perhaps something ornamental such as a vase of flowers or a pot plant. The top is supported on a carcase divided to contain one, two or three cupboards with some drawers, often arranged as a tier. Such a piece is usually raised well above the floor, perhaps on the new metal 'stick' legs. Again the sideboard may in fact be a fitment attached to the wall, raised above the floor so that close-fitted carpets can be cleaned without difficulty. Outer surfaces may be of a wood veneer, or made in a plastic counterfeit, e.g. imitating walnut. New treatments have been applied to make the top resistant to heat and spilt liquids. Sometimes, apart from the drawers which always have solid fronts, the front of the piece may be fitted with glass panels sliding sideways in grooves. Handles used include round or shaped knob forms, or thin metal bars, or again the surface may be grooved or slightly depressed to give the fingers a purchase, thus omitting handles altogether.

At the other end of the scale in the field of mass-production, sideboards are made in a great variety of designs, mainly adaptations of past styles but with a tendency to omit a second or upper portion, except when reproducing a modern version of the dresser. This not only keeps the cost down, but makes the piece more suitable for modern low-ceilinged rooms. The open partitions, sometimes used in 'open-plan' domestic interiors, are often fitted as sideboards with cupboards and drawers for cutlery. Painted in harmony with the colour scheme of the living-room, or in contrast to it, these fittings are not in serious rivalry with the production of furniture proper, i.e. the movable pieces which, after all, can be moved when their owner moves house.

CHAPTER ELEVEN

Couches, Day-beds and Sofas

These three names have each been used at different times for a comfortable piece of furniture, mainly intended for the use of one person to recline upon during the daytime. On occasion the terms 'couch' and 'sofa' have been loosely applied to the settee, a name which might with advantage be reserved for the long seat with back and arms, meant for two or more people to sit on.

In classical times, it had been an age-old custom to recline at the banquet, especially for men. The ancient Romans, with their highly developed taste for luxury, appreciated to the full the pleasure of lolling on a couch. Even when a wealthy Roman gave a dinner party, he would consider three the perfect number: he and his carefully-chosen guests reclined, each on a separate couch, about the three sides of the dining table. This left the fourth side free for the attendants to serve the wine and the dishes. Hence came the name 'triclinium' which may be freely translated 'place of three couches'. In the archaic frescoes painted on the walls of Etruscan tombs, bronzed men are depicted reclining on couches and waited upon by serving men with golden jugs of wine.

The daytime couch and the bed for sleeping on at night were in those remote ages much the same in design. It was to be a different matter in later times. During the Middle Ages, however, a period not exactly celebrated for its comforts, even in a wealthy establishment a special couch to rest on was fairly rare among the limited number of pieces of furniture. The rich man or woman evidently lay at ease on the upholstered bed of the time, propped on cushions or pillows with the bed-curtains looped up out of the way. This kind of scene may be met with in illuminated manuscripts. Occasional mention occurs of a couch which sounds like a long bench on which some cushions had been laid. By the end of the sixteenth century, day-beds as such were becoming more common. A day-bed is mentioned at least twice by Shakespeare, each time the inference being one of luxury and even of effeminacy. In *Richard III* (1594) the Duke of Buckingham, speaking of the Duke of Gloucester (later Richard III) and King Edward IV, exclaims of Gloucester:

> 'Ah, ha, my lord, this prince is not an Edward!
> He is not lolling upon a lewd daybed,
> But on his knees at meditation'
> (*Richard III*, ACT III, SCENE VII)

Buckingham was not giving a sincere estimate of Gloucester's character, but the point of the day-bed being a piece of furniture on which to lounge in idleness was made, and the Elizabethan playgoer was obviously expected to appreciate it without difficulty. In *Twelfth Night* (1600), it is Olivia, the wealthy mistress of a large household, who is spoken of by her steward Malvolio as taking her repose on a day-bed. He is indulging in one of his fanciful day-dreams of future glory for himself as her husband, but clearly the scene he describes is true to life.

A notable example, the kind of thing Shakespeare may well have had in mind, was made for the owners of Hardwick Hall in Derbyshire in 1600. This piece shows its derivation from the long medieval bench, and has a tilted panel fixed at each end to form a support for the person, the wooden framework all being painted a dark red. For these early day-beds the upholstery was more important than the frame; a long mattress with a number of cushions of graduated sizes was usually covered with some rich material, such as rose-coloured

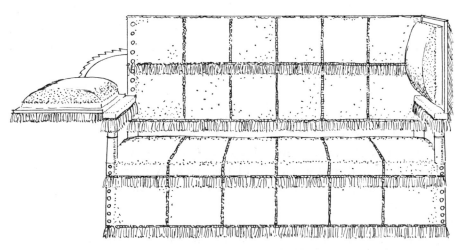

Couch with folding ends, similar to one at Knole. Early seventeenth century

damask, or even painted leather. During the early Stuart period the design of the day-bed took on a form which derived from the contemporary upholstered chairs. It now resembled a settle, having a back and open arm at each end, all fully upholstered; on each arm a tilted panel, upholstered and fitted with a cushion, gave some support.

It is doubtful whether the name of settee might not be better applied to this type of design, because of the presence of the arms. A comparable design might simply have the adjustable ends (no arms) which could be let down fully, and thus allow the occupant to lie down completely. Velvets, black or red or green, perhaps enriched with appliqué embroidery and usually finished with a tasselled fringe, still survive on one or two day-beds today and compare with entries in documents of the time. The inventory of the contents of Tart Hall (1641) which belonged to Thomas Howard, Earl of Arundel, and in those days stood near the present St James's Park in London, includes mention of a couch or two, one being covered with red damask and furnished with two long cushions '& Basis of ye same'; the clerk notes that the latter had a fringe of crimson and gold. The practice of having a 'basis' of fabric meant that the day-bed had rather a box-like appearance, the lower part being set about with material which hung nearly down to the floor. This luxurious type of finish suffered eclipse during the Commonwealth. The day-bed then had rather a plain framework similar to the chair, and a useful leather did duty for the upholstery covering.

After the Restoration, day-beds became both fashionable and popular and generally had a more decorative character, the framework becoming more important than hitherto being of walnut richly carved in the same elaborate style as the chair of the period, chairs and day-beds often being made *en suite*. These late Stuart day-beds were long and comparatively narrow with a supporting panel at one or both ends to serve as a back, usually adjustable. Many which survive have only the one panel. The framework consisted of six or eight short legs connected by deep stretchers, carved with acanthus or plain scrolls, the design of the back panel being similar in style. Caning was used for the long seat and a portion of the back. A long mattress or loose cushion, accompanied by a set of graduated pillows, completed the comfort and elegance of the piece which normally stood out from the wall; occasionally a surviving example has decorative stretchers along the ends and one side only, the other side being plain which suggests that some day-beds were intended to stand along the wall. A characteristic day-bed surviving from the 1680s has a framework of walnut, supported on spiral turned legs connected by deep stretchers which are carved with flower and scroll ornament. The adjustable head, suspended by chains, consists of two spiral uprights with a panel of canework framed in flower and scroll carving similar to the stretchers. The seat is formed of canework.

Other day-beds were fully upholstered, in keeping with the new upholstered chairs. Here the framework was formed of the usual decorative stretchers and eight short legs, perhaps of scroll form if such was the design of the stretchers. The end was fixed at a convenient slope, often scrolled and turned over at the top, whilst the long seat was fully upholstered including a long mattress covered in the same rich fabric.

Materials for these pieces were often chosen to make the day-bed *en suite* with chairs and other seats in the room, especially if it was in very luxurious style, e.g. crimson silk or blue damask. By the 1690s the framework of day-beds followed the change in style seen in chairs, notably in the use of serpentine cross stretchers and the tapered baluster legs of the late seventeenth century. A round bolster and a loose square cushion were placed at the head. One piece (c. 1695) was most luxurious, the entire framework being gilt and the head formed as an upholstered armchair; here the covering fabric was Genoa velvet in a bold pattern of green, red and golden yellow on a cream ground. A rich tasselled fringe edged the upholstery and the two large cushions. This type, with the armchair head or end, may be called a 'chaise longue' after the French term, although in contemporary accounts the word 'couch' continued to be used for the day-bed.

The fashion for reclining at ease continued in the Queen Anne and early Georgian periods, the same basic framework being used. The only difference, or development, was in the adoption of the cabriole form for the leg and a modification of the stretchers. These tended to be of a simple turned baluster type, two long central ones uniting the three or four shorter ones which connected each pair of legs. The head, if the piece was upholstered, scrolled over at the top as before, but another type had an open head designed in conformity with the contemporary chair back; for instance, one surviving example made in walnut has an adjustable head filled in with two vase-shaped splats of the type so often seen in chairs. Seats were caned or upholstered. An example at present in the Victoria and Albert Museum has a caned seat, supported on cabriole legs connected with shaped stretchers, whilst the splat back is fully in the curvilinear style

173

associated with the label 'Queen Anne'. This piece is not in walnut, but japanned in gold and silver on a brilliant vermilion ground.

Towards the middle of the eighteenth century, day-beds with open backs were designed after the Chippendale manner with open ribbon-back splats, cabriole legs and plain turned stretchers. These pieces were made in mahogany, and in some very decorative examples the carved enrichments were gilded in rococo style. Some upholstered day-beds might have a scrolled-over 'head' at each end and be furnished with a double set of cushions, graduated in size.

A number of couches of the time were designed as convertible pieces of furniture. These might have a ribbon-back of double chair form with arms, appearing as a settee in the closed position; the seat unfolded by ingenious means to rest at the far end on folding trestle-type legs, thus making a couch to recline upon. Chippendale in his *Director* and Messrs Ince and Mayhew in their book *Universal System of Household Furniture* devoted considerable attention to designing convertible couches.

In the late Georgian period, designs for day-beds appeared in Hepplewhite's *Guide* and in Sheraton's *Drawing Book*. A noticeable development is the introduction of the type known as a 'duchesse', which consisted of two 'barjier'[1] chairs placed facing one another with a stool between them. This stool was intended to be removable, so that the 'duchesse' was a convertible piece of furniture. The barjier chairs appear in the plates as tub-shaped, fully upholstered; the seats might be overstuffed or in the form of loose 'squab' cushions. The cabriole leg had of course been discarded in favour of the delicate tapered baluster leg of the period, and mahogany was recommended for the construction. Sheraton suggested that the duchesse when used in its complete form should have one long squab cushion to cover the seat entirely from end to end. This, like his convertible chaise longue (one armchair only, with extension), he thought would be an elegant piece on which a person could enjoy some repose after dinner. The person he had in mind was no doubt the lady of the house, since her husband was more likely to remain at table enjoying the pleasures of the bottle. Fine silks, perhaps in striped and floral brocaded designs, and cottons were included among the upholstery materials.

In the Regency period the traditional couch or day-bed, with its sloping and sometimes adjustable head, was completely superseded by a new type of sofa. The use of the term sofa is very suitable to distinguish this very fashionable piece introduced from France, where

[1] A term derived from the French 'bergère' (see p. 267).

the passion for 'antique' furniture originated in the early nineteenth century. The design of the sofa was based on a classical form, and consisted of a long low upholstered seat with an upholstered head or end curving over slightly at the top; the other end of the seat (at the 'foot' so to speak) rolled over back upon the seat in an upholstered scroll. A round bolster and perhaps a loose cushion were added at the head. Some of these sofas were open, but some had a curving half-back flowing down from the top rail of the head, and thus forming a long 'arm', fully upholstered, on which the lady of fashion could rest one arm in elegant style. These pieces were often supplied in pairs so that they could stand, in reciprocal manner, one each side of the chimney-piece. The short legs which supported these Regency sofas might curve outward in a style reminiscent of the sabre leg used on con-temporary chairs, the curve flowing agreeably from the framework at each end and turned in opposite directions. Sometimes a short turned leg was used but in no case were stretchers employed; the sofa was too near the floor to introduce them, and indeed they were not required.

One or two sofas were designed in the Egyptian style with cat-headed uprights to the head, and the legs made in plain or hocked animal form. A notable example of a sofa or couch in this style is in carved and gilded wood; it has a curved head framed between two lion-headed uprights which are carved with a lotus leaf motif and finish in animal legs with paw feet. The scrolled opposite end is carved with lion masks and again is supported on animal legs. There is a curved half-back, or arm rest. The sofa is upholstered in red silk damask in a floral design, and in addition has a long squab cushion throughout its length and a round bolster at the head. This piece is now in the Victoria and Albert Museum, and originally formed part of a suite of furniture which included twelve armchairs and two couches. It was made by the firm of Gillow in 1805 for Colonel Hughes of Kinmel Park in Denbighshire.

Regency sofas which were not gilded were made in mahogany, satinwood or rosewood. Ornament was sparingly used on these veneered pieces, e.g. the inlaid brass lines characteristic of the period, perhaps with an occasional acanthus or anthemion motif. Brass motifs were sometimes applied instead of being inlaid. Upholstery materials included silk fabrics with a tendency towards the use of darker colours than in the previous period.

In the first half of the Victorian era the Regency type of sofa con-tinued to be made, but was considerably coarsened in line. The frame-work tended to be more solid and the short tapered legs were round

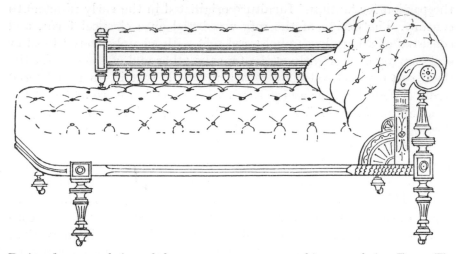

Design for a couch intended to accompany two matching armchairs. From *The Furniture Gazette*, October 1875

and rather podgy in appearance. The half-back or arm rest continued to be popular, and some pieces developed the curving rococo line to the seat and its supports. A couch or sofa on which she might rest for a little in the afternoon or early evening was often a useful adjunct to the bedroom furniture of the Victorian lady. In the second half of the nineteenth century new sofas tended to be designed, not so much for one person to recline on but more as settees, i.e. seats for several people. As life became progressively more energetic for more people, and more women took up active games, the Regency image of an elegant lady of fashion reclining gracefully on a sofa as she presided over a salon full of interesting, clever and cultivated guests faded away. Anyone in the twentieth century who wishes 'to put her feet up' does so on the contemporary drawing-room settee. The day of the traditional couch, day-bed or sofa has now been left behind, it might be said for ever, in the busy rush of modern life.

Above: sideboard of oak. Later seventeenth century.

Below: sideboard of rosewood inlaid with brass. Early nineteenth century.

Dresser of oak. Later seventeenth century.

Sideboard veneered with mahogany. c. 1795.

Above: day-bed of carved walnut. c. 1685.

Above right: 'A Grecian Squab' sofa
design by Sheraton. 1802.

Right: sofa finished with painted papier-
mâché and mother-of-pearl.
Mid-nineteenth century.

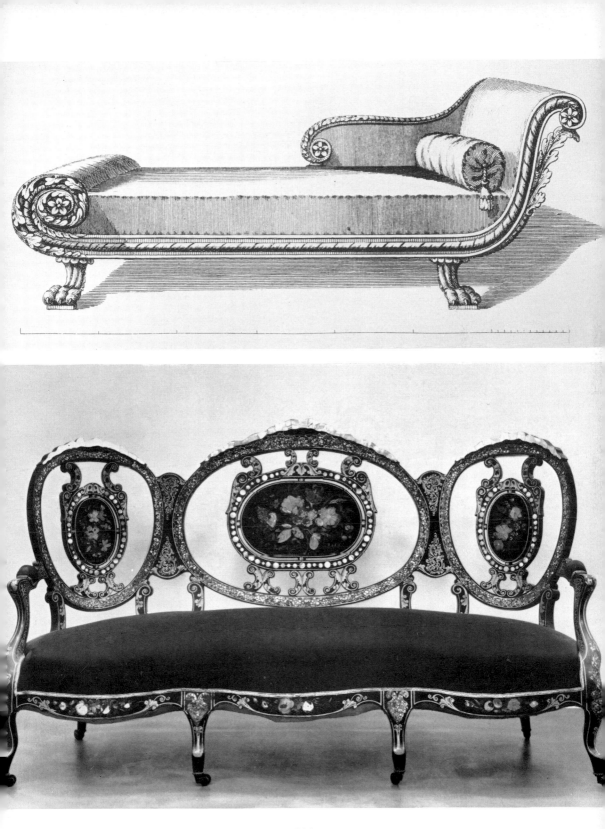

181

Bookcase of oak. Later seventeenth century.

Bookcase of painted wood,
ascribed to William Kent.
c. 1730–40.

'China Case', an engraved
design. c. 1760.

Bureau cabinet of mahogany. c. 1775.

Bookcase or cabinet of satinwood veneered and painted, with marquetry
decoration of various woods. c. 1790.

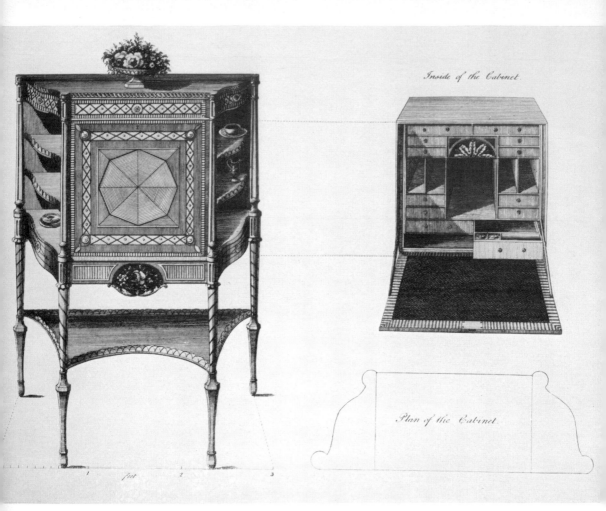

Inside of the Cabinet.

Plan of the Cabinet.

'A Lady's Cabinet', a Sheraton design. c. 1793.

Bookcase of mahogany, carved and veneered. Mid-eighteenth century.

Desk on stand, of walnut decorated with 'seaweed' or arabesque marquetry.
Later seventeenth century.

Above: bureau veneered with walnut.
c. 1715.

Right: secretaire veneered with walnut.
Early eighteenth century.

Davenport of rosewood. Early nineteenth century.

Davenport veneered with walnut. Mid-nineteenth century.

192

Above left: desk veneered with mahogany with fall-front. c. 1840.

Left: chest of drawers veneered with walnut and marquetry decoration.
Later seventeenth century.

Above: commode chest of drawers veneered with mahogany. c. 1780.

Above: commode chest of drawers of mahogany. Mid-eighteenth century.

Commode, veneered with satinwood and marquetry of various woods. Later
eighteenth century.

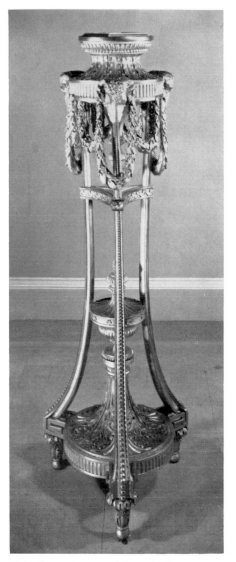

Stand of wood painted white and
gilt, designed by Adam. c. 1765.

Tripod stand or torchère of gilded
wood, designed by Adam. c. 1775.

Sideboard pedestal of carved
mahogany, with urn. c. 1765.

Stand of carved mahogany in the
style of Thomas Hope. c. 1810.

196

Frame of stained wood carved in high relief, attributed to Grinling Gibbons. Later seventeenth or early eighteenth century.

Looking-glass frame with glass border and cresting of gilded wood. End of seventeenth century.

Looking-glass frame of
veneered mahogany partly
gilded. c. 1730.

Toilet glass of green and gold
lacquer. Early eighteenth
century.

Pier glass of gilded wood, designed by Adam. c. 1770.

Tripod pole screen of carved mahogany with panel of needlework. c. 1760.

CHAPTER TWELVE

Bookcases and Cabinets

Bookcases and cabinets are classed together because they are designed to serve similar purposes, and in the main tend to have the same character although notable exceptions will be recorded. Neither piece of furniture has a long history, and indeed both came upon the scene at much the same time in England. They formed no part of the furnishings of the medieval castle or manor-house, and although cabinets are mentioned in Tudor times (e.g. in inventories) they were almost without exception imported from abroad. If not, it would seem they were made by foreign craftsmen working in England, particularly in, or very near, London. Bookcases could not come into general use until there were books to store in them, and it was some considerable time after the invention of printing before enough books were being printed and bound to make it necessary to provide enclosed shelves on which they could be arranged. The first Bibles printed in English seem to have been kept in boxes, more or less decorative according to the taste of the owner of the precious volume.

After the Restoration, however, the fashion arose for collecting books in order to form a library, and it was not long before a whole room in the larger houses was devoted to the sole purpose of keeping books on tiers of shelves arranged around the walls. Such shelving was in fact part of the interior decoration, considered and designed as such, together with the panelling in vogue at different periods. This practice continued throughout the eighteenth century and on into modern times. Not everyone had space in his house for such a luxury as a whole room devoted to books alone, but a separate piece of furniture for the purpose could be a dignified addition to any of the reception rooms. Likewise the cabinet, for keeping objects of value. At first these two pieces were distinct in appearance from one another, in that the cabinet had solid doors but the bookcase had glazed ones, which enabled the beauty of the bindings with their gold tooling to be displayed. Later, when cabinets were used for fine porcelain their doors, too, were glazed.

Both pieces of furniture began by having something of an archi-

o

tectural character, the top being finished with cornice mouldings derived from the classical orders. Both pieces were constructed in two stages, the 'case' or upper part enclosed by doors being mounted, either on a lower cupboard for the bookcase, or on an open stand, for the cabinet. At this time too, the bookcase alone was fitted with shelves, the cabinet being designed with many small drawers (for papers, jewels, etc.).

Samuel Pepys (1633–1703), the famous diarist, continually mentions buying books and having to provide somewhere to keep them. One of the earliest of English bookcases, made c. 1675, still survives, and may be seen in the Victoria and Albert Museum. It was made of solid oak by a man called Sympson, and is similar in design to the bookcases left by Pepys in his will to the library of Magdalen College, Cambridge. The Museum piece is in two stages, the lower part being nearly one-third of the total height and standing on five bun feet, three being at the front. The upper part is finished with a projecting cornice, deeply under-cut (cavetto), and carved with acanthus foliage. The interior is fitted with shelves which can be adjusted to the height required to suit the books. Both upper and lower parts of the bookcase are enclosed by glazed doors, divided into small panels by thick strong glazing bars. It is interesting to note how, as furniture design and craftsmanship became more refined, the scale of glazing bars became increasingly slighter and more elegant, reaching their most refined phase in the closing years of the eighteenth century during the age of satinwood.

The cabinet, introduced during the Restoration period, was eminently suited to show off the new and fashionable methods used to finish the more luxurious pieces of furniture. Both lacquered and veneered cabinets have survived from this time, and both were constructed with two doors, opening upon a number of small drawers, ranged in various sizes and fitted with tiny knob handles of brass. Each type was mounted on a stand. The lacquered ('japanned') cabinet was directly inspired by Oriental models and was severely rectangular in shape, without additional mouldings. The two doors were mounted with several decorative brass hinges, usually engraved, with lock plates (no handles) and angle pieces at the corners, all in similar style. These mounts gave a very distinctive character to the piece. Black lacquer, with raised designs in Chinese style, in gold and perhaps a little colour, was the decorative treatment given to the outside surface and also to the inner sides of the doors and to the drawer fronts. These cabinets, and others of polychrome incised lacquer, of Oriental or English workmanship, were usually mounted on very ornate stands of carved limewood (or of fir or pear) gilded or silvered. The cabinets were intended to stand against the wall, hence the decoration of the stands is seen to be towards the front. The legs, connected by an apron of pierced carving which included such motifs as amorini and swags of fruit, flowers and foliage, usually had a strong outward curve at the knee, and either had a scroll-top or eagle-head finish or, in the most elaborate examples, were carved as human terminal figures. The lower part of the leg was carved with acanthus foliage and usually finished in a scroll foot. Lacquer cabinets of the William and Mary period sometimes had a carved pierced cresting added to the top, in sympathy with the crested stretcher connecting the legs of the stand, which now resembled the table legs of the time in design. An example of late seventeenth-century date might be supported on legs of square tapered baluster form, connected by shaped stretchers with a finial at the centre crossing.

The top of the stand was always rebated to receive the cabinet. Sometimes at a later period, e.g. in the eighteenth century, such decorative stands, divorced from their original cabinets, were fitted with marble tops and were thus converted into side tables. This, however, was never their original purpose.

In contrast with the lacquered cabinets, veneered cabinets were not treated with gilding. Stand and cabinet alike were of walnut, forming a complete piece. The upper part, the cabinet proper, was finished with a moulded, horizontal cornice over shaped (usually convex) frieze containing a long drawer. Below were the two doors, enclosing several drawers and a small central cupboard. The cabinet was supported on a stand fitted with two drawers, with spirally-turned or baluster legs either resting on a solid plinth or connected and strengthened by flat, shaped stretchers. All flat surfaces were covered with walnut veneer, perhaps in a simple parquetry design, but very often in the more elaborate floral marquetry patterns characteristic of the period. The contrasting tones and colours of the woods, and the occasional glint of white or green-stained ivory employed in this decoration, gave these pieces a distinction and brilliance all their own. Brass mounts used on them were few and inconspicuous, compared with those on the lacquered pieces, and were limited to small handles to the cabinet drawers, and to the escutcheons on the doors which were opened by means of keys alone. Little change is noticeable in veneered cabinets at the end of the seventeenth century, save for a modification of the marquetry designs, the floral being superseded by the quieter and smaller endive type of ornament, whilst the legs to the stands followed contemporary developments in table legs.

Occasionally a cabinet was mounted on a chest of drawers. One example (dated 1688) of this type is of walnut, decorated with arabesque marquetry; the lower portion has one long top drawer over three graduated ones below, on a shaped base. Another example (c. 1700) has a double-hooded top, with tiny pedestals on it for the display of vases, a design in character with the style of the contemporary bureau-cabinet (see Desks and Bureaux). The doors open on the usual arrangement of small drawers and central cupboard, the chest of drawers below being supported on a shaped base. The piece is decorated throughout in light-toned marquetry of walnut, including delicate flowery sprays and birds on the outer surfaces, and endive marquetry designs on the interior fittings.

The fashion for collecting Chinese porcelain began during the seventeenth century, led by the Dutch and much encouraged in England by the example of Queen Mary, wife of William of Orange. One or two simple glazed cabinets for display were made, consisting of a plain two-doored piece mounted on a plain cupboard. It is evident from contemporary illustrations, for example the designs for interiors of rooms published by Daniel Marot, that this Chinese porcelain, mostly vases, and the Delftware imitations, were placed about the room on the tiered shelves of the chimney-piece, on ledges over doors and windows and on the tops of pieces of furniture, including the corners of cabinets and bureaux. It might be considered nowadays that none of these places was very safe in view of the fragile nature of the wares, but it seems to have been the fashion. Eventually mid-eighteenth-century designers turned their attention to the problem of display, soon after English factories had begun to make native porcelain with success.

Meanwhile, in the early Georgian period, the design of the bookcase was showing some developments. It began to be finished with a pediment, and the lower part, now enclosed with solid doors, gave the appearance of a pedestal to the upper portion. William Kent (1684–1748) and his colleagues, enthusiasts for Palladian architecture and ardent admirers of the work of Inigo Jones (1573–1651), turned to the interior designs of the latter for inspiration regarding such furniture as cabinets, bookcases, and presses (cupboards). Jones' designs for the architectural treatment of interior doors and chimney-pieces furnished Kent and his followers in the 1730s and 1740s with ideas, and enabled them to produce a type in which the bookcase was framed between columns or pilasters supporting an entablature and pediment above, the whole standing on, or part of, a lower cupboard. These pieces were often decorated with a considerable amount of ornament, somewhat coarse in scale and suggesting sculptured stone rather than carved wood. In some examples the front was divided into a central portion, slightly projecting, between a narrower wing on either side. The tops of these wings were connected by a curved slope or console shape to the higher central portion which was crowned by a broken pediment. One bookcase in the style of William Kent is of pinewood, carved, and painted brown with gilt enrichments. It consists of three cupboards with glazed doors, the arched central one surmounted by a broken pediment, the side cupboards square-headed; the whole framed in pilasters topped by cornice mouldings. Each pilaster has an acanthus corbel from which hang pendants of leaves carved in full relief. The lower part consists of one large cupboard, on a moulded base or plinth. The popularity of mahogany made it an ideal choice for bookcases and cabinets from 1740 onward.

Some lacquer cabinets were still in fashion and these were mounted on gilded stands supported on an adaptation of the cabriole leg. These stands were light in appearance compared with their seventeenth-century predecessors, with some use of gesso work to allow of rather delicate relief ornamentation. The cabriole leg might be carved with a mask and acanthus foliage and end in a paw foot. The design of these pieces, it must be stressed, was in a different category from the new developments carried out in mahogany.

During the mid-Georgian period bookcases and cabinets shared the same type of design, only differing from each other in scale and decorative treatment. Naturally enough, the bookcase (or library case as it was termed in the eighteenth century) tended to be large in size, even monumental on occasion; it always had a glazed upper part, crowned with a broken pediment, and a lower portion having veneered doors to the cupboards. The bookcase, if very wide, was always designed with wings, so that the pediment could be kept in proportion and not become huge and massive. This meant that large pieces were normally of the break-front type. The lower doors, sometimes quarter-veneered, had a small moulding applied to suggest a panel; sometimes this moulding was associated with a rosette or some small foliage motif. The plinth was continuous, i.e. not shaped to rise above floor level. The glazed upper part was slightly set back above the lower cupboards, thus allowing a very narrow ledge in front on which books might rest when being consulted; the edges here were slightly moulded. The glazing of the doors was usually divided into panes by astragal glazing bars, making a pleasing design of rectangles and cross bars. The cornice mouldings were refined in profile, whilst the centre portion rose in a broken pediment, sometimes of the swan-neck type.

Naturally Chippendale gave various designs for 'Library Cases' in his *Director*. Some of these are quite plain in character, but well-proportioned and relying for effect on the refinement of the mouldings and the arrangement, often in trellis design, of the glazing bars. The 'Gothick Taste' was occasionally expressed by an attempt to suggest Gothic tracery in the glazed doors, and by substituting a design of Gothic gables and pinnacles, all crocketed, for the classical pediment top.

Much more play in design was permitted when it came to display cabinets, or 'China Cases' as they were called. These like the book-cases had a glazed upper part, but here the sides as well as the front were filled with glass, and the lower part very often took the form of a stand, so that altogether the piece had a lighter appearance and was well-suited to its purpose. Here the mistress of the house could show off to advantage her finest pieces of porcelain. The 'China' Case was made in both the 'French' (rococo) and the 'Chinese Tastes', some-times the two styles being skilfully combined in one piece. The cabinet was fitted with one or two doors, according to size, but seldom attained the great width of the 'Library Case'. The frame might be carved with a key fret, and the top finished with a tiny pierced latticework gallery each side of a broken pediment. Chippendale sometimes shows the fine glazing bars slightly foliated, whilst scallops and the 'dripping' rocaille motifs were often introduced. The stand usually had four plain square legs, perhaps connected by cross stretchers and ornamented with light carving in low flat relief, such as lattice or Greek key; alternatively the legs might be pierced with lattice ornament. The stretchers were finished in similar style to the legs. To impart the fashionable touch of 'Chinese Taste', numbers of these china cabinets were finished with a pagoda top, gracefully fluted, and sometimes having gilded bells hanging at the corners. Sometimes a place was found on the top for a winged Chinese dragon. The pagoda roof motif might also be incorporated in the design of the glazing. Again mahogany was the fashionable wood used.

Hanging cabinets of veneered mahogany were also designed and made for the display of ornaments, and were carried out in rococo and 'Chinese Taste'. They usually consisted of two shelves enclosed with glass, both front and sides, and were frequently finished with a fluted pagoda roof top, whilst typical rococo motifs were again used to enrich the piece. The light, open, carved bracket appearing under the hanging cabinet was merely ornamental and had no structural function. Sometimes open shelves with open backs and lattice sides, and topped by a pierced lattice gallery and tiny central pediment, were also used for the display of porcelain.

By the later eighteenth century, or late Georgian period, the design of bookcases was becoming decidedly lighter than those of the Chippendale era, with mouldings noticeably smaller in section. Mahogany was still used to some extent, but was rivalled by satinwood when that came into fashion. Some pieces were painted, or grained in imitation of a wood, and many were made for a definite place in a particular room. In a considerable number of country houses, however, library walls were lined with bookshelves treated as 'library cases' but were in fact fixtures, and painted in key with the colour scheme of the interior. The shelves were left unglazed, and the lower part was treated as a continuous plinth with cupboards in it. In houses where Adam was responsible for the interior design this treatment was generally adopted, giving great dignity to the library, with the colour and gold tooling of the books adding their quota to the general effect. Although at Kedleston in Derbyshire the bookcases were separate items and could be removed, elsewhere, e.g. at Shardeloes and Syon House, they are fixtures. At Osterley Park House in Middlesex the library cases are open shelves, treated as breakfront designs crowned with a pediment, and painted a very pale delicate green with touches of gilding. Where satinwood was used, the result was much happier for cabinets and light bureaux than for a bookcase. For the latter the large expanse of colour tended to be rather overwhelming, and was only mitigated by the colour of the bindings seen in the upper portion which might have glazed or wire trellis doors.

Cabinets or bookcases of satinwood were sometimes part of a piece combining a desk below with a glazed portion above which had solid sides, and which might well have contained either pieces of porcelain or smaller sized books on its shelves. These bureau bookcases or cabinets were not only fairly small in size, but also showed greater refinement in design than their counterparts of the preceding periods. Pediments were abandoned, the top consisting of an elegant cornice, whilst the glazing of the doors was done with delicacy. The glazing bars were arranged in a trellis design of small squares and rectangles, and were made as fine as possible and yet able to hold the glass with safety. They took the form of a tiny astragal, or were quite flat (about $\frac{3}{8}$ inch wide). The latter might be veneered with satinwood and a dark stringing.

One example of a satinwood secretaire bookcase is of breakfront design, the upper part glazed and fitted with four shelves (adjustable) under a scalloped cornice painted with honeysuckle and other flowers. The lower portion consists of a number of drawers flanked by a cupboard (and a drawer over) at each side. The top central drawer, deeper than the others, is fitted as a secretaire with small drawers and pigeonholes, and has a fall-front opening on brass quadrant hinges to afford a surface for writing. The piece is mounted on small square tapered feet inlaid with flutes. The decoration chiefly consists of a marquetry of floral wreaths and classical urns, whilst a narrow cross-banding of tulip wood is used for the stiles and rails of the glazed doors, and for borders to the drawer fronts and cupboard doors. The brass drawer handles are in the form of paterae and rings. Another bureau bookcase of satinwood has the glazed upper part mounted on a desk supported on four gently-tapered legs. The desk has a cylindrical front, fitted with two brass knob handles over one long drawer which has brass ring handles on pierced plates. The piece is simply ornamented with borders of rosewood inlaid with light stringing.

Bookcases and cabinets of the Regency period vary noticeably in size. Some were of monumental proportions, severe in line and plain in appearance. Others again were made in one stage only, consisting of a fairly low cupboard with a narrow open shelf or two (sometimes of marble) above. A third type, not very large in size, included the secretaire bookcase or cabinet. Glazing bars began to be omitted, plain glass being used, or often brass wire trellis took the place of glass altogether and was sometimes backed by dark green gathered silk. Rosewood, mahogany, or zebra wood, gave the characteristic dark-toned appearance.

The first type, large and massive, mostly followed the 'antique' or 'Egyptian' tastes. One example of this, a large mahogany bookcase formerly belonging to Thomas Hope, has the glazed upper portion divided by sphinx-headed pilasters (not a breakfront piece however), surmounted by a plain frieze and topped by a very small cornice. The lower portion is fitted with cupboards divided by winged cat-headed hocked legs which at the same time support a ledge in front of the bookcase proper. A mahogany china cabinet in the manner of Thomas Hope is in the same severe style, but without the Egyptian adornments; here the lower cupboard also is glazed. Glazing bars are absent from both pieces of furniture.

A typical example of the second class of bookcase or cabinet is of rosewood, one of a pair; the low cupboard has two doors filled with brass wire trellis under two narrow drawers. The top is of white marble, with a narrow marble shelf above surrounded at back and sides by a minute pierced brass gallery. The low back is in rosewood, but mirror plate was frequently used instead of wood. A variant, lacking the upper shelf, has a marble top and contains three cupboards divided by narrow pilasters with sphinx (Greek) heads, and feet. These, like the applied decorative mounts, are of brass. The panel of each door, and the open sides, are filled with brass trellis, and the whole bookcase, veneered with rosewood, stands on a shallow continuous plinth.

In the third category, the secretaire bookcase or secretaire cabinet (the terms are almost interchangeable) might vary in height from four to five feet or thereabouts. The upper part consisted of either a glazed two-door cabinet, or of a tier of two narrow shelves backed by mirror plate. The lower portion, mounted on short feet, had a two-doored cupboard under the deep secretaire drawer which was fitted with a fall-front and the usual pigeonholes and tiny drawers. One such piece, of rosewood, is ornamented with a small amount of brass inlay of delicately foliated lines; the narrower upper part consists of two shallow drawers with veneered shelves above, supported at each end on brass spindles, and backed by mirror plate. In another example, of zebra wood, the doors of the upper cabinet have glazing bars designed to cross in Gothic arch style, but Egyptian sphinx heads and feet form metal mounts to the corners of the lower cupboard.

In some small Regency cabinets the secretaire fitting to the long drawer was omitted. Otherwise the general character was the same as in the combined pieces.

During the Victorian era the bookcase continued to be in the main a sober and dignified piece of furniture, but the design of the cabinet often differed from it conspicuously. Indeed, the cabinet became a piece of increasing importance, especially in middle-class Victorian households where the passion for assembling every possible kind of knick-knack gave rise to a considerable demand for extra furniture. Throughout the Victorian period the ordinary bookcase was usually made of mahogany, rather brighter in hue than formerly, and made in two stages. The upper portion was glazed, the lower cupboard was closed with two solid doors with a single long drawer over them. The

Corner cabinet. 1875

cornice was usually horizontal with no pediment, and the upper doors were filled with plain glass unrelieved by glazing bars. Surface ornament was usually non-existent.

An 'occasional' piece of furniture was the rectangular revolving bookcase. Pivoting on a low base, this had all four sides fitted with shelves and a small cupboard, room being found on one side for a tiny shallow drawer for pencils and notebook. This bookcase was generally not more than two feet wide and stood about two feet six inches high; it was a useful piece in a room other than a formal library or study, to contain its owner's favourite current reading and placed conveniently near his easy chair. The cabinet however was meant to be noticed. Early ones were sometimes low and narrow, a relic of the Regency. When Boulle-type marquetry enjoyed a short revival this was applied to some of these cabinets, the back inside often being lined with mirror plate and the doors filled with plain glass.

By the middle of the nineteenth century the prevailing craze for variety was reflected in the design of cabinets as elsewhere. The two styles labelled 'Henri Deux' and 'Renaissance' consisted of two tiers of cupboards with solid doors, and a conspicuous cornice to the upper portion. Much carved ornament, strapwork, figures and the like, is suggested in drawings which survive. Cabinets in the 'Sheraton' style became more popular, as these allowed the owner's possessions to be seen and appreciated. In general such a piece would consist of a lower part, raised on short narrow feet with a central glazed cupboard flanked by open shelves, and a more impressive upper part mostly consisting of shelving backed by mirror plate. These upper shelves were often very narrow, but the width was varied by curving in plan. Slender spindles supported them, and the top of the piece was usually finished with a cornice or some kind of broken pediment. A dark walnut or a wood painted black (ebonized) was the chief material employed.

This style continued to be popular during the early twentieth century, but a simpler type of piece gradually came into fashion. This generally took the form of a single cabinet mounted on square tapered legs, the glazed cupboard perhaps divided with a fixed central panel of glass flanked by glazed doors and the sides also glazed. The shelves inside were usually lined with a pale-coloured velvet which might form an alternative to mirror plate for the back. A very small cornice (no pediment) would finish the top. Such a piece might be carried out in mahogany with a light satinwood stringing, perhaps chequered, for the sole ornamentation. A new type of bookcase, mass-produced, appeared in the early twentieth century, consisting of a series of horizontal glazed shelves, each made separately, which could be added one above the other in varying numbers and at different times, according to the requirements of the purchaser. A separate cornice piece was provided. The bottom portion, about two feet high or even less, was usually slightly deeper in width than the main sections allowing a narrow shelf in front. A peculiarity of these sectional bookcases was that the glazed front to each section could be lifted up to a horizontal position and thence pushed back into the top of the section out of the way.

During the 1930s the average house had come to have only sitting-room and dining-room (no library or study) and even in some cases these were combined into one large 'living-room'. For bookcases at this time, open shelving, graded to take various sizes of book, was provided by the builder or interior decorator; it was often left un-glazed and was painted to match the general colour scheme of the room. Such shelving was usually fitted into the embrasures by the chimney breast or in some other suitable recess. Alternatively it might be part of a continuous fitment, of sideboard height only, or even lower, which also often accommodated a cupboard or two (e.g. for cocktail bottles and glasses). As for the cabinet, its traditional function, with rare exceptions, was practically at an end. To have large quantities of ornaments on view was now regarded as very old-fashioned, and good taste consisted in having only one or two pieces of china displayed, carefully placed about in the room to show to individual advantage. Decorative reading lamps now often filled the role of ornaments. The collecting of knick-knacks and souvenirs might continue but their display was out-of-date. The exception to this was of course the collecting of valuable pieces of antique pottery or porcelain and other objects. These naturally required safe keeping, but it was desirable that their beauty could be enjoyed.

Many people either inherited, or bought secondhand, old furniture which pleased their taste. Cabinets and bookcases came into this category, especially the cabinets needed by serious collectors of antique porcelain, silver and glass. Contemporary furniture makers were also copying, more or less faithfully, eighteenth-century pieces of this kind, including the bookcase or cabinet of mahogany fitted with glazed doors of trellis design, after the style of Chippendale. Sometimes these reproductions were only rather distant adaptations; for example, a

Cabinet and bookcase, veneered; with sliding doors to lower part optional. After a design c. 1960, similar to style of Messrs S. Hille & Co.

glazed mahogany bookcase might be made as a single piece only, without an upper portion, becoming rather a curious dwarf piece of furniture. Some very pretentious glazed cabinets and bookcases were made in light-coloured walnut, highly polished. These often consisted of an upper portion supported on cabriole legs. In general, the furniture trade was making the usual number of variants of past styles.

After the Second World War most people still did not have a separate library or study in their homes. Open shelving, fixed or bought as movable furniture, continued to be the normal way of storing books, and was of the plainest kind painted in key with the interior decoration. Cabinets, except for the collection of antiques, had become practically obsolete. Open partitions in the 'open-plan' type of interior afforded space for book shelves or the display of a vase or two, or the indoor plants which had become a great feature of fashionable interior decoration.

Modern contemporary furniture includes the importation of choice pieces from the Scandinavian countries, finely veneered. Bookcases in this genre are simple in line, low in height and not too wide, and may be fitted with sliding glass panels for doors. They may stand directly on the floor, or be supported on the fashionable 'stick' legs which are often of metal. These imported pieces have had a limited influence on native English design and manufacture.

CHAPTER THIRTEEN

Desks, Bureaux and Secretaires

At different times in history different terms have been used to describe the piece of furniture at which to sit down to write, a piece, indeed, specially designed for the purpose. Such terms as escritoire, scrutore, scriptor and secretary, all used in the past and all allied to secretaire, imply writing. Today the terms desk and bureau seem to be most commonly used.

In early times, few people outside a monastic establishment could read, let alone write, and in the medieval period the word desk was chiefly applied to the fitment with its steeply-sloping shelf or front, at which the educated person sat down to read in some monastic or collegiate library; it was therefore not a domestic piece of furniture. A certain number of small portable desks for writing were in use throughout the Middle Ages, and even in the sixteenth century they were the only kind of provision made for this purpose. A desk in the modern sense of the word was not made until the late Stuart period. These portable desks were like boxes, and in some inventories of the Tudor period the words box or desk are used for what seems to have been essentially the same thing. The feature which, strictly speaking, distinguished the desk was its sloping lid, whilst the interior was fitted with small compartments or drawers for the various necessities connected with writing, wax, pens, penknife and so on. A small desk which survives from this time (c. 1525) has a lid which contains a tray and opens upon a deep compartment with two narrow locked ones; the front drops down to disclose three very shallow drawers or tills in the bottom. The whole of the interior is gaily decorated, the fitting being of painted leather, blue and red colours predominating, with gilt patterns ornamenting the various surfaces including such motifs as the Tudor rose, the Royal arms and arabesques. This particular example has a later covering of shagreen on the exterior, but in early Tudor documents mention is made of desks and boxes covered with velvet.

During the late Tudor and early Stuart period, portable desks were chiefly made of oak, the front, sides and back being carved or inlaid in the fashion of the time. Such motifs as guilloche, rosettes, lozenges and a curling vine pattern are seen in surviving examples. One writing desk of oak, dating from the late sixteenth century and now in the Victoria and Albert Museum, is inlaid with holly, bog oak and other woods. The top and the sloping lid hinged to it are inlaid with chequer ornament in bands, whilst on the front, sides and back are designs similar in character to those used on the so-called 'Nonsuch' type of chest, i.e. panels containing representations of a building with towers and cupola. More luxurious kinds of desk are mentioned in some early Stuart inventories, being covered with fabric, e.g. velvet, and possibly enriched with embroidery.

After the Restoration, bureaux began to be made in two stages consisting of a fitted upper portion mounted on a stand or chest-of-drawers. Fine veneer, especially walnut, was used for the flat surfaces and the legs of the stand were either spiral turned or baluster shaped, being connected by shaped stretchers. The fitted portion, or secretaire, was either designed as a desk with a hinged lid opening downwards or took the form of a tall box or cabinet with a fall-front upon which to write when the piece was open. Two 'scrutores', so called in the 1679 inventory of Ham House near Richmond in Surrey, are of this latter type. Both are described as being of princewood (the old name for kingwood), 'garnished with silver', that is to say with decorative hinges, lockplate and handles. The open stands have spiral turned and vase-shaped legs, partly silvered, connected with a flat shaped stretcher. Both can be seen today, but are normally kept closed. The interior is fitted with a row of five pigeonholes at the top and a small central cupboard surrounded by small drawers, the fall-front being supported on a folding strap hinge at each side. One of these pieces is remarkable for the parquetry nature of the veneer. By c. 1700 the sloping front hinged to open forward for writing on was established. This front was sometimes supported on the gate-leg principle, but the provision of runners to pull out for support proved a more lasting expedient.

The bureau designed as a chest of drawers with a sloping top opening on hinges to form a writing surface, and disclosing a secretaire fitting of tiny pigeonholes and nests of very small drawers, proved a most welcome newcomer. It was not only made as a single piece, but also in two stages as a bureau-cabinet. The bureau-cabinet during the late Stuart period was sometimes finished with japanning, red and gold being a very fashionable colour scheme from c. 1690, or perhaps black and gold. The upper portion, or cabinet, usually had a double-hooded cornice over two doors with curved tops which opened upon a fitted interior. This consisted of a small central cupboard surrounded by drawers and tall narrow compartments for ledgers, with or without pigeonholes in addition. The bureau-cabinet of veneered walnut was similarly designed; the doors to the upper portion were sometimes veneered, or sometimes fitted with panels of Vauxhall mirror plate on the exterior. The cornice might be double-hooded, or rise in a broken swan-neck pediment with a cartouche in the centre. The sloping bureau front opened on runners in the usual way, with the interior fitted as a secretaire as already described. Another type of bureau-cabinet was composed of a plain chest-of-drawers surmounted by a flat-topped upper portion which had a fall-down front. One example of this latter type of design, c. 1685, is finished in floral marquetry; pieces of c. 1700 in date are seen to be decorated with endive or sea-weed marquetry. The bureau is usually mounted on a simple base (not a plinth) with shaped feet. Being thus raised from the floor it allowed for sweeping underneath, and also prevented the piece from being kicked or knocked at floor level.

In the Queen Anne and early Georgian period bureaux (single stage) and bureau-cabinets continued to be made, either of walnut or japanned, the more elaborate pieces having broken pediments to the cabinet; often a small figure of carved and gilded wood was perched in the centre and at each corner. Occasionally the piece was like a tallboy in design, i.e. two chests of drawers one upon the other. The difference was that in the bureau the top drawer of the lower portion was fitted with pigeonholes and nests of drawers like a secretaire, and pulled out with a fall-down front on which to write. At all times some ingenious attempts were made to contrive secret compartments in these various pieces of furniture.

The portable desk continued to be made in the eighteenth century, but could not compete with the fashionable bureaux. In early Georgian times a walnut desk fitted as a secretaire in the usual way, and having a hinged sloping lid supported when open on runners drawn out either side of a shallow drawer in the frieze, might be mounted on a stand of four cabriole legs without stretchers. These small pieces of furniture, usually veneered in simple style, may have been intended for a lady's use.

In the 1730s a single door, instead of the more usual pair, to the upper portion of the bureau-cabinet was not unknown. The curved broken pediment was beginning to be superseded by the triangular pediment, plain or broken, whilst mahogany began to supersede walnut as the fashionable wood for the construction of these pieces.

One example, c. 1735, has a cabinet with a triangular pediment, and some carved ornament as pendants each side of the single door. All the enrichments are gilded. Occasionally a fluted pilaster flanked each side of the single door.

During the mid-Georgian or rococo period mahogany bureaux were made in two stages on traditional lines, including the tallboy-bureau and the bureau-cabinet with fine veneers to the fronts in particular. The designers of the period gave their attention to the piece, and Chippendale suggests that books should now be kept in the lower portion, in cupboards formed in the 'wings'. This development, although not always carried out, was in keeping with the new trend towards having the upper portion glazed. In some examples the cabinet was fitted with a number of tiny brackets, as well as the shelf, for the display of individual pieces of porcelain. The secretaire fitting was now usually arranged as a drawer to pull out, the fall-front being supported on quadrant hinges when in use as a writing surface. A little rococo ornament appeared, perhaps in the treatment of the base (e.g. with scrolled feet) or as applied carved ornament to the cupboard door fronts, if any. The 'Chinese Taste' was expressed in the form of a pagoda top, instead of a classical-type pediment, to the cabinet and also in the lattice design of its glazed doors. Occasionally a bureau-cabinet of this period, made of mahogany, consisted of a small chest of drawers (hardly more than the old 'desk' in size) mounted on four square straight legs, and had an open superstructure of lattice work. The secretaire drawer pulled out in the usual way, whilst the open shelves intended for the display of porcelain had sides and back of intricate fretwork design suggesting Chinese Taste.

In the late Georgian period bureaux became more elegant both in size and in proportion. Some took the form of bureau-bookcases (see Bookcases and Cabinets) and were very similar to bookcases in design, except for the presence of the secretaire drawer. There was a tendency now for the lower portion to contain a two-doored cupboard under the secretaire drawer. The upper part was glazed, finished with a plain horizontal cornice, instead of the broken pediments and pagoda tops of the previous period. These pieces were supported on short tapered outward-curving feet. Fine satinwood veneer with bandings of king-wood perhaps combined with marquetry, all in contemporary taste, superseded the use of mahogany with its carved ornamentation. Sometimes use was made of painted decoration, for instance, medallions in grisaille representing some classical subject. The glazing of the cabinet doors was light and elegant, perhaps taking the form of a simple arcaded tracery. In the Hepplewhite *Guide* (1788) a distinction is made between the 'desk and bookcase' (i.e. bureau-bookcase) which has the traditional sloping front, and the 'secretary and bookcase' which has a fitted top drawer, the front letting down on quadrant hinges.

The roll-top, or tambour front, was introduced towards the end of the eighteenth century. A Hepplewhite design shows a writing table with a tambour front, with two drawers in the frieze and the whole piece mounted on four square tapered legs. The tambour encloses the usual secretaire fittings. This tambour, or cylindrical front, may also be seen mounted on tapered legs, with a glazed cabinet above; such pieces may be described either as bureau-cabinets or bureau-bookcases, according to their usage, since the shelves of the upper portion might serve either for books or to display porcelain. A bureau-bookcase of this type, c. 1790, can be seen in the Victoria and Albert Museum. It is made of satinwood, ornamented with bandings of rosewood inlaid with fine lines of a lighter wood. The upper portion is glazed, whilst the lower has a cylindrical front enclosing a secretaire fitting. Below is a long drawer, and the piece is supported on tapered legs. This is said to be in the style of Sheraton, and certainly much attention was given to the working of the tambour or cylindrical front in his designs.

Occasionally a lady's secretaire appeared, small in size and mounted on elegant tapered legs. It consisted of a drawer with a fixed top, sometimes sloping, with a smaller upper part fitted with one or two very shallow drawers and an open shelf above them. Sometimes this upper portion was separate and could be lifted off, and might for this purpose be fitted with a long thin wood 'handle' curved across the top of the open shelf from side to side. Surviving examples of this type of piece (1790–1795) include one veneered with amboyna and one veneered with satinwood.

Some designs continued to be published for the old type of portable desk, and it is thought that these box-like objects were intended for use when travelling. The top might be sloped for writing, but very often the box opened almost in half, thus forming two sets of receptacles inside. Along with the usual secretaire fittings another set might be provided for the toilet, including trays and compartments for combs and razors and perhaps a glass. One may well imagine such a piece accompanying the young milord in his coach on his travels, at hand either to assist the ministrations of his valet or to record his impressions of the scenery and the society met with. A typical example, c. 1785, would be of satinwood, the edges finished with a narrow black and white chequer banding, whilst the top and all four sides would be

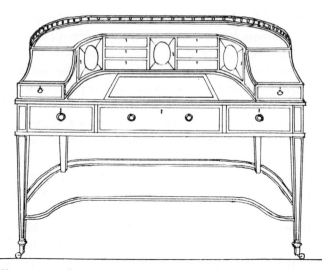

Design in Sheraton style for the type of writing table sometimes known as a 'Carlton House Table'. c. 1800

finely veneered. An oval panel, or patera, filled with a classical urn or other device in marquetry would appear on the top and front.

In the Regency period the bureau was either of the familiar cabinet type, or formed as a desk mounted on legs. The fashionable rosewood was much employed for this as for other pieces of furniture, together with the use of metal for ornamentation. A rosewood secretaire, c. 1800, which survives from these times has a tambour front and a neat little brass gallery about the sides and back of the flat top. One long and two narrow drawers are fitted into the rather shallow frieze, whilst the four tapered cylindrical legs are fluted. They are connected in this specimen by delicate shaped stretchers which join them in a concave segmental curve at front, back and sides. A typical bureau-cabinet of the period is veneered with rosewood; the upper portion comprises two open shelves, backed with mirror plate and supported on thin brass spindles, and finished with a brass gallery around the top. The lower portion has a two-doored cupboard under a fall-front secretaire drawer. The bureau stands on the short turned feet, ornamented with a little gadrooning, which were now fashionable (c. 1800). In such pieces the top of the secretaire might be of white marble in a style similar to the treatment of other Regency furniture. Again only the presence of the drawer fitted for writing entitles this kind of piece to be called a bureau or secretaire, its general appearance being so like that of a bookcase or cabinet.

219

Although portable desks were undoubtedly made at this time, again in the fashionable rosewood, they were plain with no distinguishing features.

A special piece of furniture introduced in the early nineteenth century was the rosewood or mahogany davenport, a small desk for a lady's use. This had a sloping top for writing on, usually lined with leather and hinged to the flat part of the top on which the inkstand and pen tray could be put. This flat surface was often edged with a small gallery of some kind to prevent the inkstand from slipping off. Below was a tier of drawers of equal size, which pulled out from the side of the piece, not from the front; the whole stood on short turned feet.

In the Victorian period the davenport continued to be popular. The desk part now protruded noticeably in front of the main part of the piece, its rounded corners resting on small brackets or on S-shaped supports. A small drawer pulled out on the right side and was fitted with compartments for ink bottles and pens; a tier of four larger drawers also drew out on the side. One type of early Victorian davenport was also fitted with a large slide which pulled out on either side below the frieze of the 'desk'. These Victorian davenports were usually made in the brightly-hued mahogany in fashion at the time, although an occasional specimen was ebonized and gilt.

A Victorian version of the fall-front secretaire, c. 1840, has three graduated drawers surmounted by a writing cabinet under a high flat top. The fall-front of the cabinet is surrounded by a carved moulding of bolection type. Each front corner of this piece is finished with a knobbed turned member of baluster appearance, ending in a small round foot.

During the later Victorian period a number of designs may be noted, which reflected the search for variety, aside from those pieces directly copying previous styles. One very conspicuous example was made in oak inlaid with ebony and ivory, in the form of a very wide roll-top desk with secretaire fittings, supported on two pedestal cupboards. A superstructure, divided into a central cupboard with a wing either side containing a shelf and four tiny drawers, was garnished with Gothic pinnacles and cresting. The corners of the pedestals below were finished with a carved replica of an Early English type of Gothic column complete with capital and base. Other pieces, less monumental, were made in the closing years of the nineteenth century, including a typical writing desk by Voysey. This has the spindly supports characteristic of his style, with a cabinet in two tiers, of which the lower opens as a fall-front writing surface. The flat top projects widely at front and sides, whilst the supports, continued to form the legs of an open stand, are united by thin stretchers at back and sides.

The desk with sloping front was revived in the late nineteenth century, but one example (c. 1895) shows a different proportion from that of the traditional piece. The hinged top is less wide, but is much steeper and has two narrow drawers and one long one below; the whole is supported on a low stand consisting of four slight columnar legs connected by plain narrow stretchers. Oak was used for this desk and for the Voysey piece. Another type was more like a writing table, with two drawers or one long one in the frieze; a fitting like a small cupboard, with a hinged sloping lid, was fixed either side of the writing space and these two compartments were united by a low back panel of some kind. This type usually stood on slender legs, with or without connecting stretchers. Some examples made in this style were veneered and inlaid with lines, or perhaps decorated with Art Nouveau motifs.

The portable writing desk was not unknown during the Victorian era. Made like a box, it opened in half to make a continuous slope for writing on, formed of two baize-lined trays to the interior. One of these trays usually covered its compartment only partially, leaving

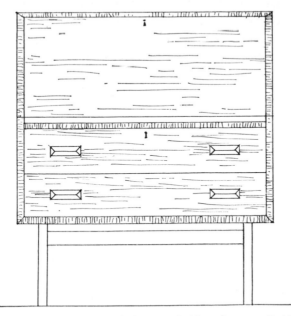

Low bureau made in the solid, or with front and sides of carcase finished in veneer. Mid-twentieth century

room for two or three receptacles for ink bottles, etc., and a hollowed (removable) tray for pens. There was often a shallow almost 'secret' drawer as well, which slid out at one end. A brass handle was usually provided at each end as had been so often in the past.

Today desks are made as replicas of various past styles, the single bureau consisting of a chest of drawers under a secretaire fitting with a sloping top being the most popular; this is carried out in oak, mahogany or walnut. The small bureau on cabriole legs has also been revived. In the 1930s a desk for writing was sometimes contrived among the fitments of the more fashionable interiors. In the 1950s a new design for a desk took the form of a fall-front cabinet, either fixed to the wall or incorporated in the open partitions which were part of the 'open-plan' house. Such an arrangement saves space where this is necessary or desirable, and the secretaire is of minimum size and proportion. The finish varies from that of painted wood to the use of more exotic veneers or their counterfeits. As for the portable desk, its place has been taken by the light-weight writing case of leather, which can easily be packed in a suitcase.

The invention of the fountain pen has banished the traditional use of pen and ink to a great extent, and therefore the need to be always provided with an ink bottle. Perhaps even more significant has been the invention of the telephone which provided a new and quicker means of communication. Ordinary letter-writing has declined, comparatively speaking, and other kinds of 'writing', e.g. business, authorship, etc., have been transferred to the typewriter.

CHAPTER FOURTEEN

Chests of Drawers, Tallboys and Commodes

The chest of drawers with its partners, the tallboy and the commode, did not come into use very early in the history of English furniture. Up to the early seventeenth century clothes were kept in chests, or in wardrobes (sometimes called presses). Shakespeare, in whose plays lively illustrations of Elizabethan life are so often found, says in *Henry V*: 'silken dalliance in the wardrobe lies'.

Indeed, the clothes worn by both men and women at this time were not only bulky, but also made of comparatively thick fabrics, so that it would have been difficult to fold them up into drawers. Household linen, too, was kept in chests or in presses. Some chests, it is evident, might in late Tudor days have had a drawer in the base, thus being precursors of the real chest of drawers which was to develop from this type of piece.

By the middle of the seventeenth century, well-to-do people were beginning to keep their clothes or linen in a hybrid piece of furniture which was part cabinet, part chest of drawers; that is to say, there might be a long top drawer with two doors below enclosing several other drawers. Sometimes, on the other hand, the top of the piece might have a lid, opening as in chests, with one deep drawer opening at the bottom of the piece. The fronts of doors and drawers alike were, in important pieces, ornamented with mitred mouldings making a geometrical kind of pattern, often surrounding central panels, perhaps octagonal or hexagonal in shape, which projected from the general surface of the piece. At this time (c. 1650–1665) solid oak was used, with very often split-baluster decoration applied to the stiles. Inlaid ornament is also sometimes found, of bone or ivory with mother-of-pearl. Sometimes the drawers opened only with a key, sometimes with ring handles. The sides of the drawers had horizontal grooves in them, whereby they could slide in and out on bearers which were fixed to the carcase. This method was discontinued after the Restoration when runners were normally used.

During Charles II's reign, the chest of drawers, like many other specialized pieces of furniture, was definitely established, although at first it was chiefly found in the richer households. Clothes were becoming increasingly elegant and made of finer materials; together with dainty accessories to dress they could mostly now be kept with greater convenience, filed away so to speak, in the new chests of drawers. Although an occasional piece might still have the top hinged like the lid of a chest, the usual arrangement consisted of two short top drawers over three long ones of gradually increasing depth, the bottom one being the deepest. This not only provided different depths of container suited to different kinds of clothes, gloves and so on, but also had a better appearance. The simple base was often cut to form neat bracket feet. These pieces are usually found to be about two feet eight inches high by about two feet deep, and varying from three feet to three feet six inches in breadth.

The colourful finishes characteristic of fine furniture of the Restoration period show to great advantage on many chests of drawers, especially the fine walnut veneer and marquetry decoration, eminently suitable for these flat surfaces. Very occasionally the drawers might be raised on a low stand, with spiral-turned or baluster-shaped supports connected by shaped stretchers, similar in design to the stands provided for some Restoration cabinets (q.v.). The stand may sometimes have marquetry decoration in keeping with the chest of drawers. In marquetry work, the veneered rectangular top was usually divided by broad bands of walnut veneer (cf. table tops), perhaps cut in 'oyster pieces', giving an oval centre panel and four near-triangular corner panels, all five being filled with a design in marquetry. The drawer front had near-oval panels, usually two to each drawer, also filled with marquetry, but the sides of the chest of drawers were normally covered with plain veneer, perhaps quarter-cut to make a pattern, whilst the back would not be veneered at all, since this piece of furniture was designed to stand against the wall.

At first floral marquetry was in fashion, perhaps with a small bird or two among the naturalistic sprays of tulips, carnations, lilies and daffodils. Carried out in strongly-contrasting woods, sometimes with green-stained holly, bone or ivory for some of the small leaves, the design was set in a darker wood veneer (e.g. ebony), giving a most brilliant effect. Gradually, however, more subtle effects were developed with less powerful contrasts, whilst at the same time the floral patterns were being abandoned in place of a fine and delicate type of formal ornament known as foliated arabesque, and sometimes in this connection called 'sea-weed marquetry', a term which gives some indication of its small scale and frond-like appearance. This style of marquetry is typical of the late seventeenth-century pieces.

Meanwhile, another decorative treatment was being introduced, i.e. japanning, which developed into a fashionable amusement and occupation for ladies, stimulated by the publication in 1690 of *A Treatise of Japanning and Varnishing* by J. Stalker and G. Parker. The colour scheme adopted in this work was black for the background, and gilding for the moulded ornamentation which was raised in slight relief. These little motifs tended to be Chinese in style, with pagodas, trees, flowers, mandarins and the like, loosely sprinkled about the surface with no real attempt at formal symmetry. These japanned chests of drawers, like the veneered pieces, might likewise be raised on a stand supported on the baluster-type legs of the period. Contemporary with these rather exotic types of decoration were some pieces made with only a simple veneer, the figured walnut being inlaid with narrow light-coloured lines of holly, or boxwood or sycamore, tracing geometrical patterns. All these later seventeenth-century pieces have few mouldings, and where there is no stand the drawers rest on a simple base, usually cut to form bracket feet at the corners. Throughout the second half of this century where handles were fitted to drawers, they were of drop-pear shape depending from a single rosette, and were usually accompanied by cartouche-shape escutcheons to the keyholes. Handles and escutcheons were normally of brass, silver being reserved for the very rich pieces (see Mounts).

The double chest of drawers, or tallboy, appeared at the end of the seventeenth century, providing more accommodation but with the upper drawers somewhat out of reach. The tallboy might well be six feet high, the width being about three feet six inches and the depth about two feet. It was made in two separate parts, the upper fitting into the lower and held there steady by one or two simple horizontal mouldings on the lower part. The upper part consisted of three very narrow top drawers over three long ones, and was surmounted by straight cornice mouldings following a somewhat concave profile, or else it was finished with a curved broken pediment. Another kind of top consisted of the hooded cresting similar to the curved tops of the great state beds of the time (q.v.). The lower portion contained two narrow drawers over two long ones, mounted on bracket feet. Above the top drawer or drawers of this lower portion a long pull-out slide might be fitted. It is thought this was intended for the use of the valet or servant when brushing clothes. These tallboys were usually

Q

Tallboy or double chest of drawers
with walnut veneer. c. 1720–30

veneered with finely-figured walnut, perhaps a burr walnut, cut and
arranged to make a symmetrical pattern on the drawer fronts which
were usually fitted with swan-neck drop handles on decorative mounts
(to protect the veneer from marking) which matched the escutcheons.
These mounts were of brass.

Meanwhile chests of drawers continued simple in design; veneered
with walnut the carcase was now of pine, but the drawers were still of
oak. Fluted pilasters sometimes decorated the front corners which
might be canted, a feature occasionally appearing also on tallboys.
Single half-round mouldings, usually of cross-banded walnut, were
used to divide the drawers from each other, and two parallel half-
round mouldings were here used slightly later. From c. 1725 a cock-
bead moulding was often used on the drawer edges themselves, the
frame being left plain. If the chests of drawers were mounted on a
stand, the stand would be supported on cabriole legs without connecting stretchers, in accordance with the style of the time, as seen on
chairs and tables. Although the majority of fine pieces are found to be
of walnut veneer, oak was used by country joiners who sometimes
continued to make chests of drawers in a rather outmoded style.

226

By the middle of the eighteenth century, the traditional chest of drawers had gone somewhat out of fashion; or rather, the term 'commode' was introduced from France where it denoted a low piece of furniture fitted with drawers, which at this time was designed in the ornate rococo style with ormolu mounts lavishly used, swirling across the front. It is evident, from Chippendale's *Director* (first published 1754), that the term commode was widely used in England for almost any decorative chests of drawers. If the term must continue in use today it is well, though this is to some extent a compromise, to reserve it for those English-made pieces which show French influence to some extent. These may either sit square to the ground, perhaps on bracket feet with a serpentine front, or may be more elaborate (nearer to the French model) with curved sides combined with modified cabriole legs. Mahogany having succeeded walnut as the fashionable wood, from 1750 it is found used for the simpler commodes with a fine-figure mahogany veneer (sometimes called 'fiddle-back') for the drawer fronts and top. Inlay or marquetry are not used, decorative effects being achieved by a small amount of carving, perhaps consisting of some acanthus foliage to the canted corners which set off the serpentine line of the front. These corners were sometimes of modified console shape, tapering downwards and carved with fluting. Usually the drawers, three or perhaps four in number, extended now across the full width of the piece increasing in depth as usual, and the veneered drawer fronts are found with a very small cockbead edge. The long top drawer was sometimes fitted with small compartments and lidded boxes, 'with a dressing drawer complete' as Chippendale says. When this drawer was pulled out a small mirror within could be tilted up on a ratchet in the centre. The whole piece could therefore serve the lady of fashion at her complicated toilet, since dressing tables fitted with a number of drawers had not yet been developed.

Other, often smaller, mahogany commodes of the mid-eighteenth century might be plain rectangles in shape, consisting of three long drawers mounted on cabriole legs with claw-and-ball feet. Although, like the serpentine-fronted mahogany commode, these pieces were intended by their simplicity for only a modest place in the house, they were frequently fitted with brass handles and mounts of quite extravagant design, which were immensely in vogue at the time.

The more extravagant type of commode, in the 'French Taste', with its curved front and sides, its bowed projecting corners finishing in cabriole supports with scroll or acanthus feet, was made in the

1770s in satinwood veneer with marquetry of various woods, marquetry having returned to favour again. The ornamental motifs employed, floral bouquets or garlands of foliage, were loosely displayed, that is, they were not enclosed tightly in panels as in Restoration work. The colours of the marquetry were softer and less contrasting in effect than formerly. Some contrast might be afforded by the use of cross-banded mahogany of light tone, used as border to the whole front and to each side. The lavish mounts of the rococo French originals were, if used at all on English pieces, much modified and simpler altogether. In some of these English pieces the front may be fitted with drawers with rococo brass handles, or have hinged doors opening only with a key, enclosing shelves.

Tallboys continued in use during the second half of the eighteenth century. Made of mahogany, a typical 'chest upon chest', as one lady described it in a letter, resembled the ordinary chest of drawers having a serpentine front with canted corners. These might be shaped as Corinthian pilasters with fluting, or might be carved with pendants of flowers and fruit. Sometimes the corners were decorated with 'Chinese' latticework patterns, in which case the frieze was similarly carved. The drawers were finished with a bright mahogany veneer, and in many instances they were fitted with elegant brass handles and plates, rococo in style. Later (c. 1780 onward) tallboys inclined to become gradually more severe, and are sometimes found with the top shaped as a swan-necked pediment.

The design of commodes had meanwhile attracted the attention of Robert Adam, and his neo-classical taste can be seen clearly reflected in various examples. Most of his commodes were straight-fronted or rectangular in form, the straight lines being in keeping with the classical motifs of ornament used by him. These commodes, like the satinwood examples in 'French Taste', were highly decorative, and similarly intended for display in the saloons, rather than for more utilitarian use in bedrooms. Made in satinwood they, too, were decorated in the revived marquetry, soft-toned woods of delicate contrast being used to express the fluting, urns, paterae, swags of husks tied with ribbon and sprays of laurel or acanthus leaves.

About 1780 it became fashionable to place commodes under looking-glasses (pier glasses) between the windows of saloons, and here they were often semi-circular in plan. Some were of satinwood veneer with marquetry, and others again were finished with lacquer (japanning) of black and gold, or painted in delicate colours. Again Robert Adam's influence can be found in the motifs of ornament used. All these pieces

Design for a dressing chest, presumably to be veneered with satinwood and lines of ebony stringing. From Sheraton's *Drawing Book* 1791–94

tended to be about three feet high and about five feet wide, and were raised from the floor on small square tapered feet, often fluted. About 1785, small corner (quadrant plan) commodes were made in pairs for corners of rooms, and were in similar taste to those placed under the pier glasses. Hepplewhite and Sheraton included commodes in their books of designs.

Late eighteenth-century chests of drawers continued to be of mahogany, of plain figure on a pine carcase, but with oak for the drawer linings. These were often rectangular in plan, and sometimes decorated in neo-classical taste with painting or carving. Hepplewhite's designs for 'Dressing Drawers' appear to be mainly very simple in style, although an exception may be found with a serpentine front made more decorative with some inlaid and painted ornament. He suggests that 'single' chests of drawers should be three feet six inches long by one foot eight inches deep; in the case of double chests (i.e. tallboys) they should be five feet six inches high. The top drawer of single chests of drawers of the late eighteenth century may be found fitted for writing as well as for the toilet; sometimes the drawer might be intended for use as a secretaire only, with the drawer front falling down and sustained by metal quadrants at the sides. Here the height of the chest of drawers would be modified to allow for sitting in comfort to write.

From about 1795, chests of drawers for bedroom use were often bow-fronted, made of mahogany and standing about four feet high, with two narrow top drawers over five long ones. The drawer fronts were often edged with narrow cross-banding and lines of stringing, and were fitted with oval brass plates with plain drop handles. Here the feet might turn outward at the corners, the line being similar to that of the Regency sabre leg.

229

During the early nineteenth century, the bow-front continued, sometimes found with the corners designed as spirally twisted columns (usually without capitals) ending in turned feet. Lion-mask handles with rings were sometimes fitted to the drawer fronts, or round brass knobs. Rosewood was occasionally used for chests of drawers in Regency times, but during the early Victorian period mahogany prevailed, shapes becoming more and more cumbersome in appearance with no use of inlay, but with occasional rather heavy carving. Mouldings also were coarse in outline. The tallboy was in keeping, and both pieces were intended for the middle-class bedroom of the newly-prosperous manufacturing classes who were becoming the buyers of the new, mass-produced factory furniture.

These Victorian chests of drawers were fitted with plain round wood knob handles, and were not specially connected with the toilet. Indeed, the Victorian woman made no use of cosmetics which were now severely frowned on by moralists. The toilet glass was set on a narrow table with only two shallow drawers in the frieze, the wardrobe being fitted for clothes. By the 1860s, however, the dressing table had arrived and was well established, being composed of a number of drawers with the toilet mirror attached. This piece therefore largely supplanted the chest of drawers for personal use, which itself might only be found in the gentleman's dressing-room. Otherwise, he shared the wardrobe. This usage continued into the twentieth century.

Factory-made furniture in general was produced in variations of traditional styles, but after the First World War the slight improvements in taste in furniture design, fostered by one or two firms, found some expression (among other pieces of furniture) in the occasional small chests of drawers, narrower and rather higher than formerly, intended for the man's use since wardrobes were becoming mostly mere hanging cupboards, or were designed as painted fitments and forming part of the room itself. These chests of drawers were often in the now fashionable limed oak, to go with the new light colour schemes, and were fitted with simple wood knob handles. For the nursery, now receiving more attention, there were gaily-painted pieces.

After the Second World War, chests of drawers, low and wide, might be separate pieces of furniture, the height being lessened to meet the desire for a more spacious feeling in the lower-ceilinged rooms of new dwellings. Some drawers were incorporated in one long low piece which might also include small cupboards for millinery, and special small drawers for dress accessories and for the cosmetics now freely in use again. This rather composite piece of furniture might stand flush with the floor, or be raised on 'stick' legs of metal to allow for cleaning underneath. Here the name of chests of drawers would be an anachronism, although mass-production continues to supply traditional types of furniture, either in modified traditional styles or in the more austere designs of contemporary flavour, derived and copied from Scandinavia and Italy. Modern plastic materials, sometimes impersonating marbles or traditional wood veneers, are used here as in other furniture. Handles may be of plastic or of lacquered brass, and in rarer cases may be absent altogether. Where this is so, slight depressions to fit the hand are made on the drawer front to allow the drawer to be pulled out as required. The tallboy and the commode, it might be said, have now vanished from the scene and have no part to play in mid-twentieth-century life.

CHAPTER FIFTEEN

Stands

From the Restoration period onward numerous types of stand, useful or ornamental or both, have been made at various times. There have been stands for lights, ornamental vases or busts, or for bric-à-brac, and splendid carved stands made to support lacquer cabinets. Among more utilitarian pieces were stands used in connection with meals, such as dumb waiters or tiny elegant stands for the Georgian tea-kettle. The washing-stand for about two hundred years was a necessity, and perhaps last to appear was the imposing Victorian hall-stand. The design and making of most of these objects followed the general character seen in other pieces of furniture, the same woods, decorative treatment and ornamental motifs being used where suitable.

In the late seventeenth century whilst the marquetry cabinet was in fashion, the stand which supported it was usually similar in design to the side table with the same spiral-turned legs and shaped flat stretcher. Lacquer cabinets of the period were placed on more important stands, of carved limewood, pear or fir, usually gilded but sometimes silvered. In the Restoration years the supports were shaped either as an eagle-head, a human terminal figure or a scroll; curving boldly outward at the 'knee' these were carved with acanthus foliage and ended in a scroll foot. They were connected by a front 'apron' carved and pierced, composed of swags of foliage, flowers and fruit, sometimes including also amorini, after the Grinling Gibbons school. In the 1690s the design was modified, the supports taking the form of square tapered legs united by crossed stretchers. Sometimes a carved wood cresting was added to the lacquer cabinet and repeated as an apron between the front legs.

The rage for lacquer cabinets expiring in the early Georgian period, the occasional stand required for one resembled the decorative side table of the time. The supports followed a cabriole form, perhaps carved with a mask at the knee and ending in a paw foot. Ornamental detail worked in gesso was restrained, with only the lightest touches of acanthus sprays or scale pattern.

Stand of carved and silvered limewood to support cabinet of black and gold lacquer.
c. 1680

Movable stands for lights had a longer history beginning in the
later seventeenth century. 'Blackamore' stands usually imported from
Italy, and named guéridons after the black Moorish page-boys who
waited on women of fashion, were exotic objects. A Moorish figure
held up a candlestick in either hand and such guéridons were placed,
often in pairs, to light a hall or staircase. A much simpler candlestand
became popular in Charles II's reign. Fairly small, it had a circular or
octagonal top on a plain or spiral baluster support raised on a tripod of
scrolls. These pieces were made in walnut or elm. Others, finished in
embossed silver, were made in pairs to go *en suite* with the elaborate
mirrors and side tables found in some very rich households, and were
ornamented with similar motifs, e.g. acanthus leaves. Occasionally a
cipher, perhaps with crown or coronet, indicated the owner. A famous
example of such a suite is to be seen at Knole in Kent. A little less

extravagant were the suites made of ebony embellished with silver plaques. By the turn of the century numerous stands for lights were made of carved and gilded wood for state apartments, some quite tall. The top was often circular, edged with a kind of lambrequin ornament supported on a vase shape rising from the tapered shaft; this ended on tripod feet of elaborate broken scroll type.

A tripod stand of the early Georgian period has an octagonal top on a vase carved with acanthus leaves supported on a straight square shaft, ornamented with the classical fret or key pattern and interrupted by an ornamental boss about half-way. The solid baluster form was more general, however, with double-scroll feet later transformed into an outward curve perhaps carved near the base of the shaft with masks and foliage. During the mid-Georgian period tripod stands were made of mahogany as well as of gilded or japanned wood, and presented a light and graceful appearance. The shaft was often opened out into scrolls and curves, with a variant of the cabriole form for the tripod feet. Some suggestion of the prevailing Chinese or Gothic Tastes was introduced in the form of lattice or cusping. Another type of shaft was the tall slender baluster, perhaps fluted or otherwise ornamented like the bedposts of the time.

Metal branches for the candles were sometimes attached to Georgian candlestands. Robert Adam made use of these in his neo-classical tripod stands. These consisted of three tall ram's-head supports, curved or straight, with a central decorative vase or column and surmounted by a classical urn fitted with two gilded ormolu candle branches curving out from it. The stand sometimes had a triangular plinth. Mahogany, and gilded, painted and japanned wood were all fashionable with an occasional example to be found of satinwood decorated with marquetry. Sometimes Adam's tripod stands were painted in harmony with his interior decoration, e.g. pale pink or eggshell blue with the motifs picked out in white matching the treatment of the walls and ceiling. These decorative stands were sometimes placed in alcoves; some carried candle branches, others again were fitted with a circular top sunk and lined with metal, for a lamp.

In the early nineteenth century Regency stands showed details such as goats' heads and lions' feet superseding Adam's motifs. 'Blackamore' stands reappeared, the figures half ebonized. Other designs included a bronze figure holding up an ormolu candelabrum, all poised on a tripod stand perhaps composed of the figures of three cranes supporting the circular top. Another Regency stand was based on a classical prototype in which the round top rested on three cat-headed animal legs standing on a solid triangular base. These were usually of carved mahogany.

Immensely important changes were soon to supplant oil lamp and candle, and with the advent of gas and electricity during the Victorian period the decorative stand of tradition lost its function. The modern reading lamp finds a ready place on any convenient piece of furniture, or may be designed as a standard (i.e. floor) lamp on its own account.

Contemporary with eighteenth-century candle stands were the pedestals and 'terms' intended to carry weightier objects, such as heavy vases or busts. Both types were designed to stand against the wall and were fashionable additions to the Palladian interior. The pedestal derived its form from the plinth of the classical column, and the 'term' from the boundary stone of classical times. This 'term' had consisted of a human bust (without arms) forming the top of an inverted obelisk. The Georgian piece had a male or female head of classic aspect under a flat top with Ionic volutes; the tapered 'obelisk' body might be decorated with scale ornament or formal sprays, and was finished with four scrolled feet or a flat square base. William Kent is known to have designed both 'terms' and pedestals (1730s and 1740s). These might be entirely gilded, but one pedestal survives made of mahogany with only the carved enrichments gilded, i.e. acanthus leaves and drapery swags.

In the later eighteenth century Adam, too, designed pedestals for busts ornamented with such typical motifs as pateras and festoons of husks, often gilded on a painted ground. Some Adam stands were like triangular cupboards, of mahogany with a marble top; the frieze was fluted, the corners had a ram's-head mount and the two sides in view were decorated with pendants and festoons. These were very much in keeping with the low pedestal cupboards usually square but occasionally circular, used as urn stands either side of his sideboard table. All might be painted in colours to match the interior decoration with or without some gilding.

From the beginning of Victoria's reign there was no place in the new villas of the rising middle classes for such imposing pieces as pedestals or 'terms', the small ornaments in vogue being more suitably displayed on the light stand called a whatnot. This piece, introduced earlier in the nineteenth century, consisted in its Regency form of three open rectangular shelves supported on slender uprights. In the Victorian period whatnots became more elaborate and were often intended as corner pieces. They were fitted with all manner of small shelves, somewhat erratically placed, and perhaps had small

Urn stand of mahogany. c. 1760

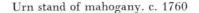

insertions of mirror plate in the shaped back. The whatnot disappeared with the change in taste of the twentieth century.

In the Georgian dining-room the portable stand known as a dumb waiter was much in use from c. 1740. It was placed near the table to hold bottles of wine, extra glasses, etc., especially at supper or on other occasions when servants were not in attendance. The dumb waiter, of mahogany, consisted of three (sometimes four) circular trays of graduated sizes arranged in tiers on a central stem. This stem was usually built up in triple vase form mounted on tripod feet. Most pieces were plain, the trays perhaps given a moulded rim to prevent the bottles from slipping off. Occasionally a dumb waiter was of more elaborate design; one example c. 1765 has three trays sexfoil in plan, bordered with delicate fretwork 'galleries' on a triple vase stem. The tripod feet are finished in the French scroll or volute in the rococo taste.

Sheraton at the end of the eighteenth century made designs for more pretentious types of dumb waiter. One drawing shows a spider-legged stand with four feet carrying two circular trays, the lower one fitted with four tiny drawers and galleried compartments. A mahogany example, c. 1810, has a lyre-shaped support on four spider legs with three graduated oblong trays on a slender stem above. Each tray has a hinged flap at back and front to increase the width. Changes in social customs eventually made the dumb waiter obsolete.

Standing trays were provided in the eighteenth century, mostly for butlers' use in serving wines. The commonest form by the mid-Georgian period was a rectangular mahogany tray placed on an X-shaped folding stand of light and simple construction. The sides of the tray might be pierced with a simple design allowing a grip for the hand on each side. A rarer example might be more decorative, the tray's edges and the folding supports alike being composed of pierced fret or trellis ornament. In the late eighteenth century the butler's tray might be oval, painted with some simple design, or of papier-mâché with painted designs on a black ground. For the oval tray the stand, perhaps gilded, might be made on the gate-leg principle, the supports consisting of four round tapered legs in Adam style. From about 1800 the rectangular mahogany tray with plain sides only pierced for handles was long popular, together with its folding stand of turned and ringed supports connected by stretchers of the same type. In more modern times the advent of the dinner wagon or trolley running on castors provided an up-to-date substitute for the traditional dumb waiter and for the standing tray, and indeed also for the stand for plate and cutlery, all at one and the same time.

These cutlery stands had something of a vogue during the later years of the eighteenth century. Of mahogany, they had a top which was either circular or oblong with one circular end; it was surrounded by a gallery of small spindles or by solid sides to contain a stack of plates, and was supported either on a tripod or on four plain legs perhaps connected by a low shelf. These plate stands, also used for extra cutlery, were at hand like the dumb waiter for informal suppers.

When tea became a fashionable refreshment in the Queen Anne and early Georgian period it was not long before small stands were made for the kettle, the teapot or the urn. These stands were either of the tripod variety or supported on four slender legs. An early example might be of walnut, the circular top mounted on a tripod with a plain vase-shaped stem. Stands of mid-eighteenth-century date had a circular or rectangular top with or without a minute pierced latticework gallery, whilst the tripod support had a vase-shaped stem carved with acanthus and feet ending in the claw-and-ball or scroll motif. Others had a square top edged with a pierced gallery, or finished with a serpentine 'tray' top. Here a tiny slide for teapot or cup was fitted into the frieze and the four legs were usually straight, connected with cross stretchers. Mahogany was used for these pieces and for the more elaborate examples of later date.

In the Adam period his influence was evident in the slender tapered supports, and the fluted frieze with its patera ornament under the rectangular shaped top. A light shelf might be fitted at a low level on late eighteenth-century examples, some of which were veneered with satinwood c. 1785. Stands for tea were superseded soon afterwards by the small occasional tables which were to become so popular during the Victorian era, and were to be supplemented further by the cake stand with its tiers of plates which could be handed around at afternoon tea in Edwardian drawing-rooms. By this time reproduction furniture made in factories included a certain amount of these small tripod stands of mid-Georgian type, which were used for the twentieth-century guest's after-dinner coffee cup or cigarette ashtray.

Washing-stands first appeared specifically designed for the purpose in the mid-eighteenth century. It would seem that before that time small tables were utilized for the temporary placing of the basin. An example of c. 1740 date is mounted on slender cabriole legs, the body of the piece having a top to lift off, a drawer in the lower part and at least one pull-out side at each end, presumably for candles. Chippendale produced designs for 'Bason Stands' (1762) and bills refer to pieces made of mahogany or rosewood or japanned in green and gold. Many mahogany basin stands were of commode or cupboard type on short square legs. The hinged top opened in two halves thus providing a useful tray at each side, each supported on angle brackets. The inner top was pierced to receive basin and toilet dishes. The cupboard under was fitted with two doors and there was often a drawer above or below this. Stands intended for shaving were similar in design, but with the addition of a small mirror which could be raised after opening the top. A more fragile type was the tripod stand in three tiers. The top tier was an open rim for the basin, half-way down was a triangular 'box' fitted with a tiny drawer, and the lowest tier was a circular shelf dished for the soap container. Slender curved supports appeared at each level, the tripod itself finishing in claw-and-ball feet or rococo scrolls.

In the later Georgian period some open stands had four legs; here the square or oblong top usually had waved edges and was fitted in the usual way for basin, etc. There was a shelf mid-way and a lower one (shaped) for the sunk soap receptacle. Some pieces were designed for corners. One example of painted wood, c. 1780, is mounted on three outward curving legs, whilst the convex front has a small central door.

The top, in two hinged layers, can be raised to form a back. Sheraton's ingenious mind suggested various designs; for example a corner stand with a two-door cupboard on short curved feet has an upper cupboard enclosed with a vertical tambour shutter. Within are seen the usual fittings for the basin and other dishes together with a small drawer suspended across the back corner. The front presents a serpentine curve to the room.

All these Georgian elegancies gave way in the early Victorian period to a plain design, usually intended for the use of two people sharing a bedroom. Marble tops were large enough for two sets of basin and ewer side by side, and this practice continued until piped water to the bedroom hand-basin came into popular use about 1930. The Victorian stand was first made in brightly-coloured mahogany with or without a splash back, and perhaps with a drawer in the frieze. An open shelf at a lower level accommodated the slop pail. Supports were straight or S-scroll and very solid. In the second half of the Victorian period the wash-stand formed part of the three-piece bedroom suite, and followed the variants in materials and styles offered at the time. Style chiefly showed in the design of the back which might have a broken pediment (imitation Chippendale), and when mirror plate was much in fashion that was introduced in small panels. Sometimes the back was tiled but the top was almost invariably of marble. A double cupboard below sometimes fulfilled the function of a night table. The wash-stand went out of fashion with the increasing provision of proper bathrooms in many houses, and had vanished by mid-twentieth century from all up-to-date homes.

The hall-stand may be briefly described. This came into general use in the Victorian period and was a factory-made piece designed to accommodate a quantity of hats, coats, sticks and umbrellas belonging to family or guests. Made of woods varying in price for different classes of customer, the hall-stand was generally provided with side rails to control the umbrellas and a central portion containing a drawer for clothes brush, gloves, etc. The back was fitted with a mirror and hat pegs and the bottom shelf with metal trays. Some illustrations in contemporary trade papers show this composite object fitted with extra shelves for potted plants, besides extra mirrors. The hall-stand became outmoded in the twentieth century when space-saving became important and certain social changes took place. Formal 'calling' declined and invited guests left wraps in a bedroom, whilst umbrellas if wet (sticks were no longer carried by men) were left at the front door in a diminutive stand fitted with a drip-tray.

A number of other pieces of furniture, e.g. the revolving bookstand, the canterbury to hold music and the desk or stand for music or reading are hardly important enough for more than a passing mention in this book.

CHAPTER SIXTEEN

Frames for Pictures and Mirrors

It is perhaps debatable whether pictures and looking-glasses may in fact be considered as furniture in the ordinary sense. They might well be thought of rather as forming part of the interior decoration; certainly their presence or arrangement on the walls of rooms can create various effects and the looking-glass in particular has had an important role to play in this respect. Nevertheless, a short account is acceptable here, if only to show how changing styles affecting furniture in general have also affected the design of frames. In the case of the picture the frame has usually been intended, however rich its treatment, to take second place to the picture itself. For the looking-glass, on the other hand, the design of the frame has always been of the first importance. It is therefore simpler to trace the story of each separately. Neither was in existence in England during the Middle Ages, and since pictures were first to appear and indeed preceded looking-glasses (except for foreign importations) by nearly a century, it is logical to speak of their design first.

Picture Frames

Pictures to hang on the wall were late-comers in the furnishing and decoration of the English house, indeed even of Royal Palaces. The colourful pageantry of tapestries, throughout the medieval period, supplied in rich measure the place which pictures take today. Those people who could not afford woven tapestries used instead painted cloths which imitated them in subject and colouring. By early Tudor times, however, numerous references to pictures occur in Royal inventories with portraits taking pride of place. These were often painted on wood panels and entered as 'tables'. A portrait of Henry VIII (c. 1520), now in the National Portrait Gallery, is a simple rectangle in a soft-wood frame which is painted to imitate grained wood with some touches of gilding. Graining, or marbling (perhaps red 'veined' with green), seems to have been quite a common practice with some gilding added to heighten the effect, but frames of 'black Ibonye' with silver mounts are also mentioned.

During Elizabethan and Jacobean times portraits were being hung in the long gallery so characteristic a part of the great houses, and for these it was fashionable to have frames elaborately carved with scrolls or even perhaps with a terminal figure each side. Colour and gilding further enriched such ornamentation which, together with the splendid dresses worn by the sitters, made a truly decorative whole. On one example (c. 1585) a cherub's head is carved at the top of the frame, whilst in another (c. 1620) there is a crown over winged amorini forming a kind of cresting. Picture frames were therefore becoming really important and by c. 1635 it was decided, after some dispute, that they were to be made by 'Joyners' rather than by 'Carpenters'. A great number were for large, full-length life-size figures, alone or in groups.

Charles I's patronage of the arts did much to stimulate the making of fine frames. Not only did he encourage such artists as Van Dyck to accept portrait commissions in England, but he spent much time bringing together the finest collection of works by such famous masters as Titian and Leonardo. Occasionally, as at Wilton House, family portraits and other pictures were set in fixed frames or panel mouldings which were an essential part of the interior decoration, a style fostered by the classical influence in architecture introduced by Inigo Jones. For movable pictures there was a vogue for plain frames of wood veneered with red or yellow tortoiseshell. This was combined with rippled or waved mouldings of ebony or ebonized wood (beech or a softwood). During the Commonwealth black frames were preferred, but tortoiseshell continued after the Restoration with 'counterfeit' tortoiseshell not unknown.

The love of luxury so characteristic of this later period naturally encouraged the making of richly carved and gilded frames once more, which might follow the 'auricular' type of ornament. This was a type of scrolling motif based on the curves of the human ear, which was repeated in flattish relief and gave a moderately curved edge to the frame. The series of portraits which hang in the long gallery at Ham House are framed in this manner. Other frames were carved with scrolled foliage and sprays sometimes forming a repeating pattern, and in some examples the decoration might be pierced to some extent. 'Fixed' pictures continued to form part of the interior decoration, e.g. over doorways, whilst a tall portrait set in narrow mouldings found a place over the chimney-piece. This setting was often given extra importance by the presence of applied carved ornament, the work of Grinling Gibbons or his followers, with sprays and drops of foliage, flowers, etc., in very realistic style. Gibbons' command of this kind of carving enabled him to provide his clients with movable frames of similar character, many for mirrors but others destined for pictures.

During the Queen Anne and early Georgian period picture frames, like mirror frames, were influenced by the architectural trends prevailing in some furniture designs. The outline might be a plain rectangle broken only at the top, to allow for a kind of cresting formed by two scrolls. A repeating pattern of egg-and-dart moulding or gadrooning was used to enrich the four sides next to the picture itself. This gave something of the effect of an architectural architrave. By mid-eighteenth century this rather severe character gave way to the rococo style now in fashion. The outer edge of the frame exhibited the freedom given by rocaille ornament, and the carving might well be pierced setting off the opposing curves of the design. Sometimes trophies of war, hunting, music or the sea were incorporated, perhaps forming a central motif at the top or introduced at the corners. It would seem that these pleasant fancies were adopted according to the nature of the picture, e.g. Neptune with trident and anchor for the portrait of an Admiral, and so on. Chippendale in his *Director* (1762) gave a number of designs for picture frames.

When Robert Adam came upon the scene he favoured a return once again to clearer lines, with the rectangular frame now delicately carved with tiny fluting and perhaps given added interest by a cresting, for example a plaque set between festoons of husks or bay leaves made in compo. Another device was formed of winged sphinxes. Frames of elliptical shape were also popular, perhaps designed as branches crossing at the top or carved more simply with reeding, ribboned at intervals. There seems to have been some use of papier-mâché for the enrichment of frames but this treatment, as well as the use of carved wood, was superseded from c. 1775 onward by the use of compo for the decoration which could allow the motifs to be smaller in scale and more delicate in modelling.

Although it is known that both Gainsborough and Reynolds liked simple and not very wide frames for their portraits, their sitters usually preferred to provide their own. In the Regency period the portraitist Sir Thomas Lawrence (1769–1830) had a certain type of frame named after him. These Lawrence frames consisted of an upright oval (for the picture) cut in a rectangular frame, spandrels thus being formed at the corners. The whole was decorated with soft rococo-type ornament done in compo and gilded. This type, seen in the 1820s, continued to be popular in the early Victorian period.

243

Middle-class prosperity in the nineteenth century was reflected in an imitation of the aristocratic way of life which included the display of family portraits, usually on the walls of the dining-room, and the buying of other pictures or engravings for other public rooms. Gilded frames, somewhat rococo in character, were popular for the largest and most important pictures, whilst steel engravings in large white card mounts might be put in a plain ebonized frame lightened with one gilded moulding only. Pictures painted in water-colour were also mounted in white card in a very narrow gilded frame. The various texts, 'God Bless Our Home', 'Thou God Seest Me', etc., favoured by the pious, were printed in coloured Gothic letters and placed in the narrow so-called 'Oxford' frame. In this type each end of the plain moulding projected at all four corners, making a kind of cross. Some pictures, or the painted plaques which were often the work of an amateur artist, might be framed in red plush.

In the newer, smaller, rather cottage-type villas of Edwardian England pictures tended to be smaller than before, often being coloured reproductions and not real paintings. The traditional portrait painted in oils began to be superseded to some extent on the rise of the newer and cheaper art of photography. Scattered about on the tops of pianos and occasional tables were photographs in silver frames, more or less ornate, standing amongst the rest of the bric-à-brac. Between the two World Wars etchings by contemporary artists had considerable popularity and these delicate prints, usually in white or cream mounts, were set in very narrow black frames. Frames of limed oak, in tune with some of the furniture of the 1930s, were thought suitable for the lighter tones and brighter colours characteristic of the modern school of painting.

As the twentieth century went on and particularly after the austerities of the Second World War, the demand for pictures was varied, part of the desire for more colour in the home. Frames were designed in a great many ways including a modified rococo type for oil paintings. This might be of limed oak perhaps with some colour rubbed in, but much use of real gilding was too expensive for most purses. The coloured plates (flowers or birds, etc.), taken from eighteenth-century books and used as pictures, were sold ready-framed according to the taste of the 'art' shop or interior decorator supplying them. These frames, not too wide, often had one or two mouldings tinted to pick up the main colour in the print, sometimes combined with a strip of flat mirror plate. The mount might be white or coloured, or even 'marbled' after a fashion.

There was a short vogue in the 1950s for a 'box' type of frame, the wood being set at a sharp angle to the plane of the picture and showing a very narrow edge, straight or gently waved. These box frames might be finished in a wood veneer, or painted white or some other colour.

The enormous mid-twentieth-century pictures, often of the type classified as 'action painting' with their violent colours and insistent kind of design, were all too likely to dominate or quarrel with any attempt to frame after traditional methods. Here a plain black or plain white frame was often found to be the most satisfactory solution.

Mirror Frames

The making of frames for looking-glasses as they were originally called, was naturally dependent on the provision of the glass itself. In England it was not until the seventeenth century that an attempt was made to master the art of making fairly large sheets of glass and treating them to give a reflection. Indeed it was not until after the Restoration that any real progress was made. It is interesting to note, too, in surviving bills, that for a long period the charge for the glass was much higher in proportion compared with the charge for the frame, even if the latter was very decorative.

A factory set up at Vauxhall under a patent held by the Duke of Buckingham c. 1670, met the increasing demand for looking-glasses with great success. These were quickly and firmly established among the important furnishings of rooms, contributing to the extravagantly luxurious style of living encouraged at Court and imitated elsewhere. A presentation to a Royal personage often took the form of a looking-glass; one in a silver frame, now at Windsor Castle, was presented to Charles II by the citizens of London. In state apartments and public rooms the favourite place for the looking-glass was between the windows; otherwise it might be placed opposite to them or over the fireplace. Looking-glasses of the Restoration period were usually square or cut as an upright rectangle, and were set in a decorative frame which might be surmounted by a semi-circular panel with pierced carving forming a cresting about the top. Some such frames were finished in a simple veneer of walnut or perhaps of tortoiseshell; others were made in the prevailing taste in marquetry, e.g. with designs of flowers and birds set in a dark-toned wood. Lacquer was occasionally employed, usually the incised type which might be of English workmanship, or contrived by cutting up panels of Oriental work to fit. The marquetry looking-glasses, like those in the extravagant embossed silver frames, might be made *en suite* with a decorative side table which was set against the wall under it. Sometimes a pair of light stands for candelabra in similar taste accompanied such an arrangement. Some looking-glasses had frames of glass, a very expensive treatment. It might be more accurate to say that such were not strictly speaking frames at all; rather were they borders of mirror plate. This treatment was similar to that of the fixed looking-glasses made up in panels, and screwed to the walls between the windows of great saloons. The movable mirror and upright rectangle hung on the wall might have the glass borders finished with mouldings of silver with elaborate mounts of silver placed at each corner, and at intervals along the top, bottom and sides.

Silver was used for very opulent frames. One of c. 1680 date has the glass set in a rectangular frame entirely overlaid with silver which is richly embossed with floral designs. The cresting is lavishly ornamented in the same style incorporating a cipher in a small cartouche. In some such pieces a crown or a coronet, denoting the rank of the owner, may accompany the cipher. At Knole in Kent there is a whole suite of silver pieces including looking-glass, side table, two guéridons and a pair of sconces to hang on the wall. The influence of the gifted carver Grinling Gibbons was naturally felt in the design of looking-glass frames. The upright oblong glass was held in a frame

Frame for looking-glass veneered with 'seaweed' or arabesque marquetry. c. 1700

of carved limewood which was composed of most realistic ornament in full relief. This would include all the typical Gibbons motifs, flowers, fruit, olive sprays, foliage, corn on the cob and the half-open pea-pod, etc., sometimes with strings of beads flung about in trails. There was no clear or formal outer edge to these frames which closely resembled the great carved 'drops' used in interior decoration, e.g. either side of the panel or portrait in the upper part of the chimney-piece of the period. These frames, highly naturalistic in treatment, may also have been used for pictures.

Towards the end of the seventeenth century looking-glasses increased in height, tending to become tall and narrow, the oblong plate perhaps set in faceted borders which were made up of great numbers of small pieces of glass, blue and white, each shaped and bevelled. This type of design was inspired by Venetian originals which were copied at Vauxhall and elsewhere. One such tall glass, of c. 1700, has a hooded (or arched) top and is set in a narrow glass border which has been decorated on the back in gold and blue ornament, in the arabesque style of the French furniture designer André Boulle.

During the first part of the eighteenth century changes began to be noticeable. Marquetry, lacquer, silver and decorative glass went out of fashion and frames were of carved wood and wholly gilded, or else were veneered with some additional emphasis given by some touches of gilding applied to significant parts of the ornament. Gesso was used to allow for more delicate relief in certain parts of the design. This technique was in keeping with that used on other types of furniture, e.g. tops of side tables and stands. The glass itself continued to be rectangular and the frame, mainly flat, was often finished with a pediment. This was scrolled, broken or fantastically shaped; sometimes it was so elaborately treated that the top hardly resembled a pediment at all. The lower edges of the frame might also be cut about in cunning shapes, giving a total effect of considerable grace. An example of c. 1725 might have a shaped frame finished with a broken swan-neck pediment in which a decorative cartouche or a carved scallop shell would be set. The enrichments would be gilded, the main part of the frame being of walnut veneer. In another example of this type a carved basket of flowers is set in the broken pediment. The edge of the frame, where it met the glass, might be carved with a small egg-and-dart moulding.

By the 1730s a more pronounced architectural character might be evident; formal architrave mouldings, perhaps 'offset' at the corners, framed the glass, being surmounted by frieze and cornice with a broken pediment above. These pieces, classical in feeling, suited well the taste for Palladianism made fashionable by William Kent and his colleagues and followers. Such looking-glasses were gilded throughout. One design, illustrated in the *Gentleman's and Builder's Companion* (1739), showed a Corinthian column either side of the glass with a full entablature and broken pediment above. Some examples had a full triangular pediment. The flat part of the architrave frame might be finished in gesso with a fret or wave ornament running in slight relief on a matted surface. Less usual, and capable of more varied treatment, were those looking-glasses of oval form set in somewhat baroque frames of carved and gilded pine. Here the design might be rather free in outline. One such glass, c. 1740, in the style of William Kent, is conspicuous for the bearded mask at the top surmounted by a coronet from which spring three ostrich feathers (badge of the Prince of Wales), the whole set against carved shell ornament and the remainder of the frame composed of acanthus foliage and festoons. Another in the Kent manner was designed with a half-figure (winged female) each side, and was enriched with cornucopias, foliated scrolls, shells and acanthus. Many looking-glasses made during the first half of the eighteenth century were fitted with a pair of candle branches to the lower part of the frame.

By mid-century the Palladian style of Kent was superseded in the fashionable world of taste by the new rococo inspired from France. This found its most charming and effective expression in the design of looking-glasses and wall lights. Wall mirrors now became very light and open in treatment, the glass being oval, rectangular or fantastic in outline, whilst the carved and gilded wood setting (it can hardly be called a frame) relied upon the use of various scrolls and curves combined with floral or foliated ornament for its design. The rage for the 'Chinese Taste' was successfully expressed by the introduction of Chinese figures or exotic birds, placed among the scrolls and foliage with elegant effect. The mirror plate might be oval or variable in shape, the frame much cut about and often pierced in places to show more of the glass. The whole design was balanced, although not necessarily strictly symmetrical. Candle brackets were often incorporated, scrolling outward like leafy stems and ending in a calyx shape for each candle. The prominent designers of the period hastened to show their ingenuity in devising many variants on this theme. One typical piece in this manner is composed of light rococo scrolls, the glass appearing between some of them, and set with flowers and leaves and two elegant birds resembling cranes. A vase of flowers surmounts the top with roses and sprays loosely curving out and downward from it. Attempts were also made to express the 'Gothic Taste' in the design of frames by the introduction of such motifs as cusping, tracery and pointed arch forms. Rococo or mid-Georgian looking-glasses were intended to be hung between windows in the traditional way, but designs were also adapted for chimney-glasses or overmantels, to be placed above single-stage fireplaces.

In the late Georgian period the influence of Robert Adam was felt in the design of looking-glasses as in other furniture, especially those pieces intended for state apartments. The term pier glass became fashionable for the mirror which was hung over its accompanying pier table. Adam's wall mirrors, like his chimney-glasses, soon showed an abandoning of the swirling rococo character, and the adoption of more controlled lines associated with an oval or tall oblong glass. The light frame was usually carved with minute fluting, and the piece decked with his typical ornamental motifs such as the classical urn, festoons of husks, or *garrya elliptica*, bows of ribbon, etc. In his later work these devices became so light and airy that they had to be carried out, not in wood, but in wire composition. They might be added as a cresting to the frame or form a dominant part of the design as a whole. Examples of Adam's oval and oblong mirrors can be seen in the State Apartments at Osterley Park House in Middlesex.

A most striking change took place in the design of looking-glass frames during the Regency period. The glass itself was circular and convex, thereby at once diminishing the reflection and intensifying it. Light appeared to be concentrated and colours strengthened, all of which made quickly for great popularity. Naturally the frame of gilded wood was made circular to enclose the glass, and it was generally the practice to put a carved eagle at the top and some carved acanthus leaves at the bottom of the frame. The eagle, its wings partly spread, is often seen with its head lowered and perhaps with one or more round balls or beads depending from its beak. It may perch alone on the frame or be accompanied by acanthus leaves. The main moulding of the frame was usually hollowed (cavetto) and studded with a number of small round balls, black or gilded. The outer moulding was often enriched with reeding, perhaps ribboned for extra interest. Sometimes these convex looking-glasses were fitted with a pair of simple candle branches; these branches are occasionally seen

Frame for looking-glass of carved and gilded wood. Regency period

hung with cut-glass prism drops similar in style to those seen on the glass chandeliers of the time.

During the Victorian period looking-glasses came to be termed 'mirrors', a shortened form of 'mirror plate'; the traditional name only survived in the great houses of the aristocracy and gentry. The middle classes were growing in numbers and prosperity, and in a typical house the tendency was to have a fixed glass over the chimney-piece rather than to have individual frames hung on the walls of rooms. Pictures of the early Victorian era show this clearly; immense sheets of mirror plate are represented in narrow gilded frames, the plain vertical sides rising to a top shaped in a sweeping curve. Throughout the century the walls of rooms continued to be crowded (it can scarcely be called decorated) with pictures, steel engravings and curios of all kinds, in such a disorderly manner that there was no significant place for a wall mirror other than over the fireplace. By the time of the 1863 Exhibition mirror plate was being introduced into the design of every possible piece of furniture, not only (legitimately) of the bedroom suite but also the sideboard, display cabinet and hall-stand. The large overmantel mirror was now regarded as old-fashioned, and in its place there was a smaller mirror surrounded by various small shelves for the display of ornaments and bric-à-brac. With the advent of gas and soon afterward of electricity for lighting, the old custom of adding candle branches to mirrors was abandoned during the Victorian period. Mirrors indeed ceased to be the splendid decorative objects which in past times had displayed such fine qualities of lively design and superb craftsmanship. In the last years of the century there was a short-lived vogue among the middle classes for having mirrors which had been decorated by a daughter of the house with artistic leanings. The glass was painted on the outer surface, in oils, with some realistic subject, such as a branch of apple blossom perhaps with a bird's nest among the leaves, which spread across but did not obscure reflections. The frame might be covered with red or green velvet or plush, the shape being an upright oblong.

During the first half of the twentieth century mirrors were being mass-produced in greater variety by the manufacturers, and after the First World War the frames took a number of different shapes, an oval hung horizontally being among the most popular. The frame was usually unpretentious in design, and might be of wood (fumed oak) or of chromium plate. As top-heavy sideboards and cabinets began to be superseded by lower pieces of furniture and walls themselves became less crowded, there were once again more places available for mirrors. During the 1930s there was a fashion for mirrors which showed no frame at all, and these were designed in what might be called a modernistic manner. A very characteristic shape was rectangular with the corners stepped or broken, and the surface of the glass cut to a certain extent to give a pattern. The glass might be clear or tinged with a peach colour. These twentieth-century pieces were not fixed to the wall with plates like their predecessors, but were often hung by means of chains, which were visible, from the picture rail. There was also during the first half of the twentieth century, a certain amount of 'reproduction' work going on in furniture factories including small mirrors designed in the style of the Queen Anne and early Georgian period, and others imitating the convex Regency period piece. The traditional candle branch, however, tended to be omitted in the age of electricity.

After the Second World War mirror frames were again produced in considerable variety, manufacturers competing in the range of designs offered to the public. These designs continue to include several versions of traditional shapes as before, the mirror surface being rectangular, round or oval, and the character of the frame is limited by methods of mass production.

CHAPTER SEVENTEEN

Mounts

Under this heading come all those additions to furniture such as handles and hinges which mainly fulfil a practical purpose, and a small category of applied ornamental details. Handles and hinges were generally made of metal, e.g. wrought iron and gilded brass, during the historical periods but in the twentieth century new materials, at any rate for handles, were introduced. Handles in particular have often been considered as part of the design of a piece, and have on occasion been influenced by changes in style in general. Surface hinges on medieval furniture were usually of wrought iron including the plain butterfly hinge and the long strap hinge, whilst end handles were fitted to the travelling chest. Ornamental iron bands in more or less elaborate scrolling patterns may be seen on the fronts of some medieval chests or cupboards, whilst edges may be strengthened by plain flat corner straps. On the richly-carved furniture of Elizabethan and Jacobean times mounts were not important features, although the wrought-iron H-type hinge and the 'cock's-head' hinge may be noted on cupboard doors. Keys rather than handles were used for opening.

After the Restoration brass superseded iron and handles became increasingly decorative. Hinges were soon to become insignificant and indeed to disappear altogether from view, with the notable exception of the hinges applied to lacquer cabinets during the later seventeenth century. These were made like broad short straps, the ends fancifully shaped and the surface coarsely engraved. Five at least were placed fairly close together on each door, and these together with protective angle plates, corner plates and huge double lock plates all similarly ornamented, enriched the piece considerably after the Oriental fashion. Silver mounts, embossed and chased, are sometimes seen on Restoration marquetry furniture, as corner plates, escutcheons (keyhole plates) and handles, but brass was to have the monopoly until the early Victorian period. Designs were cast from moulds, thus being quickly reproduced, whilst a finish was imparted by polishing, and gilding or lacquering to prevent tarnishing. Birmingham,

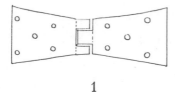

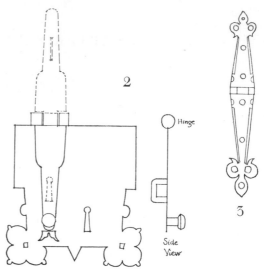

1: 'Butterfly' hinge of wrought iron, from oak cupboard, early sixteenth century. 2: Hasp lock and plate of wrought iron, from oak chest, mid-sixteenth century. 3: Double strap hinge of wrought iron, from oak desk, c. 1600

for ages a centre of the iron industry, soon developed fresh importance as a centre for this new work in brass.

In the late seventeenth century and early eighteenth century drop handles, the pear drop or acorn types depending from a circular mount, and escutcheons of cartouche shape slightly ornamented were made. These mounts were superseded in early Georgian times by the familiar loop handle, mounted on a flat shaped plate which

1: Escutcheon of brass from cabinet, late seventeenth century. 2: Ring handle of brass from cabinet, late seventeenth century. 3: Drop handle of cast brass, late seventeenth century. 4: Drop handle from table, late seventeenth century. 5: Drop handle of cast brass, early eighteenth century. 6: Escutcheon of pierced brass from clock, c. 1685

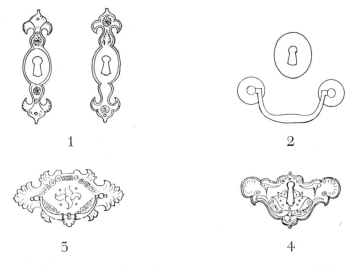

1: Escutcheons from cabinet doors, late seventeenth century. 2: Plain escutcheon and loop handle from bureau-bookcase made by Samuel Bennett of London, early eighteenth century. 3: Loop handle with engraved brass plate, from writing cabinet, early eighteenth century. 4: Escutcheon of engraved brass from writing cabinet of Queen Anne period

preserved the veneered front of the drawer. This plate, like the matching escutcheon, was soon supplied cut out in the centre in a decorative manner, giving an effect of strap or scroll design. The loop handle, sometimes seen with a moulded centre in the earlier years, maintained throughout most of the eighteenth century a plain form merely with a 'swelling' to aid the hand to seize it. In the mid-eighteenth century plates were discarded in favour of 'roses' and the current taste for rococo ornament was reflected in the design of these, as witness not only actual examples surviving but also drawings published by Chippendale (*Director*, 1762 edition). Commodes of bombé form, made in imitation of French originals, were given the

1: Escutcheons from cabinet doors. 2: Escutcheon, with pierced pattern, with loop handle of brass from the same cabinet, first quarter eighteenth century

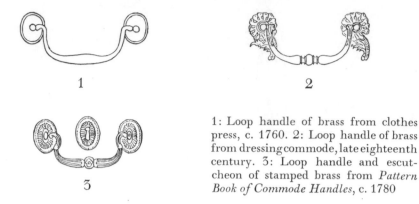

1: Loop handle of brass from clothes press, c. 1760. 2: Loop handle of brass from dressing commode, late eighteenth century. 3: Loop handle and escutcheon of stamped brass from *Pattern Book of Commode Handles*, c. 1780

same ormolu mounts, e.g. the protective sheaths to the sharp edges of the corners, but these may well have been of French workmanship.

Matthew Boulton established his celebrated Soho Factory near Birmingham in 1762 and did much fine work in metal. During the later eighteenth century Adam's fondness for such motifs as the ram's head, festoons of husks, etc., often resulted in their introduction as decorative mounts to his commodes, candle stands and decorative tables. Much of this work is attributed to Boulton's factory. Meanwhile, towards the end of the century brass loop handles were again being fitted with back-plates often an oval shape, now of sheet brass, the ornament being stamped. Alternatively, stamped roses resembling paterae are seen with escutcheons *en suite*. Cast loop handles of the late eighteenth century were sometimes more elaborate than the plain 'swelled' type generally in vogue during the Georgian period.

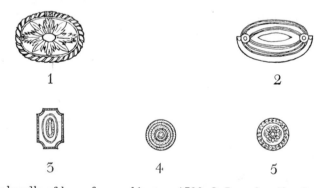

1: Oval ring handle of brass from cabinet, c. 1790. 2: Loop handle of stamped brass from Pattern Book, 1790–1810. 3: Escutcheon of brass from Pattern Book, 1790–1810. 4: Knob handle of brass from Pembroke table, late eighteenth century. 5: Knob handle of brass from Pattern Book, 1790–1810

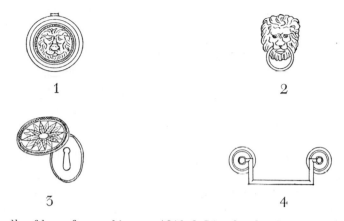

1   2

3   4

1: Ring handle of brass from cabinet, c. 1810. 2: Lion-head and ring handle of brass from secretaire, c. 1810. 3: 'Concealed' escutcheon from Pattern Book, c. 1814. 4: Rectangular 'loop' handle of brass from Victorian Pattern Book

During the early nineteenth century the loop handle gave way to some extent to a brass knob handle. Another type, a ring handle depending from a lion's mask, was also much employed. Regency furniture was notable for a limited use of applied metal ornament including such motifs as the Greek anthemion, the water leaf design and the patera, as well as the Egyptian sphinx head.

On furniture of the early Victorian era plain wood knob handles were popular, and the lively contrast of brass against wood was eclipsed for a time. In the second half of the Victorian period handles suitable to the factory-made imitations of traditional furniture were provided including cheap brass loop types, but mostly with the omission of gilding. Handles on furniture in Art Nouveau style might be of wood.

During the 1920s and 1930s handles were made of all kinds of materials including metal (brass, or chromium plate, etc.); glass (clear or coloured, plain or 'cut'); and plastic in various colours or combinations of colour. Designs might follow traditional patterns, or essay a kind of 'modernism', e.g. a simple bar set close to the surface of door or drawer front. In the mid-twentieth century there was also a vogue for having no handle of conventional type at all. Instead a recessed groove or other form of grip for the hand may be seen. This reflects to some degree the modern idea of getting rid of excrescences held to collect dust and thus cause unnecessary work.

CHAPTER EIGHTEEN

Miscellanea

Certain classes of furniture, e.g. bed, table and chair (and until c. 1700 the chest), had been basic necessities in furnishing for centuries, whilst other classes such as the cabinet, the bureau, the mirror and the chest of drawers at first appeared as luxuries and then became established as near-necessities in many houses and in most walks of life. Rather outside these two categories, however, come a small number of objects which for one reason or another have made only a short appearance on the scene, or have only been introduced in very recent times. Such pieces can be given but a brief mention in a book of this scope, and they are here brought together under the heading of miscellanea. Among those which almost belong more to the past than to the present are keyboard musical instruments, long-case clocks, tripod fire-screens and toilet glasses, whilst those which rank as twentieth-century innovations include television sets, and radio and cocktail cabinets.

It is a matter of debate whether the keyboard musical instrument, although it had for a time its own place in the domestic scene, can properly be called furniture. The long-case or grandfather clock on the other hand was a necessity in most households from c. 1700 to fairly recent times. A helpful clue to period here can be derived from the wood or wood veneer employed, or in the use of some particular kind of marquetry pattern. The long-case clock and its colleague the barometer, romantic survivals from the past, have been largely superseded respectively by the broadcasting of time signals by radio or telephone and by modern developments in weather forecasting.

The tripod pole-screen of the eighteenth century is seen to echo the type of support used for the contemporary tripod table. The movable panel (usually filled with petit point embroidery) which afforded protection from the fire, was an upright rectangle in mid-Georgian times; in the later eighteenth century it might take an oval or circular shape, whilst the tripod was superseded by a circular or triangular weighted base. Victorian fire-screens had a panel ('banner') suspended by cords from the pole, like a picture from a picture-hook.

In modern times the cheval type of screen, occasionally in use during the first half of the eighteenth century, was revived. This cheval screen had consisted of a panel (sometimes of curved rococo outline) fitted between or upon two upright supports mounted on short feet. A modern version, with the panel filled according to the taste of the individual owner, is sometimes used nowadays as a summer decoration before the empty hearth or the unwanted fixed gas or electric heater. On the whole the original function of the fire-screen has been rendered unnecessary by modern methods of central heating.

Small toilet glasses stand a little apart. Before they became established in the Victorian period as a fixed part of the dressing table they had been made, from the late seventeenth century onward, as separate pieces of furniture; they usually stood on a convenient small table (which was often prettily draped) or on a chest of drawers. In early pieces the frame was a simpler, unpretending version of the contemporary wall mirror, and swung between two uprights which were usually mounted on a small box stand fitted with a drawer or two for toilet requisites. In some cases the stand had a sloping top which opened forward for writing on, disclosing minute pigeonholes and a nest of tiny drawers in emulation of the bureau or secretaire. Most toilet stands were veneered with walnut but some were finished with lacquer. In the mid-Georgian period the frame followed the fashionable curves of the rococo 'French Taste'; unhappily, few examples have survived. In the later eighteenth century toilet glasses were set in an oval or shield-shaped frame mounted on a stand veneered with mahogany or satinwood. These were succeeded by the simple wide rectangular mirror of the Regency period, which in turn was followed by the toilet mirror of early Victorian date, rather more clumsy and massive. In the twentieth century a small toilet mirror with hinged side wings appeared, when the draped dressing table of the Georgian era came into fashion again. In the mid-twentieth century small toilet mirrors with adjustable wings might be fixed to the wall in very small bedrooms. Others, often circular and unframed, were mounted with a ball-and-socket fitting on a metal rod, and may be seen fixed in pairs to the very low set of drawers serving as dressing table in ultra-modern style.

Numerous smaller objects, of minor importance in the story of furniture, were from time to time, and especially during the Georgian period, added to the furnishing of the house. Among these were the cellaret and winecooler, placed near or under the sideboard table in the dining-room; the 'cat' or tripod rest (often of metal) put to keep plates or food hot before the fire; various kinds of racks, e.g. the spoon rack seen in the kitchen; decorative hanging shelves for displaying china, and brackets on the wall for a bust or vase. A quantity of small boxes and caskets were in use for keeping delicate things like kerchiefs, gloves and laces, and the useful caddy or canister for tea bottles. More significant perhaps, since they had a definite place on the later eighteenth-century sideboard or sideboard table, were the pairs of knife-boxes and urns for cutlery. The boxes were tallish with the front usually slightly serpentine in plan and sloping lids. The urns were of classical form, and were made so that the tops rose on a central metal support to give access to the contents. Both types might be found in veneered mahogany or satinwood.

Between the two World Wars one or two quite new pieces of furniture were introduced as a result of social change or technical invention. First came the cocktail cabinet of the 1920s when the American habit of taking a mixed alcoholic drink before a meal became popular. Often the host mixed the drinks himself immediately in the living-room and here stood a small cupboard, usually of two tiers. The lower one contained the various bottles of wine and spirits, the upper opened to show an inviting array of glasses, and cocktail shaker and various extras such as cocktail sticks, stuffed olives and cocktail cherries. A convenient arrangement was for the lid to open upward, and the front to fall forward on hinges at a suitable level to give extra space for the little ceremony. In the more impressive cabinets this upper portion was often lined with mirror plate. Sometimes a touch of 'period style' was attempted by introducing cabriole legs ('Queen Anne'), or by the use of decoration that recalled the Chippendale style. Walnut or mahogany veneers were commonly used, or alternatively, lighter finishes during the 'off-white' vogue fashionable in interior decoration in the 1930s.

Technical advances and innovations were responsible for the arrival of the radio cabinet soon after the conversion of the primitive gramophone (with its clumsy horn) into a large lidded box with louvres to emit the sound. The two were soon to be combined into one piece of case furniture, the radiogram, which sometimes included a storage space for records. Designed as a low cabinet, its height consonant with the task of changing records and needles (until this was made automatic), the radiogram contained the two pieces of equipment side by side under one long lid. This piece, and the television viewing set of the 1950s and later, stands on the borderline between furniture and equipment; together they hastened the disappearance of the piano, and the television set in particular was to displace the latter as a status symbol.

The television set has its own importance in the field of modern design, since its shape is controlled quite noticeably by its function and it has no real traditional ancestor. At first rather heavy and solid in character, a cabinet type piece surmounted by the small oblong screen, the television set has become in more recent years a neat upright rectangular box of shallow depth, made in a number of different plastic or synthetic finishes. Like the more important and imposing type of sound receiver (as distinct from the transistor set) the television set may either be portable, or given a place in the fitments seen in the modern domestic interior.

Period	Character
Late Tudor and Early Stuart c. 1560–c. 1660	Sturdy, with rich carved ornament on important pieces; bulbous supports common
Later Stuart c. 1660–c. 1700	Shapes become more convenient and more refined; carved ornament conspicuous; spiral turning; some Oriental motifs
Queen Anne and Early Georgian c. 1702–c. 1740	Simple pieces in rather curvilinear style, with cabriole leg a great feature; architectural pieces in 'Palladian' style for great houses
Mid-Georgian or Rococo c. 1740–c. 1765	French, Chinese and Gothic 'Tastes'; French rococo curves often blended with Chinese motifs or hints of Gothic tracery; era of typical Chippendale chair back
Late Georgian, or neo-classical c. 1765–c. 1800	More controlled lines, curves giving way to rectilinear; Adam's classical motifs pervade ornament; variety in chair design; cabriole leg superseded by tapered support, square or cylindrical
Regency c. 1800–c. 1830	Heavier proportions, resulting from study of 'the antique'; Greek, Roman and Egyptian motifs a strong feature in much fashionable furniture; convex looking-glass an innovation

Chart

Materials and Techniques	Names and Events
Oak, used in the solid; limited use of walnut and elm; inlay of holly and bog oak, some mother-of-pearl	
Walnut, solid and as veneer; various woods in marquetry; lacquer, gilding and silvering; gesso for delicate relief; caning; limewood for carving; use of upholstery established	Grinling Gibbons (1647–1720); master carver; name associated with realistic type of applied ornament (flowers, fruit, etc.) for interior decoration which in turn inspired work for decorative furniture
Walnut, solid or veneer; with limited amount of carving; marquetry and silvering out of fashion; red lacquer more popular than black-and-gold of previous period; mahogany introduced c. 1725; much gilding; use of paint to imitate stone or marble for structure; coloured marble or scagliola for table tops	William Kent (1685–1748); chief exponent of Palladianism
Mahogany, in solid or veneer; discreet and refined carving; walnut declines	Thomas Chippendale (1718–1779); his *Director* published 1754, 1759 and 1762
Mahogany and satinwood, solid and veneered; marquetry and painted decoration; some use of black-and-gold lacquer; less use of marble	Robert Adam (1728–1792); his *Works* published 1773 George Hepplewhite (died 1786); his *Guide* published 1788 Thomas Sheraton (1751–1806); *Drawing Book* published 1791/3
Rosewood and mahogany; some use of zebra wood; beech painted black and gold; brass inlay for ornament; carving returns; marquetry out of fashion	Sheraton's *Drawing Book* in 1802 Thomas Hope (1770–1831); *Household Furniture* published 1807 George Smith published his *Household Furniture* 1808

Period	Character
Victorian c. 1830–c.1900 early	Imitations of Regency; mixture of 'Louis XIV' and 'Louis XV', called 'old French style'; also 'Elizabethan' vogue, a misnomer; all fairly heavy and solid in character;
middle	'Early English', or pseudo-Gothic phase;
later	confusion of ideas derived from past styles; tendency to slighter and more spindly character
Twentieth century early	Modifications and reproductions of previous historic styles, notably Jacobean, Queen Anne and, to some extent, Chippendale and Sheraton; collecting of 'antiques';
1930s	Modernism, or the 'functional' in vogue; revolt from tradition; straight lines, no ornament;
1940s	austerity during Second World War; 'utility' design;
c. 1955	recovery, with return to some traditional shapes, but simpler styles copied from Scandinavia and Italy; 'stick' furniture

Materials and Techniques	Names and Events
Rosewood and mahogany; amboyna; solid preferred to veneer; some heavy carving; no marquetry;	
	Great Exhibition 1851 William Burges (1827–1881)
use of period woods, oak, walnut, mahogany, satinwood revived; canework, rattan, bamboo, bentwood, cast-iron, brass; mirror plate in cabinet-work	William Morris (1834–1896) Art-Workers' Guild formed 1884
All traditional woods and finishes;	First Daily Mail 'Ideal Home' Exhibition held in 1908
tubular steel; laminated wood; some exotic woods for veneer for ultra-expensive work; shortage of timber; use of building board; plastic imitations of wood veneers; coloured enamel; heat- and water-resisting finishes	

Glossary

Acacia Yellow wood with brown markings; used to some extent in the eighteenth century for bandings.

Acanthus Plant with leaf having strongly-serrated edges; the leaf in conventional form much used as an ornamental motif; of classical origin, e.g. on Corinthian capitals and used from the Renaissance period onward, chiefly as carved ornament, in architecture and the decorative arts.

Adam, Robert: 1728–1792 Famous architect and interior decorator, who also designed furniture in a distinctive style.

Amboyna Tree native to the West Indies; the wood has a bird's-eye figure of golden brown colour; used in the later eighteenth century as a veneer and for decorative banding in marquetry.

Ambry, or aumbry Somewhat archaic term, applied to a small cupboard used for storing food; formerly the aumbry was used in churches for storing the sacred vessels.

Amorini (Ital.) Winged cupids or small gods of Love, much used for decorative motifs on furniture during the late seventeenth and early eighteenth centuries.

Anthemion Conventional ornamental motif derived from the honeysuckle flower; of classical Greek origin and revived by Robert Adam in his designs.

Apron, or apron piece Shaped piece depending from the seat rail of a chair, settee or stool; also seen on certain stands for chests of drawers; chiefly found on early eighteenth-century furniture.

Arabesque A linear type of symmetrical ornament which came to Europe from Islamic art via Venice and Spain; allied with *Grotesque* (q.v.) in English decoration by c. 1700.

Arcade, arcaded Series of arches supported on piers or columns; used as carved decoration on furniture, e.g. during the Elizabethan and Jacobean periods.

Architrave Architectural feature consisting of several mouldings which, with the frieze immediately above and the cornice on top, formed the classical entablature in architecture; the architrave was essentially the beam which spanned the space from one column to the next; architrave mouldings were used alone as frames to doorways and windows in classical and Renaissance architecture, and were adapted as frames for looking-glasses in the eighteenth century.

Ash Tree native to Britain; the wood greyish-white to pale yellow in colour; flexible, e.g. the 'bend of ash' used for the back rail of Windsor chairs in the eighteenth and nineteenth centuries.

Astragal Small moulding, semi-circular in profile; used on furniture as an applied moulding, and noticeable for the glazing bars of eighteenth-century book-cases and cabinets.

Back-stool Term used in the later seventeenth century for a plain chair without arms.

Bail-handle Brass drop handle introduced in the later seventeenth century; of oblong shape, straight or curved, hanging from a knob or rosette fixed to the drawer front.

Ball foot Turned foot, somewhat spherical; used during the late seventeenth century.

Baluster Small carved or turned column, sometimes of vase form; in architecture several balusters with a hand-rail form a balustrade; balusters are found in a modified form as supports in furniture, e.g. for legs and stretchers in chairs and tables, occasionally as the back uprights to a chair; see also *Split baluster*.

Banding A band, of contrasting colour or material, used as a decorative element, especially in veneer and marquetry; see also *Cross-banding* and *Stringing*.

Barjier, burjair Eighteenth-century English adaptation of the French term *bergère*, for an armchair with closed sides; first used c. 1725.

Bead, or beading Narrow semi-circular moulding; see also *Cock-bead* and *Reeding*.

Bead-and-reel Decorative moulding derived from classical architecture; it consists of three small 'beads' alternating with a long 'reel'; used on eighteenth-century mahogany furniture.

Bead-moulding Decorative moulding, formed by cutting the 'bead' into a continuous series of beads or 'pearls'; found on eighteenth-century mahogany furniture.

Beech Tree native to Britain; wood of light brown colour with grain of close texture; in the Regency period beech was used for furniture painted black ('japanned').

Bergère See *Barjier*.

Bergeries From French *berger*, shepherd; term denoting pastoral scenes of shepherds and shepherdesses; frequent subject for French tapestries and adapted for coverings for seated furniture; found on some Adam furniture.

Bevel Sloped surface, e.g. bevelled edge, as found on looking-glass plates.

Birch Tree native to Britain; wood has a pale yellowish tint when polished.

Bog oak Black in colour; used for inlaid motifs in Elizabethan and Jacobean furniture.

Bombé Term for the shaped outline of carcase furniture with swelling or bulging fronts (and sometimes sides); e.g. English imitations of French commodes of the Louis XV period.

Boulle, André Charles: 1642–1732 Celebrated French cabinet-maker; his name is particularly connected with the marquetry of brass and tortoiseshell used in his workshop as a decorative veneer to furniture; imitated by *Gerreit Jensen* (q.v.), and by English cabinet-makers in the Victorian period.

Bow-front Horizontal convex segmental curve; e.g. to commodes and chests of drawers made during the second half of the eighteenth century.

Boxwood Pale yellowish-white in colour; very hard and smooth; used for bandings in veneer or inlay; sometimes stained green.

Bracket Supporting member, usually carved, projecting from a vertical surface; made in the eighteenth century as an individual object, secured to the wall to carry a decorative vase or a bust.

Bracket-foot Used at the corners of the base to cabinets, chests of drawers, etc., thus raising the piece from the ground; found on early eighteenth-century pieces.

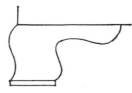

Breakfast-table Term used by Chippendale; small folding oblong table on four legs, with a shelf underneath

usually enclosed by latticework on three sides; the folding leaves supported on brackets when extended.

Breakfront Term used when the front of the piece (e.g. a bookcase) is in more than one plane; bookcases of the mid-eighteenth century were often divided into three parts, the centre portion being two or three inches forward of the sides or wings.

Buffet A form of sideboard; in the early twentieth century this term was erroneously applied to the open *Court cupboards* (q.v.) of the Elizabethan period.

Bulbous Descriptive of the turned supports to beds, cupboards, tables, etc., in which a large bulb-like swelling is a noticeable feature; seen in furniture of the Elizabethan and Jacobean periods.

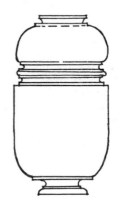

Bun foot Resembles a flattened globe (see *Ball foot*) used during the later seventeenth century.

Bureau By eighteenth-century definition this piece had a sloping front (like a desk) which hinged to drop outward and rest upon two pull-out runners or sliders, thus forming a surface to write on and disclosing the desk fittings of pigeonholes and nests of drawers; contrast with the *Escritoire* (q.v.) which had a flat front (called scrutore in the late seventeenth century).

Burr Term for a rather irregular figure in veneer, e.g. burr walnut; burr wood, obtainable from various trees including elm, maple, oak, walnut and yew, was selected from the malformations which grew out from the trunk of the tree.

Cabinet Piece of furniture containing drawers or shelves, enclosed by doors which may be solid or glazed, or filled with wire trellis.

Cabochon Ornamental motif, usually carved; oval or round, convex or concave and generally with a leafy border; seen on the 'knee' of the cabriole leg of chairs made in the 1740s.

Cabriole leg Distinctive shape, curving sharply outward at the 'knee', then curving inward and out again to end in

a foot which may be one of several types, e.g. claw-and-ball, paw, club, hoof or scroll; commonly used during the eighteenth century until superseded by the tapering leg of Adam's neo-classical style.

Caduceus Ornamental motif, consisting of two serpents twining about a rod and symbolizing 'Medicine'; of classical origin and revived during the Regency period; perhaps carved.

Calamander Wood imported from Ceylon and in use from c. 1780 for nearly fifty years; used for decorative veneer work, appearing as a mottled brown with black streaks.

Candlestand A tallish, light-weight stand, sometimes very decorative; popular during the eighteenth century for vases and busts as well as for candelabra.

Candle-slide Thin, narrow pull-out piece of wood, fitted with a small brass knob handle; usually seen on the bureau-cabinet of the first half of the eighteenth century.

Canework Used for the seats and back panels of chairs and day-beds during the second half of the seventeenth century; in fashion again in the Regency period, and at intervals during the nineteenth century and in modern times.

Canopy Term sometimes used for the solid top or ceiling characteristic of important beds during the historic periods;

sometimes called a *Tester* (q.v.); may be of carved panelled wood (e.g. Elizabethan and Jacobean); of wood covered in a decorative fabric (e.g. late Stuart and early Georgian); or of material draped on a metal frame (e.g. nineteenth century).

Canted Term used of a surface which is bevelled, chamfered or splayed, e.g. the front corners of a chest of drawers of the Chippendale period.

Canterbury (*a*) Stand with shaped top, to hold plates, knives and forks, designed in the late eighteenth century to accompany the supper table; (*b*) stand, specially divided to hold sheets of music.

Caqueteuse, or caquetoire Term borrowed from the French, and applied to an open armchair of mid-sixteenth-century date popularly supposed to have been reserved for women's use.

Carcase The basic framework of a piece of furniture such as a chest of drawers or a cabinet, particularly before the addition of a veneer or other form of decoration.

Carlton House table Writing table mounted on legs, which has a raised back and sides all fitted with small drawers and cupboards or pigeonholes; fashionable to a limited extent at the end of the eighteenth century.

Cartouche Decorative motif resembling a sheet of paper partly unrolled, often with fancifully-cut edges; on this surface a cipher, a coat of arms or other design may be added; used as a carved orna-

ment in the centre of a broken pediment to cabinets, bookcases and looking-glasses during the eighteenth century.

Caryatid Female statue used as a support, e.g. for decorative stands and tables; derived from the classical original which took the place of a column; sometimes used in pilaster form, e.g. on seventeenth-century pieces.

Castor Small wheel fitted to the feet of chairs, stands, tables, etc., to ensure easy movement; introduced towards the end of the seventeenth century.

Cavetto moulding Hollow moulding, about a quarter-circle, found as part of the cornice to certain taller pieces, e.g. tallboys.

Cedar Imported from N. America and the West Indies and usually known as red cedar; popular in the eighteenth century to line drawers, boxes and trays in wardrobes.

Cellaret Primarily a case for wine-bottles, usually lidded, and lined with lead; the term appeared in the mid-eighteenth century; it is also used for the deep drawer lined with lead and divided for wine-bottles, which was a feature of sideboards of the late eighteenth century and throughout most of the nineteenth century.

Celure See *Tester.*

Chambers, Sir William: 1726–1796 Practised as an architect in England after travelling in China; in 1759 he published a book of designs of *Chinese Buildings, Furniture, Dresses, Machines and Utensils.*

Chamfer Bevel or splay, to the edge of a surface, e.g. to a moulding, to the stiles or rails in panelled chests, etc.

Chequer or checker Type of decoration, using squares of contrasting tone or colour, e.g. inlaid ornament, c. 1600.

Cherry Wood of reddish colour; used for inlaid ornament in the seventeenth century.

Chesterfield Over-stuffed settee, of the type popular in the 1920s.

Chestnut Wood used as a veneer; like birch, chestnut was used as a cheap substitute for satinwood (for which it may be mistaken) at the end of the eighteenth century.

Cheval glass A looking-glass swinging between two vertical supports on shaped feet; used for the toilet, and especially in fashion from the late eighteenth century into the Victorian period, until it was superseded by the addition of a mirror to the door of the wardrobe.

Chevron Ornamental zigzag repeating pattern, derived from medieval heraldry; found on inlaid seventeenth-century pieces.

Chiffonier Term for a sideboard with two doors below enclosing shelves, used in the mid nineteenth century; also sometimes applied to the high tallboy of the later Victorian period.

'Chinese Taste' Term especially popular in the 1760s, after the published designs of Chippendale and others; it chiefly consisted in the introduction of Chinese motifs, e.g. the pagoda, combining them with Western shapes; applicable to the other decorative arts as well as to furniture, and today objects in this manner are referred to as chinoiserie.

Chip-carving Form of decoration achieved by the direct use of gouge and chisel, making shallow cuts and resulting in somewhat geometric designs;

flourished especially during the sixteenth and early seventeenth centuries, e.g. on the fronts of chests.

Chippendale, Thomas: 1718–1779 London cabinet-maker; published a comprehensive book of designs, *The Gentleman and Cabinet-Maker's Director*, in 1754, with further editions in 1759 and 1762; produced pieces in the French (rococo), 'Chinese' and 'Gothick Tastes' then prevailing; he also carried out work to the designs of Robert Adam in the neo-classical style.

Cipher or cypher Interlaced initials (monogram) frequently used as an ornamental motif.

Claw-and-ball foot Probably originated in China, where it may have represented the three-clawed foot of a dragon clutching the sacred jewel; introduced into England from Holland in the late seventeenth century, and much used with the cabriole leg in the first half of the eighteenth century.

Club foot Formed by thickening the leg to make a foot; often had a small disc carved under it to rest on the floor; chiefly used on furniture of the early eighteenth century.

271

Cluster-column leg Term for a design giving the appearance of a cluster of columns ; found in some furniture made in the 'Gothick Taste' of Chippendale's time.

Cock-bead moulding Small moulding used for the edges of drawer fronts; convex or half-round in section; much used from c. 1730 to the end of the eighteenth century.

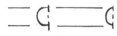

Coffer From the Old French *cofre-fort*; chest or strong box used during the medieval period for holding such valuables as money, jewels, etc.; in modern times rather a fanciful name for any 'antique' chest.

Coffin-stool A modern term, applied in error to the small oak four-legged stool with stretchers of late sixteenth- or early seventeenth-century date.

Column In architecture, a vertical structural support consisting of base, shaft and capital, usually conforming to one of the classical orders or in Gothic style; occasionally used in a modified form in furniture; see *Pilaster*.

Commode French term for any kind of chest fitted with drawers; some were made in England at the time of Chippendale and Adam; those closely imitating the French style were bombé in form, others might only have a curved front; in some pieces the drawers were enclosed by two doors.

Composition, or 'compo' Mixture of whiting, resin and size, which could be cast into moulds to make patterns; resembles the gesso of Italian origin; this could be used for details too delicate for carving in wood; cf. much eighteenth-century furniture.

Confidante, or confidente Term borrowed from the French, to denote an upholstered settee to which a seat had been added at each end; illustrated in Hepplewhite's *Guide*, 3rd edition, 1794.

Console Bracket, usually shaped like an S-scroll; mainly found as a decorative feature in eighteenth-century furniture.

Console table Small side table, usually fixed to the wall and with the support(s) designed to give something of a bracket effect; some may be seen designed with a dolphin or eagle motif for support; since the favourite position was between the windows of a saloon, the console table was a kind of pier table.

Copland, H.: fl. mid-eighteenth century. Published *A New Book of Ornaments* in 1746, consisting of designs for cartouches and details of ornament; collaborated with *Matthias Lock* (q.v.) on a further volume in 1752; some chair designs by Copland appeared in a book by *Robert Manwaring* published in 1766; Copland is said to have been in business in Cheapside.

Coquillage From the French *coquille*, shell-fish; term used to describe a shell-like pattern which was combined with other rococo motifs; in its simplest form it is seen on mid-eighteenth-century furniture in rococo or 'French Taste', e.g. on the seat rail of various pieces.

Corbel Architectural term for a small projecting bracket supporting other members, cf. 'console' in furniture.

Cornice In architecture, the top members of the classical entablature, which project above the plain frieze; sometimes the cornice was used alone, e.g. in some Queen Anne period houses; this feature was adopted for furniture from the late seventeenth century onwards, as the crowning member of such pieces as bookcases, cabinets and looking-glasses.

Couch An upholstered seat for reclining, similar to a sofa, with head end only and half-back.

Court cupboard Piece consisting of two tiers of open shelves; the word court is allied to the French *court*, short; court cupboards were introduced in the early sixteenth century and were popular until the Restoration.

Cradle Small enclosed cot for a baby; usually fitted with a hood and mounted on rockers; popular from the Middle Ages until recent times; now displaced by the modern open cot on castors.

Credence From Italian *credenza*; type of side table on which dishes were placed preparatory to service at table; in form, a cupboard on legs, perhaps with an open shelf below; term used in the later sixteenth and early seventeenth centuries; few examples have survived and the word is practically obsolete.

Cresting Ornamental feature added to the top of a piece of furniture, e.g. across the top rail of a Jacobean armchair, or above the Restoration period looking-glass.

Cross-banding Band or border, in which the figure of the wood runs across the width; seen in veneered furniture.

C-scroll Descriptive term for an ornamental motif, cf. in the carved back of a Restoration period chair.

Cusping The small pointed arcs of Gothic tracery; seen as decoration in furniture, e.g. Chippendale period chairs, etc., in the 'Gothick Taste' and Victorian Gothic Revival furniture, as well as in carved medieval furniture.

Cylinder-front Roll-top cover, e.g. to a bureau or secretaire; see *Tambour*.

Cypress Reddish-coloured wood, close-grained, hard and durable; popular for chests and other storage pieces, especially in the sixteenth and seventeenth centuries when it was held to resist worm and to protect (by its odour) the contents from moth.

Damask Rich figured (i.e. patterned) material, originally of silk; used for upholstery; the design usually woven in the same coloured thread, and of conventional character, employing flowers, fruit, etc.

Darly, Matthias: fl. c. 1750–1778 Designer and man of varied activities; called himself a 'Professor of Ornament', engraved certain plates in Chippendale's *Director*, and published some works of his own, e.g. *A Compleat Body of Architecture, etc.* in 1770.

Davenport Small desk, with sloping top for writing (which lifts like a box lid), and having drawers opening from the side; popular during the first half of the nineteenth century.

Day-bed Ancestor of the Regency sofa and the twentieth-century divan; had a headpiece (sometimes adjustable) at one end, but no back, and intended for one person to recline on during the day; popular from the time of Queen Elizabeth I to Queen Anne.

T

273

Deal General term for the wood of various conifers; in furniture mainly used for carcase work, e.g. cabinets, chests of drawers, etc., to a limited extent in the eighteenth century; used for very cheap furniture in the Victorian period and the first half of the twentieth century.

Deudarn See *Tridarn*.

Diaper work Conventional pattern, consisting of some motif, e.g. a tiny flower or even a mere dot, in repeating squares or diamonds forming an all-over decorative treatment.

Dinner waggon Two-tiered or three-tiered piece, usually rectangular and moving on castors, used for the conveyance of plates, cutlery, etc.

Dished Term implying a sunken surface, e.g. the seat of a chair dished slightly for a loose cushion, or the small sinkings in the eighteenth-century card table top in which counters or money lay during play.

Divan Idea derived from the East; a long upholstered settee without back or sides, popularized chiefly during the twentieth century; comparable to the divan bed.

Dolphin Used in richly-decorative furniture, notably during the eighteenth century; the dolphin often being a conspicuous feature, e.g. in the design of elaborate chairs, or as the main support to console tables.

Draw table Term for the type of dining table which is fitted with leaves, one to pull out at each end to increase space at mealtimes; first popular in Elizabethan days.

Dresser Originally a side table, consisting of two or three horizontal drawers with cupboards or an open shelf (potboard) below, and surmounted by a number of very narrow, backed shelves above, on which rows of plates (pewter, earthenware, etc.) or dishes could be displayed; the modern term 'Welsh dresser' is incorrect, the type having no connection with Wales; see also *Tridarn*.

Dressing table Unknown in its modern form (i.e. as a combined piece with chest of drawers, etc., with mirror attached) until the end of the eighteenth century, but established during the Victorian period.

Duchesse Hepplewhite's definition (*Cabinet Maker and Upholsterer's Guide, 1788*): 'Two Barjier chairs, of proper construction, with a stool in the middle.'

Dumb-waiter During the eighteenth century it consisted of three tiers of circular shelves diminishing in diameter, supported on a tripod stand which stood near the dining table at supper-time, for plates, etc.

Ebony Black wood, chiefly used in furniture for decorative treatment, e.g. as inlay, veneer or marquetry details, at various periods.

Egg-and-dart Repeating ornamental motif, derived from classical architecture and adapted in the decorative treatment of furniture, notably during the eighteenth century.

Elm Hard wood, the grain irregular in appearance; used for chairs and tables in Tudor times, and for seats of Windsor chairs in Georgian and Victorian days.

Endive marquetry Sometimes called 'seaweed' marquetry, the pattern resembling in its flowing arabesque lines

the delicate leaves of the endive plant; seen in walnut furniture c. 1700.

Entablature Constructional feature in classical architecture; originally the horizontal structure resting on columns and divided into architrave, frieze and cornice; also used as crowning part of a building; used in furniture as ornamental feature to cabinets, bookcases, etc. of eighteenth-century classical taste and in later periods.

Escallop Or scallop shell; ornamental motif used variously, especially during the eighteenth century, e.g. on the 'knee' of the cabriole leg.

Escritoire One of several names for a desk or bureau fitted for writing; scrutore (seventeenth century) and secretaire are similar.

Escutcheon (*a*) Derived from heraldry; in furniture a shield often carved for decorative purposes and perhaps to carry a crest or cipher; (*b*) metal plate placed to protect a keyhole.

Etagère From the French; a small light stand fitted with a shelf or two, for the display of small ornaments or use as a work table; term used in the nineteenth century.

Farthingale chair Modern term used by dealers for an upholstered chair with a broad seat and low back, without arms; of early seventeenth-century date.

Fauteuil French term; armchair with upholstered back and seat.

Feather-banding See *Herring-bone banding*.

Festoon Piece of drapery, or string of leaves or flowers, hung in a horizontal curve; used as a decorative motif on furniture, carved or painted, or in marquetry work, notably during the eighteenth century; swag is an alternative term.

Figure Name given to the natural marking seen in wood; term used especially in connection with the choice woods used in making the finest furniture.

Finial Small decorative feature, added as a terminal ornament to a piece of furniture, e.g. a knob on the back upright of a chair, or the intersection of crossed stretchers or on the top of a pole screen; takes various forms at different periods.

Fir Wood known to have been used during the eighteenth century for the carved and gilded parts of very decorative tables (with marble tops); several examples in the style of William Kent have survived.

Fluting Ornamental treatment derived from the classical column, consisting of parallel vertical grooves separated from each other by a sharpish edge; found in furniture as decoration, inlaid, painted or carved, to the frieze rails of tables and to supports to chairs, etc., especially during the second half of the eighteenth century.

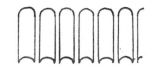

Foliated Using a leafy form, e.g. a foliated scroll.

Foot Deliberate shaping to the end of the leg of a table, chair, stand, etc., and found in many different forms during the past; these include: bun, claw-and-ball, French scroll, hoof, spade and pied-de-biche.

Footman Small stand of polished steel, about twelve inches high, consisting of a top of open bars supported on shaped legs; to stand before the fire holding plates to keep them hot.

Form Long seat with no back; especially popular during the early seventeenth century to seat several people at the long dining table.

French polishing Medium consisting of shellac dissolved in methylated spirits with colouring matter added; gave a high meretricious polish to furniture and was easily affected by heat or wet; not in use until the late eighteenth century; modern methods of proofing against spoiling by heat and liquids have supplanted this.

Fretwork Form of ornamentation, resembling trelliswork or small interlacings, usually geometrical; used either as perforated decoration or on a solid foundation; usually of laminated construction but sometimes seen cut on the solid; used for pierced fretwork 'galleries' to table tops, pierced fretwork stretchers, and as solid ornament for friezes of tables and for chair legs; much in vogue in the Chippendale period, notably in pieces in the 'Chinese Taste'.

Frieze Central horizontal member of the entablature of classic architecture, and usually plain and flat; made a fine field for decorative treatment; found in furniture as part of the top to cabinets, etc.; gives its name to frieze-rail; found ornamented with carving, painting or inlaid marquetry during the historic periods.

Frieze-rail Horizontal member under the moulded edge of the top to a table, chest or stand.

Gadroon A carved repeating ornament, usually of convex form; may be vertical or slightly twisted; much used on Elizabethan and Jacobean furniture, e.g. on drawer fronts and supports for tables and chairs.

Gallery Used to form a protection to the edge of a table, cabinet top, etc.; takes the form of a tiny balustrade or a trellis fret, in wood or metalwork, during the eighteenth century and Regency period; term also applied to the metal supports at the back of sideboards, late eighteenth century.

Galon Thick ribbon or braid, used to make an ornamental edging to curtains and pelmets and also as a finish to other upholstery, e.g. seat coverings; very fashionable during the early eighteenth century, and made of silk, or gold or silver thread.

Games table Eighteenth-century piece with top, reversible to disclose an inlaid chess-board, and sometimes removable altogether to reveal a board underneath marked for backgammon.

Gate-leg table Table with fixed top supported on four legs, with a hinged leaf on each side supported, when extended, on the 'gate' principle, the gate being either single or double; the top usually oval or circular when fully extended; first introduced mid-seventeenth century and popular for half a century.

Gesso From the Italian, plaster or chalk; made up of chalk and size and easily moulded or carved into designs, and then painted or gilt; cf. the 'compo' used for much of the gilded furniture of the early eighteenth century; revived in the Adam period.

Gibbons, Grinling: 1648–1721 Celebrated carver of decorative woodwork which is very realistic in character, including such motifs as cherubs' heads, bunches of flowers, fruit, leaves, peapods, wheat ears and the like; his work greatly influenced the style and standard of carving of his period, not only in interior decoration but also in furniture, e.g. frames for looking-glasses, decorative stands for cabinets and so on.

Gilding The ornamentation of furniture, wholly or in part, by the use of gold leaf or gold dust; frequently used as a finish to fine furniture for Royal palaces and the state apartments of the aristocracy during the historic periods, and to frames for pictures and looking-glasses generally during the eighteenth and nineteenth centuries.

Gillow, Robert: 1703–1773 Founded a factory for furniture making at Lancaster; notable designer and cabinet-maker; firm later traded as Waring and Gillow.

Girandole Decorative branched candlestick, designed to hang on the wall; sometimes seen in conjunction with mirror plate, especially during the eighteenth century when it was usually gilded.

Goodison, Benjamin: died 1767 Cabinet-maker working in London, who supplied a quantity of furniture for the Royal

palaces, as well as for Holkham in Norfolk and elsewhere.

'Gothick' Taste Eighteenth-century term for furniture distinguished by the use of Gothic motifs, chiefly tracery; vogue probably introduced by Horace Walpole of Strawberry Hill fame; pieces in this style were made in limited numbers (mid-eighteenth century), as it was not very popular; Chippendale and others published designs labelled 'Gothick Taste'; not to be confused with Victorian furniture of the Gothic Revival.

Grandfather clock Popular, but erroneous, term for *Long-case clock*, q.v.

Griffin or gryphon Fabulous monster of classical antiquity; it combined the head and wings of an eagle with the hind part, legs and tail of a lion; a notable decorative motif, usually carved, in the work of Robert Adam and in some Regency pieces.

Grille Term applicable to the openwork brass lattice or trellis used instead of glazing, e.g. for bookcases or cabinet doors on Regency furniture.

Grisaille Term descriptive of the use of a grey monochrome in painting; a decorative treatment seen in some furniture, e.g. painted grisaille medallions allied with marquetry, in satinwood furniture of the late eighteenth century.

Gros point, petit point Tent-stitch embroidery used to make a decorative furnishing fabric, resembling woven tapestry; in petit point, smaller-sized stitches are used than in gros point; both types may be used in the same piece of work to enhance the effect, e.g. the central or more delicate design may be in petit point, the decorative surround in gros point; chiefly used from the late sixteenth century to the mid-eighteenth century; revived in the Victorian era, notably as Berlin woolwork, using somewhat garish colours and rather tasteless designs, carried out in a coarser stitch than during the earlier period; used in the twentieth century mainly in connection with reproduction furniture.

Grotesque Decoration of classical origin, revived in Renaissance Italy after its rediscovery on the walls and ceilings of 'grottoes' (actually half-buried ruins of various types of Roman buildings); a characteristic design consists of a number of small 'pictures' framed as medallions or rectangular tablets, suspended amongst a light and fanciful arrangement of foliated scrolls and fabulous and semi-human creatures; in England, used chiefly in interior decoration; only occasionally seen, in a modified form, in a few painted or marquetry pieces of the later eighteenth century.

Guéridon or torchère French term for a small table, stand or pedestal, used for candelabra, etc., chiefly during the eighteenth century.

Guilloche Repeating ornamental motif of classical origin, and taking the form of a running band of interlacing circles, sometimes with a conventional motif at the centre, e.g. a rosette; in furniture, found carved at recurring periods from the later sixteenth century onward, and painted or veneered in the later eighteenth century.

Gumley, John: died 1729 Maker of furniture and frames for looking-glasses; pieces signed by him or by his partner James Moore (died 1726) are to be seen in the State Apartments at Hampton Court Palace; his mother, Mrs Elizabeth Gumley, was also concerned in the business.

Haig, Thomas: fl. 1771–1796 Worked in partnership with Thomas Chippendale; later with Chippendale the younger (Chippendale, Haig & Co.).

Harewood Term used for sycamore which has been stained a greenish-grey colour; used for decorative bandings of veneer in marquetry furniture of the late eighteenth century.

Harlequin table A piece fitted with several conveniences, usually concealed, and thus perhaps serving as both dressing and writing table; it may contain a small looking-glass raised by a spring, or a range of small drawers and pigeonholes raised by a mechanism; such examples appear among designs by Thomas Sheraton about the end of the eighteenth century.

Hepplewhite, George: died 1786 Furniture maker established in London; his widow published *The Cabinetmaker and Upholsterers' Guide* (1788, 1789, 1794); designs associated with his name show some elegance and curvilinear tendencies, e.g. chairs with shield- or heart-shaped backs.

Herring-bone banding Decorative border, chiefly used in veneer or marquetry work; two narrow strips are laid together at opposing angles, hence term; sometimes called feather-banding.

Hocked leg Curved leg, shaped like the hind (or hock) leg of an animal; appears in Regency furniture, e.g. legs to chairs, sofas, etc.

Holly A hard, white wood; used for decorative work, white or stained, e.g. as inlay in Elizabethan and Jacobean furniture.

Honeysuckle Ornamental motif, see *Anthemion.*

Hoof foot The use of animal hoofs, cloven or solid, as feet on furniture is of great antiquity; introduced into English furniture at the end of the seventeenth century and seen on the early, or transitional, type of cabriole leg.

Hope, Thomas: c. 1770–1831 Writer and amateur furniture-designer; published *Household Furniture and Interior Decoration* (1807); a devotee of the Regency style in its most severely-classical and archaeological form; furniture designed by him has survived.

Horsehair cloth Upholstery fabric, woven from the mane and tail hairs; used for seated furniture in the later eighteenth century and throughout the nineteenth century; usually black but sometimes found dyed in other colours.

Husk ornament Conventional motif, derived from the bell-shaped flower of the *garrya elliptica*, several being strung together in diminishing sizes to form a festoon or pendant; much used on furniture in the Adam and Hepplewhite styles; used carved, painted or in marquetry.

Ince, W. and Mayhew, J.: fl. second half eighteenth century Partners in London firm of cabinet-makers and upholsterers, and also published various designs, e.g. the *Universal System of Household Furniture* (c. 1762).

Inlay Method of decorating a surface by cutting hollows in it forming a design, and filling in with some materials in contrast, either in texture, tone or colour, or all three; in furniture, inlay may be done by using, for example, metal, ivory, mother-of-pearl, or tortoiseshell or woods contrasting with the general ground; much used in Elizabethan and Jacobean furniture, e.g. with holly for the light and bog oak for the dark parts of the design—against the oak of the piece; not to be confused with *Marquetry* (q.v.).

Ivory Tusk of the elephant, walrus, etc.; used for decorative work in furniture, e.g. in marquetry work of the later seventeenth century and later eighteenth century.

Japanning English term for the decorative process used in imitation of Oriental *Lacquer* (q.v.); introduced during the later seventeenth century; at first varnish was used, but later a mere coat of paint on which motifs were painted in gold answered to the same name.

Jardinière From the French; a decorative stand for plants or flowers; popular in the later eighteenth and early nineteenth centuries.

Jensen, Gerreit: fl. c. 1680–1714 Name variously spelt, e.g. Garrett Johnson; cabinet-maker and glass-seller; his work included some examples in marquetry imitating the style of the Frenchman, André Charles Boulle.

Johnson, Thomas: fl. mid-eighteenth century London carver and designer who published (1755) *Twelve Girandoles* and (1756/8) *One Hundred and Fifty New Designs*, following the French Taste.

Kauffmann, Angelica: 1741–1807 Swiss painter working in England for fifteen years from 1766 onward; designed and painted decorative panels for interior decoration schemes and for furniture, mainly figure subjects in neo-classical taste; noted for her connection with Adam's work.

Kent, William: 1684–1748 Man of many parts, architect, painter, sculptor and designer; his decorative furniture was massive and elaborate in design, much influenced by the current Venetian style.

Key pattern Alternative name for a 'Greek fret' repeating ornament; seen as low-relief carved ornament to the frieze rail of tables, etc., mid-eighteenth century, and sometimes seen in late eighteenth-century marquetry decoration.

Kidney table Table with kidney-shaped top, designed for the sitter to face the concave side; alternatively a knee-hole pedestal type table with drawers under a similar top; introduced at the time of Sheraton; popular in modern times for small dressing tables.

Kingwood Decorative wood from Brazil, showing distinct contrasting markings; used in marquetry and veneer; first appeared in England, but at that time called 'prince's wood'; used for cross-banded borders in the late eighteenth century.

Knee-hole Descriptive of writing tables or bureaux, designed with a central portion recessed between two pedestals of drawers for the convenience of the person seated at them; first introduced in the early eighteenth century.

Knife-box Small decorative piece, but with a practical purpose; either designed as a box with a sloping hinged lid, or as a classical urn with the top rising on a central sprung support; used in pairs in the later eighteenth century, either on the sideboard table itself or one each on the accompanying pedestals; also on early sideboards proper; table cutlery was placed inside the knife-box in a vertical position with the handles uppermost.

Knob, or ball turning Descriptive of the turning of legs and stretchers; chiefly in use during the seventeenth century and then superseded by spiral turning.

Laburnum Wood yellow to reddish-brown in colour and streaky; used for decorative veneer, e.g. in 'oyster-piece' work of the late seventeenth century and early eighteenth century.

Lacquer Decorative process originating in the Far East and based on the use of a natural varnish; in raised lacquerwork the ground is coloured (black, green, blue or vermilion) with the raised motifs gilded; in incised lacquerwork the design is polychrome; both types were copied for English furniture, especially in the later seventeenth and early eighteenth centuries.

Ladderback Type of chair back formed of horizontal slats or rails; used at various times, the Chippendale type being the most distinguished.

Lambrequin French term for pelmet; sometimes found in furniture in a modified form as an ornamental motif.

Laminated wood Thin layers of wood glued together before use; in the central layer the grain runs in the opposite direction; much used today in default of solid wood, for panels, etc.

Latticework Construction in wood or metal, of criss-cross design; used variously in furniture.

Laurel Leaf of the bay tree used in classical times for wreaths and garlands; motif derived from antiquity and used in the ornamentation of furniture, notably during the second half of the eighteenth century.

Lignum vitae Wood from the West Indies with a dark brown and black streaky figure; used to some extent in seventeenth-century furniture, in the solid and for veneer.

Limewood Very popular for decorative carved work due to its fine white grain, especially in the later seventeenth century when Grinling Gibbons set a high standard of craftsmanship; used for the elaborately carved and gilded, or silvered, stands made for lacquer cabinets of the period.

Linenfold Panel decoration of late Gothic period, representing a fold or scroll of linen. Probably introduced into this country through Flemish influence.

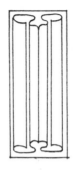

Lion mask Ornamental motif, usually carved, e.g. on the 'knee' of the early eighteenth-century cabriole leg; revived as a decorative feature on Regency furniture.

Livery cupboard Name given to a cupboard formed with openwork panels or balustered doors which allowed for ventilation; in such a piece food could be stored temporarily, especially the refreshment allowed at night in medieval times; examples survive from the sixteenth and early seventeenth centuries.

Lock, Matthias: fl. mid-eighteenth century Designer and carver who published various works, including *A New Drawing Book of Ornaments* (c. 1740), in the rococo manner; with H. Copland he also published designs in neo-classical taste, e.g. *A New Book of Ornaments* (1768).

Long-case clock Correct term for the type popularly called a grandfather clock; constructed to accommodate pendulum and weights; introduced soon after the Restoration, continuing to be made until near the end of the Victorian period.

Lotus Egyptian motif revived on Regency furniture in the Egyptian style, chiefly as an applied metal mount.

Lozenge Decorative motif, diamond-shaped; popular in carved and inlaid work of the early seventeenth century.

Lunette A semi-circular or fan shape, used as a decorative motif, sometimes alone or repeating, plain or intersected, or even foliated; seen as a carved motif

in work of the Jacobean period; appeared again usually painted or in marquetry during the late eighteenth century.

Lustre Contemporary term for the glass chandeliers of the later eighteenth and early nineteenth centuries.

Lyre-back Name given to chairs in which the design of the back consists of an adaptation of the classical lyre, a

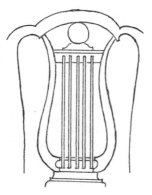

stringed musical instrument not unlike a small harp but symmetrical; seen in designs by Adam and Sheraton.

Mahogany Wood imported from the Spanish West Indies, introduced for furniture in the early eighteenth century, increasing in popularity after 1720, until rivalled by satinwood in the later eighteenth century; its use revived in the Victorian period; varies in colour from a golden to a reddish-brown offering a fine figure for veneered work, and in the solid suitable, because of its toughness, for very refined carving, e.g. on mid-eighteenth-century furniture.

Maple A white wood, used from the seventeenth century; sometimes stained for marquetry work; 'bird's-eye' maple is a distinctively figured veneer popular in the Victorian period.

Marble Found in most shades of colour, plain, mottled or variegated; takes a high polish; very fashionable for tops of decorative tables during the eighteenth century; white marble was used for tops to Regency cabinets and Victorian wash-stands.

Marot, Daniel: died c. 1718 French designer, working mainly in Holland as a Huguenot refugee; attached himself to William of Orange and visited England in 1694 and 1698; had some influence on the design of decorative furniture of the more elaborate kind, notably the extremely tall state beds of the period.

Marquetry Process of laying together pieces of veneer to form a design, using contrasting woods, perhaps with the addition of bone or ivory, white or stained green; introduced in the later seventeenth century and popular for about 25 years; revived by Robert Adam; *André Charles Boulle* (q.v.) gave his name to a particular type which was imitated by *Gerreit Jensen* (q.v.) and again to some extent during the nineteenth century in both France and England.

Mask Ornamental motif consisting of a formal representation of a face, either natural or distorted, e.g. human (especially female), lion, satyr, etc.; appeared on furniture during various historic periods.

Matted Decorative treatment of a flat surface by small dented marks, making a kind of texture, employed to enhance the raised, flat type of carving such as strapwork, e.g. on Elizabethan and Jacobean furniture.

Medallion Oval or circular form enclosing a motif, emblem, etc.

Monogram Entwined initials, sometimes used as a decorative motif on furniture where the piece has been made specially for one particular client; see also *Cipher*.

Morris, William: 1834–1896 Artist, designer and poet; his work all inspired by medievalism; chiefly remembered for his designs for woven tapestry, embroidered hangings and printed chintzes and wallpapers, all of a quality much superior to the mass-produced work of the period.

Mounts Additions, usually of metal, e.g. hinges, handles and lockplates, primarily for a useful purpose; also the elaborate enrichments such as the ormolu decoration applied to French furniture of the seventeenth and eighteenth centuries, a practice used only to a limited extent in England during the later eighteenth and early nineteenth centuries.

Nulling Another term for *Gadroon* (q.v.).

Oak The chief wood in use in England for furniture throughout the Middle Ages until the middle of the seventeenth century; after that time used for carcase work for veneered furniture; revived again for solid furniture in modern times; both native and imported timber (from Scandinavian countries) has been used; brown in colour with a distinctive grain.

Olive wood Yellow in colour with dark veining; sometimes found used in parquetry work, e.g. at the time of William and Mary.

Ormolu Gilded bronze; much used during the seventeenth and eighteenth centuries by the French for decorative mounts to furniture; used in England to only a limited extent, e.g. on commodes in the French style in the 1770s.

Ottoman Term for a long stuffed seat, such as a divan, with no back or arms; name imported from the Near East, fashionable in England, c. 1800.

Oyster piece, or oyster shell Descriptive name for a type of veneer obtained by the use of transverse slices of the bough or root of the tree, the markings then having this resemblance; laburnum and walnut chiefly used for the purpose, especially for the wide borders to marquetry panels, e.g. for cabinet doors, drawer fronts and table tops during the later seventeenth century.

Pad foot Shape resembling the *club foot* (q.v.), especially when set on a small flat disc.

Pagoda Building of Far Eastern origin with distinctive roof, curving sharply upwards at the eaves; a notable element in 'chinoiserie' and 'Chinese Taste', in English furniture and the decorative arts at various times.

Palmette Conventional decorative motif resembling the formal *anthemion* (q.v.), but based on the palm leaf; of classical origin; sometimes anthemion and palmette are used alternately to form a running band of ornament, e.g. in Adam interior decoration; occasionally appears in marquetry furniture of the same period.

Papier-mâché Artificial product (paper pulped and bound with some resinous medium), capable of being moulded to the desired form, e.g. smaller articles such as trays, boxes, etc.; such pieces were lacquered in black or a bright red or green, sometimes with additional decoration in gold, mother-of-pearl or painting; this style was in vogue during the second half of the eighteenth century; during the first half of the nineteenth century 'bronze' effects were popular, either alone or with some other ornamentation such as mother-of-pearl.

Parquetry Type of veneering in which the design is based on geometrical forms, as opposed to *marquetry* (q.v.) in which floral or sea-weed motifs make more naturalistic patterns; *oyster-piece* (q.v.) veneer, used alone or with floral marquetry, may be referred to as parquetry; parquetry was chiefly in use during the later seventeenth and early eighteenth centuries.

Patera Originally the round shallow dish used for drinking in classical times; in furniture and the decorative arts the patera is a flattish disc, round or oval, plain or filled with leaves or petals (if the latter, sometimes called a rosette); carved, painted, or used in marquetry; a favourite Adam motif.

Patina The surface effect seen on furniture as a result of the passage of time together with domestic polishing.

Paw foot Used on furniture from very early times, e.g. in ancient Egypt, and continually revived; chiefly found in fashionable English furniture during the first half of the eighteenth century, usually the lion's paw; also used to a limited extent in Regency furniture in which Egyptian motifs appear.

Pear Lightish colour brown and lacks figure; was used, stained black, as a cheap alternative to ebony in the early nineteenth century.

Pear drop (*a*) Handle; small pendant form somewhat pear-shaped, of metal; introduced in the Restoration period; (*b*) ornament; pear-shaped, appearing as a continuous band of small carved drops or pendants; e.g. to mouldings above

the frieze in furniture of the later eighteenth century.

Pedestal (*a*) Part of a knee-hole writing or dressing table, the cupboards or drawers on each side of the knee-hole being termed a pedestal, e.g. a pedestal of drawers; (*b*) separate piece of furniture, e.g. the stand containing a *cellaret* (q.v.) and supporting an urn, used each side of a sideboard table, at the time of Robert Adam.

Pediment (*a*) Triangular or segmental finish above the cornice, cf. the gable end of the classical temple; in furniture, used to finish cabinets, bookcases and wardrobes, notably those designed by William Kent (1730s), Chippendale and others (mid-eighteenth century); also used as top to looking-glasses during the first half of the eighteenth century; variants include: (*b*) the 'broken' pediment in which the raked (sloped) mouldings stop before reaching the apex, the space so left often being filled in with a carved cartouche; (*c*) 'swan-neck' or scrolled pediment, i.e. a broken pediment in which the mouldings follow a double curved outline, instead of a straight or segmental one.

Pembroke table Small table with an oblong top, the long side leaves being supported when extended on small brackets; in use during the eighteenth century; in contrast to *Sofa table* (q.v.).

Petit point See *Gros point.*

Piano stool For use at a keyboard musical instrument, the height often being adjustable; introduced in the late eighteenth century; in its heyday during the Victorian and Edwardian periods when playing the piano was a fashionable accomplishment.

Pie-crust table Modern name given to a certain type of small tripod table, usually of mahogany, in which the round top has a moulded edge made up of ogees and scrolls giving a broken but regular outline; this was similar to the rims on the large silver salvers of the same date; made during the mid-eighteenth century.

Pied-de-biche foot From the French, hind's foot; shaped like a cloven hoof; seen in pieces of c. 1700 date.

Pier glass Eighteenth-century name for the looking-glass hung on the wall-space between windows (i.e. the pier).

Pier table Eighteenth-century name for the table placed directly under the *pier glass* (q.v.); sometimes designed in keeping with the looking-glass.

Pigeonholes Small open compartments arranged inside the writing desk or bureau; in use from c. 1700 onward.

Pilaster Equivalent of a *column* (q.v.) but not free-standing, i.e. in architecture it consists of a flat strip, usually rectangular in plan forming part of a wall, but having base, shaft and capital, as in the column; used in furniture of an architectural character, e.g. in the work of William Kent and Thomas Chippendale, and seen carved on the fronts of large bookcases and cabinets; used in a very modified form on some late eighteenth-century pieces.

Pine Conifer tree, the timber usually being called *deal* (q.v.).

Pinnacle Vertical feature in Gothic architecture, being an upright terminal, e.g. on the top of a buttress usually carved with crockets; seen occasionally in furniture of the 'Gothick Taste' and of the Victorian Gothic Revival.

Plaque Small ornamental tablet, square or rectangular; may be of metal, porcelain, pottery, etc. in furniture; plaques of Wedgwood pottery were occasionally used on late eighteenth-century furniture; Sèvres porcelain plaques were a notable feature on French furniture in the Louis Seize style.

Plinth In classical architecture the square part of the base to the column or pilaster; in furniture the low base, plain or decorative, which supports such pieces as chests of drawers, bookcases, cupboards, etc., raising the body from direct contact with the floor; typical of much furniture of an architectural character, especially during the eighteenth century.

Pokerwork Means of decorating wood, using heated metal tools and sand; popular in the Victorian period.

Pole screen Usually consists of a tall rod supported on tripod feet, and carrying a panel, e.g. of embroidery, which could be raised or lowered as required; in use from the middle of the eighteenth century until the early Victorian period.

Pot-board Open shelf, just above the floor, e.g. to a dresser.

Press Seventeenth-century term for a cupboard intended to contain clothes or books; in more recent times it refers to open bookshelves.

Prince of Wales' Feathers Three ostrich feathers (badge of the Heir Apparent to the Throne); motif used in the late eighteenth century, notably in chair backs in the Hepplewhite manner.

Purple wood Imported from Brazil; the purple hue changes to brown on exposure; sometimes used for veneers and bandings, e.g. on satinwood furniture of the later eighteenth century.

Quadrant Quarter-circle band of metal, e.g. brass; used on the pull-down fronts of secretaires to support them in the horizontal position for writing upon.

Quartetto tables Nests of four small tables graduated in size to fit within each other, and designed (except the smallest) with three stretchers only to permit drawing out; Sheraton published designs for quartettos; the term is now nearly obsolete, although nests of tables (often three in number) are made today in varying styles.

Quatrefoil Four-leaved; decorative motif originating in Gothic tracery; carved on furniture of the medieval period; e.g. the front of a chest; likewise *Trefoil* (q.v.).

Rail Horizontal structural member, e.g. the seat rail of a chair, the frieze rail of a table.

Ram's head Ornamental motif of classical origin; a special feature of Adam's work; used variously, e.g. as a metal mount, a carved and gilded ornamentation, a painted motif or in marquetry veneer; of later eighteenth-century date.

Reeding Decorative feature formed by the grouping of 'reeds' side by side making a kind of ribbing; sometimes seen carved with a light ribbon twisted round at intervals; in furniture, tapered supports to chairs, tables, etc., were occasionally reeded, e.g. in the late eighteenth century, the Regency period and during the Victorian period.

Ribbon-back Descriptive term derived from certain of Chippendale's chair designs which he labelled 'Ribband Back'; the openwork back is carved with an elaborate arrangement suggesting twining ribbons of watered silk with bows; mid-eighteenth century.

Rococo Term used for a fantastic type of ornament derived from the French decorative arts (Louis Quinze style), which includes such motifs as shells, rockwork (*rocaille*) and leafy C-scrolls; there is a noticeable tendency to lack of symmetry; this term is used today for a characteristic period style (using much of this ornament), but which Chippendale and his contemporaries who practised it called 'French Taste'.

Rosette A conventionalized rose, used as a decorative motif; see also *Patera*.

Rosewood Timber imported from Brazil; also obtainable from India; light to warm brown in colour; strongly-marked but with an even grain; popular for furniture-making during the Regency period.

Roundel Round disc, or medallion; e.g. the circular medallion enclosing a head carved in profile, used as an ornamental motif in sixteenth-century furniture.

Rush, rushes Marsh or water-side plant, the stems or leaves of which have been used for various purposes when plaited; rush-seating has been used for the cheaper or simpler types of chairs at different periods from the middle of the seventeenth century to the present day.

Sabre leg Descriptive term for a chair leg fashionable in the Regency period; it curved in and outward again sharply; after the shape of a sabre.

Sarcophagus See *Wine Cistern*.

Satinwood Timber imported from both the West (c. 1760) and East Indies (c. 1780); of yellow colour, sometimes beautifully figured; used for fashionable veneered furniture, often with marquetry or painted decoration, during the later eighteenth century; its use was revived in the mid-nineteenth century for mass-produced furniture, e.g. bedroom suites, etc.

Satyr, satyr mask Originally a woodland deity of the classical period; the satyr's head or mask (human with goat's ears and expression) was used as an ornamental motif on English furniture (c. 1730–c. 1740), e.g. carved on the 'knee' of the cabriole leg.

Scagliola Composition (plaster of Paris, marble chips and colouring) made in imitation of marble; fashionable material for tops of decorative side tables during the eighteenth century.

Scaling Surface ornamentation resembling over-lapping fish scales; delicately carved and used to fill in backgrounds; seen on gilded furniture, e.g. mid-eighteenth century.

Scallop shell See *Escallop*.

Screen Used for two purposes from medieval times onward: to ward off draughts and to protect from the heat of the fire; in modern central heating conditions its use is practically obsolete.

Scroll foot Curved like a volute, and seen on cabriole legs in the 'French Taste' of the Chippendale period.

Scutore, scrutoir See *Escritoire*.

Seaweed marquetry See *Endive marquetry*.

Secretaire, secretary See *Escritoire*.

Serpentine front A horizontal curve (i.e. in plan) given to the fronts of some commodes, sideboards, etc.; usually the central part of the curve is convex set against a concave curve on each side; seen in furniture of the second half of the eighteenth century.

Settee To be distinguished from the *sofa* (q.v.); long seat which may be called an extension of the chair, the back sometimes appearing as two or more chair backs combined, either open-back or fully upholstered; introduced in the

Restoration period and continued to present day in various styles.

Settle A bench with a high back and an arm at each end, sometimes winged; used in kitchens, farmhouses and inns in times past.

Sheraton, Thomas: 1750–1806 Notable for the furniture designs he published, especially his *Cabinet-Maker and Upholsterer's Drawing Book* (1791, 1793, and 1802) and his *Cabinet-Maker's Dictionary* (1803); his style showed elegance, with straight lines, using satinwood with marquetry veneer; his later work showed some Regency influence.

Shield-back Descriptive term for a chair back design, much favoured by Hepplewhite in the 1780s.

Sideboard Dining-room piece; fitted with cupboards and drawers to contain cutlery, dishes, etc. for the service of meals; first designed as a composite piece in the later eighteenth century.

Slat Term sometimes used for the thin horizontal bars of a chair back, e.g. in the Chippendale ladderback chair.

Slide Pull-out shelf, e.g. the small one for a candle on a bureau, or the larger one for brushing clothes on a chest of drawers or commode; both types in use during the eighteenth century.

Sofa Distinct from the *settee* (q.v.), being similar to the day-bed in purpose, i.e. for one person to recline on; inspired by classical furniture it was a fashionable Regency piece and continued in the Victorian period in ordinary homes.

Sofa table Table with oblong top and a small leaf at each end, supported on brackets when extended; first introduced and popular in the Regency period.

Spade foot A short tapered foot, used on the square tapered supports to furniture of the later eighteenth century.

Sphinx Winged monster with woman's head and lion's body, of Greek mythology; a decorative motif used by Adam in the later eighteenth century; on Regency furniture an Egyptian sphinx head with the typical Egyptian wig head-dress sometimes appears.

Spindle Very slender turned baluster, variously used, e.g. grouped to fill in the open door-panel of a livery cupboard.

Spiral turning Descriptive term, cf. for legs, stretchers, etc. of furniture of the Restoration period in which the typical 'barley-sugar' twist was much used.

Splat The central vertical part of an open chair back; e.g. in the Queen Anne period (solid) and in the Chippendale style (pierced); takes many forms.

Splay Set at an angle.

Split baluster Self-explanatory term for a decorative motif used as applied ornament, e.g. on various pieces of furniture in the mid-seventeenth century.

Squab Loose cushion, much in use before properly-upholstered furniture became general.

S-scroll Descriptive term for a carved ornamental motif in use at various times during the historic periods.

Stalker and Parker Authors of *A Treatise of Japanning and Varnishing* dated 1688.

Stick-back Informal name for the traditional Windsor chair.

Stick furniture Modern term for furniture with stick-like supports, often of metal, in vogue in the mid-twentieth century.

Stile Vertical constructional member in case furniture, particularly in pieces framed up in panels, e.g. a chest front, cupboard door, etc.

Strapwork Decorative carved pattern, in flat low relief, consisting of interlacing bands; a characteristic ornament seen on furniture from about the middle of the sixteenth century to the middle of the seventeenth century; a more delicate variant is seen on pieces of mid-eighteenth-century date when it might be called fretwork.

Stretcher Constructional member, usually horizontal, uniting the legs of chairs, tables, stands, etc.; took various forms at different periods.

Stringing Extremely narrow line, or lines, of veneer, e.g. the light and dark stringing seen on eighteenth-century satinwood furniture.

Swag See *Festoon.*

Sycamore Wood of very fine grain, yellowish-white in colour, used in veneer, e.g. in floral marquetry of second half of the seventeenth century; later, stained greenish-grey, it was called *Harewood* (q.v.).

Tallboy Double chest of drawers; introduced c. 1700, popular throughout the eighteenth century and during the first half of the nineteenth century.

Tambour top, tambour front Flexible top fitted to a desk and acting as a lid ('roll-top'); consists of narrow slats of wood mounted on canvas; introduced in the later eighteenth century; Sheraton called bureaux designed with such lids 'Cylinder' desks.

Tapestry Fabric specially woven, originally and chiefly to make a decorative hanging, usually of a pictorial nature; of very ancient origin; in the eighteenth century the French used tapestry for upholstery, for chairs, settees, etc., and this practice was imitated by Adam.

Teapoy Small table usually tripod, but sometimes four-legged, which had a top lifting to disclose compartments for tea-caddies; popular in the late eighteenth and the early nineteenth centuries.

Tester The canopy or ceiling to a bed; at one time the terms celure and tester seemed interchangeable.

Thuja Wood imported from Africa; rich brown in colour and notable for its 'bird's-eye' figure; used (but rarely) as a veneer in the early eighteenth century.

Till Tiny drawer or compartment provided in a piece of furniture, e.g. in a chest, often for purposes of concealment.

Toilet glass During the historic periods took one of two forms: (*a*) small looking-glass, usually mounted on a range of small drawers but intended to stand separately on a small table or other suitable pieces of furniture; (*b*) narrow looking-glass which swings between uprights standing on the floor and called a *Cheval glass* (q.v.).

Torchère See *Guéridon.*

Tortoiseshell Back plates of the sea-turtle; used in marquetry, especially by *André Charles Boulle* (q.v.), who combined it with metal; sometimes used for veneer to frames for looking-glasses, e.g. during the later seventeenth century.

Towel horse Bedroom piece; consisting of a light framework of cross-bars and uprights on which to hang towels; in use from mid-eighteenth century until recent times, becoming almost obsolete when bathrooms became more common.

Tracery In architecture, particularly Gothic, the bands of stone which fill in, in various patterns, the pointed arch-heads of windows; in furniture, seen used decoratively, pierced or carved, in a modified form in medieval and early Tudor furniture; a favourite motif in furniture of the 'Gothick Taste' and of the Victorian Gothic Revival.

Trefoil Three-leaved; seen in Gothic tracery; see also *Quatrefoil*.

Trestle Light, usually movable, support, mostly in pairs, e.g. for a trestle table.

Trestle table Consists of a separate board or top laid on trestles, the whole being easy to dismantle and lay aside if required; usual form of dining table in medieval and early Tudor times before the framed ('joined') table was established.

Tridarn Three-piece cupboard, consisting of a two-tiered cupboard surmounted by a small open dresser; a two-tiered cupboard without the dresser was called a 'deudarn'; popular in the Welsh and border counties, the deudarn from c. 1600 to c. 1800, the tridarn (introduced in the later seventeenth century) throughout the eighteenth century; both pieces were superseded to some extent by the English farmhouse dresser with its higher range of shelves.

Tripod table Small table usually with a circular top, often hinged to tip up to save space, supported on a central column with three feet; fashionable during the mid-eighteenth century, frequently being called a 'pillar-and-claw' or 'claw table', where the feet were of the claw-and-ball type; see also *Pie-crust table*.

Truckle, or trundle bed Low bed which could be pushed under a large one when not in use; mostly intended for children or servants during the earlier historic periods.

Tulip wood Imported from Brazil; striped brown and red and much esteemed for veneering, e.g. *cross-banding* (q.v.); used during the eighteenth century and the Regency period.

Tunbridge ware Term for pieces finished in a particular type of veneer, made up of small fragments of wood forming a kind of mosaic pattern, geometrical, floral, etc.; the industry began in Tunbridge (hence the name) in the mid-seventeenth century, but the type of veneer is seen used on later pieces, e.g. Regency period.

Turkey work English term first used about the time carpets were first being imported in quantities from the Near East (Henry VIII and Cardinal Wolsey were notable collectors); in furniture, the name denoted an upholstery fabric formed by knotting wool threads on a canvas base to form a pile; seen on some chairs of the first half of the seventeenth century.

Turning Shaping by means of a lathe, e.g. for the legs, stretchers, etc. of chairs, tables and other furniture at various periods; took many different forms, including baluster, bulbous, knob (Tudor to mid-seventeenth century) and spiral (later seventeenth century); ousted by the cabriole leg and (later eighteenth century) the square tapered leg.

Urn Shape of classical origin; in furniture, a large container of wood, vase-shaped, used to hold cutlery or lined with lead for hot or iced water; usually it stood on a special pedestal, a pair of each being arranged to accompany the sideboard table in the Adam dining-room; superseded when the sideboard proper was perfected.

Valance Drapery arranged horizontally, e.g. as a pelmet to a window or hanging to the tester of a bed; occasionally carved in wood and painted (sometimes to imitate drapery realistically in the eighteenth century); in use as a fabric at all periods.

Velvet Rich silk fabric with a short close pile, used for furniture upholstery in various ways until recent times when real silk was superseded by fabric made from test-tube fibres.

Velvet, Genoa or Genoese Silk velvet of particularly sumptuous design, often with a cut-pile pattern; used for bed-hangings, chair covers, etc., notably c. 1700 and for furniture designed by William Kent.

Veneer Thin 'skin', usually of some finely-figured wood, applied to the basic carcase to give a decorative effect; used alone or in conjunction with *marquetry* (q.v.); was a fashionable finish to English furniture in the Restoration period, and was used to a greater or lesser extent throughout the eighteenth century and succeeding periods.

Vile, William: died 1767 London cabinet-maker in partnership with John Cobb; made furniture, mostly of mahogany, for the Royal residences and elsewhere.

Volute Flat spiral scroll; seen in classical capitals (except the Doric) and hence on certain pieces of furniture in which columns of classical derivation have been introduced into the design.

Walnut Tree growing in England from the mid-seventeenth century, but the wood was used for furniture from the Tudor period; the fine figure is seen to advantage in the veneered furniture of the Restoration period and the early eighteenth century; superseded by mahogany after c. 1740.

Whatnot Series of open shelves mounted on a light stand for books, china ornaments or 'whatnot'; introduced in the later eighteenth century and became a very popular piece of furniture (sometimes a corner piece) in Victorian parlours and drawing-rooms, when the passion for displaying small knick-knacks was at its height.

Windsor chair No direct connection with the town of Windsor; made entirely of wood, the various parts being dowelled into one another; the back mainly consists of turned spindles fitted into a 'bow' (curved top rail), the legs and stretchers also usually of spindle form; the seat ('saddle-shaped') of elm, the 'bow' made of a bend of ash or yew, the remainder of beech; popular during the eighteenth century and made with modifications in the nineteenth century and modern times; High Wycombe in Buckinghamshire for long the chief centre of production.

Wine cistern, wine cooler Tub of decorative design, lined with lead, intended to hold bottles of wine on ice or in iced water; fashionable in the eighteenth century when it usually stood under the sideboard or sideboard table in the dining-room; see also *Cellaret*.

Wing-chair Easy chair, usually upholstered, with ear-pieces or 'wings'; popular at most periods from the later seventeenth century onward.

Yew Timber used in England from very early times (e.g. by medieval archers for their bows); reddish-brown in colour, hard and springy; used for the constructional parts of some country-made pieces of furniture in the sixteenth century and for parquetry (seventeenth century), and veneer work in the seventeenth and eighteenth centuries; used for the 'bow' of some eighteenth-century Windsor chairs; sometimes used for drawer knobs.

Zebra wood Imported from S. America; very strongly-streaked in light and dark brown; used for veneer, e.g. cross-banding (late eighteenth century), and occasionally seen used over an entire surface, e.g. in the Regency period.

291

Bibliography

BRACKETT, O. English Furniture Illustrated. (Revised edition.) 1950.

DUTTON, R. The Victorian Home. 1954.

EDWARDS, H. C. R. Georgian Furniture. (V. & A. Museum Picture Book.) 1951.

History of English Chairs. (V. & A. Museum Picture Book.) 1951.

Shorter Dictionary of English Furniture. 1964.

EDWARDS, H. C. R. and JOURDAIN, M. Georgian Cabinetmakers. 1946.

EDWARDS, H. C. R. and MACQUOID, P. Dictionary of English Furniture. 1954.

EDWARDS, H. C. R. and RAMSEY, L. G. G. (Editors). *Connoisseur Period Guides.*

Tudor Period. 1956.

Stuart Period. 1957.

Early Georgian Period. 1957.

Late Georgian Period. 1961.

Note In these four volumes furniture is included among the chapters devoted to the decorative arts.

FASTNEDGE, R. English Furniture Styles, 1500 to 1830. 1955.

GLOAG, J. A Short Dictionary of Furniture. 1952.

HARRIS, EILEEN. The Furniture of Robert Adam. 1963.

HARRIS, M. The English Chair. 1948.

Old English Furniture. 1947.

HAYWARD, HELENA. Thomas Johnson and English Rococo. 1964.

HEPPLEWHITE. Furniture Designs. (Reprint of the *Guide*.) 1955.

JOURDAIN, M. Regency Furniture. 1949.

Stuart Furniture at Knole. 1952.

English Furniture of the Georgian Period. 1953.

ROGERS, J. C. English Furniture. (Revised edition.) 1950.

SHERATON. Sheraton Furniture Designs. (Reprint.) 1945.

SYMONDS, R. W. English Furniture from Charles II to George II. 1929.

Furniture Making in 17th Century and 18th Century England. 1955.

Victorian Furniture. 1962.

YARWOOD, DOREEN. The English Home. 1956.

VICTORIA & ALBERT MUSEUM PUBLICATIONS.

History of English Furniture. 1955. (P. Ward-Jackson.)

Note A number of individual picture books (*English Tables*, etc.) are also put out by the Museum, and may be bought either at the Museum or from H.M.S.O. Bookshop.

Index

Illustrations indicated by italics